A FUTURE FOR
SOCIALISM?

HAROLD WELLS

A FUTURE FOR SOCIALISM?

POLITICAL THEOLOGY AND THE "TRIUMPH OF CAPITALISM"

TRINITY PRESS INTERNATIONAL
Valley Forge, Pennsylvania

Copyright © 1996 Harold Wells

All rights reserved. No part of this book may be reproduced, stored in a retrieval system, or transmitted, in any form or by any means, electronic, mechanical, photocopying, recording, or otherwise, without the written permission of the publisher.

Trinity Press International, P.O. Box 851, Valley Forge, PA 19482-0851

Library of Congress Cataloging-in-Publication Data

Wells, Harold.
    A future for socialism? : political theology and the "triumph of capitalism" / Harold Wells.
        p.   cm.
    Includes bibliographical references and index.
    ISBN 1-56338-129-X (alk. paper)
    1. Socialism, Christian.   I. Title.
HX51.W37   1996
335–dc20   95-52254
                                                                  CIP

Printed in the United States of America

96   97   98   99   10   9   8   7   6   5   4   3   2   1

For my Father
Lorne A. Wells
my first teacher

Contents

CONCLUDING THEOLOGICAL REFLECTIONS

Preface

This book is intended to be a modest contribution to an enormously important debate in theology: Does Christian faith lead us in one political direction rather than another? More specifically, does our Christian faith lead us in the direction of "socialism," as so many major theologians of this century — Rauschenbusch, Barth, Tillich, Moltmann, Soelle, Gutiérrez, Míguez Bonino, Radford Ruether — have suggested? Do the present collapse of communism and the "triumph of capitalism," as well as the current crisis of democratic socialism in many places, mean that "Christian socialism" has lost its credibility? Is there a future for socialism at all? This is an interdisciplinary study, an exercise in Christian political theology that draws heavily upon the information and insights provided by historians and social scientists.

I am happy to acknowledge that I would not have launched into this particular project except for the invitation of Dr. Ken Ranney of Grand Prairie, Alberta, Canada, to participate in a Northern Alberta ecumenical seminar held at the United Church in Grand Prairie, for which a paper on "Christian socialism" was originally prepared. I am grateful to him for prompting me to think theologically about social and political structures under the conference title: "What would the world be like if we lived the way God wants us to live?" When I was first confronted with this question, it was immediately obvious to me that, of course, it would be a socialist world.

If I may identify the background and bias that predisposed me to this answer: My own sympathy for socialist politics no doubt can be traced back to my childhood as part of a working-class family in the city of Hamilton, Ontario, and to the intelligent class consciousness of my father; also to certain friends and teachers who were my companions or mentors while I was an undergraduate at McMaster University. Professor George Grant, that great Canadian philosophical and political guru, who at that time called himself a socialist and was fond of affirming his faith in "the blessed Trinity," was a superlatively provocative teacher and had a lasting influence on my thinking. Those were the early days of the New Democratic Party, when the achievements for Canadian society of its predecessor, the Cooperative Commonwealth Federation (C.C.F.), were highly visible. In the summer of 1962 I had the good luck to be appointed, as a student minister, to work in the city of Regina, Saskatchewan, and so found myself in the midst of one of the most exciting political battles in Canadian history. The C.C.F. government of the province of Saskatchewan, the first "socialist" government in North America, had finally (after nearly twenty years in power) brought in universal, government-sponsored medicare, to which the physicians had responded by a walkout. People feared for their health, since only emergency medical services were provided. The Liberal and Progressive Conservative opposition parties opposed the legislation vigorously and had the backing of most of the media, as signs were set up at the provincial borders: "You are now entering the Red Province." I can vividly recall the bitter divisions that existed within the community, the church, and even within the household in which I was billeted. At the same time, the former premier, T. C. (Tommy) Douglas, the main architect of medicare, was running for election to the federal parliament as new leader of the New Democratic Party, and this young student minister had the privilege of meeting him and working for him in a very humble "knocking on doors" capacity. Douglas's personal defeat in that election was heartbreaking (no doubt more so to me than to Douglas), and the defeat of the new party in Saskatchewan soon afterward convinced me that this was a movement and a party that was willing to fight against great odds with the most powerful forces in society, and to lose if necessary, while pursuing worthy social objectives.

Later, as a young pastoral minister of the United Church of Canada in northern Ontario, I was politically active in a minor way in the fledgling New Democratic Party. My concern with political theology was particularly stimulated by years in southern Africa (1976–81) where at the National University of Lesotho I encountered many Marxist students and colleagues. Those were tumultuous political years for that region, beginning with the massacre at Soweto in 1976 and the murder of Steve Biko in 1977, proceeding through the Zimbabwe civil war to its culmination in independence in 1980, and the ongoing struggle against apartheid in South Africa. A Marxist analysis of apartheid was predominant on that university campus: it was capitalism — in this case the love of cheap black labor and a high margin of profit — that kept apartheid firmly in place for so long, bolstered by the requisite economic investment and hypocritical public disapproval of the western/northern nations. "It was truly the capitalist nations of the west that killed Biko!" the campus radicals proclaimed in 1977, and with good cause. The enemy was rhetorically identified as "The Three Big C's: Colonialism, Capitalism, and Christianity." Both racism and religion were seen as ideological functions of capitalist profiteering, and Christianity had been complicit in the pacification of African peoples in the face of colonial expansion and exploitation. I was moved by the commitment and high aspirations of so many students and colleagues who longed for "socialism," seeing their struggle as a quest not only for racial equality, but as a fight for a qualitatively different society — a truly cooperative, nonexploitative social order. Sometimes, in their need to find an alternative to the reign of capital, they became blind, I felt, to the failures and atrocities of Soviet-style communism. At the same time, Christian faith on that campus was deep and vital and the church very strong among students and faculty, many of whom carried on a love/hate relationship with Christianity. Christian faith, despite the church's complicity with colonialism, had given dignity, hope, and joy to many of them. As a Christian chaplain and lecturer in Theology and Ethics, I was constantly challenged by students who cherished their Christian faith and held it together with political commitment to freedom and justice, to think through the relationship of faith to politics and ideology. The connection of Christianity and socialism was always at the center of this concern. For several years I taught courses on Christian Faith and Marxism, on Liberation Theology, and on social and political ethics; happily I was forced, in that context, to delve into history and the social sciences. Colleagues there, such as the Marxist economist Michael Sefali, challenged spiritualizing Christian thought with the hardheadedness of historical materialism in Marxist/Christian public debates in which I was sometimes a protagonist. Dominican Father Peter Sanders and Anglican Father Michael Lapsley (later the victim of a letter bomb from apartheid South Africa because of his engagement in that struggle) were helpful in the process of thinking through the possibility of a "Christian Marxism." But I was sad on a recent visit to Lesotho to find that the eager hope for socialism has been replaced for many by a wizened resignation to the "triumph of capitalism." In the wake of the collapse of "socialism" in the east, many of the young revolutionaries (though certainly not those mentioned above) have quietly settled into a resigned acceptance of "the way things are in the world." I am told that the same malaise has settled in upon much of the left in some parts of Latin America. It infects us here in Canada as well, where the once heroic New Democratic Party, when it gained power in Ontario, seemed unable to implement very much of its social democratic agenda.

It will soon be evident in these pages that I am defining socialism very broadly, including within this large concept most of the theories and practices that have called themselves by this name. I adopt, then, a pluralist approach to socialist thought, rejecting the widespread usage of the term that limits socialism to Marxism or to east European, Soviet, or Chinese communism. Toward the end, on the basis of the book's accumulated argument, I shall propose a definition of socialism that I think may be helpful and clarifying. Meanwhile, under the category of socialism I am exploring and reflecting upon many of the systems of thought and political practice that have placed a higher value on community than on individual economic rights, that emphasize cooperation more than competition, and that strive to empower and dignify human beings as workers over against the power of privately controlled capital. Fundamental to all socialism is the conviction that *capital is made for humans and not humans for capital.* Human beings should control capital, and not the reverse, lest capital reign as the great idol. For a long time it has seemed obvious to me (though I recognize it is not obvious to everyone) that a democratic socialist political attitude and commitment best coheres with Christian faith. This is the thesis I shall argue, contrary to the views of, for example, a theologian like Michael Novak, who attempts to make the case for "democratic capitalism."

Some disclaimers and defenses are in order. First, this is unapologetically a theological work. The argument is clearly and explicitly based in Christian faith. It is an instance of "faith seeking understanding," and "faith seeking praxis," i.e., faith seeking to find its way to clarity of commitment and action in the political sphere. It is Christ-centered and biblical, as well as contextual and liberationist in its theological stance. Because of the brevity of this work it does not pretend to be a thorough or definitive theological treatment of socialism, nor a major account of the history of socialism or Christian socialism. Nevertheless, the net is cast broadly, taking note of socialist stories in many parts of the world, drawing upon the efforts of historians, economists, political scientists, sociologists, and others. Interdisciplinary thought is not new for theology. Theologians have traditionally paid much attention to philosophy, as they still should. Today these other disciplines must also be consulted. It is impossible, otherwise, to make a case for the practical viability of various kinds of socialism — a case that must be made if a political theological/ethical argument is to be put. Without attention to empirical socio-political realities, our political theology is condemned to remain abstract, vague, and irrelevant. This of course embroils the author in the treacherous waters of other people's disciplines, a risky affair indeed. But I feel strongly that such perilous interdisciplinary journeys must be made. Is the truth not one, after all? How will we find wisdom if we remain fastidiously behind our artificial disciplinary walls, refusing to listen to each other or make the effort to learn from each other? Surely we must put aside our academic fear of putting a foot wrong and dare to ask the "big questions." The large and long view must be attempted, if we are not to remain, like little Jack Horner, safe in our cramped disciplinary corners.

I shall not be so pretentious as to suggest that this book is an exercise in "world-systems analysis." However, it benefits from the insight of the likes of Immanuel Wallerstein, who, as a historian and social scientist, insists that the basic unit of analysis must be the historical system as such, and the world-economy, not a single state or society. It is obvious that we do in fact live within a single world-system. "Contextual" studies, including contextual theology, must now be "global" in their perspective (though more local contexts still deserve attention). Further, the neat division of intellectual labor, against which Wallerstein protests, would separate not only the different branches of social science from each other, but also social scientists from historians, and historians from philosophers, ethicists, and theologians. This book attempts to link these disciplines to theology, to bring broad-based theological perspectives to bear upon political questions, and to rescue political theology from its safe, but boring neutrality.

In these pages I do carry on a conversation with a great many thinkers of various disciplines, past and present, who have considered the relation of political hope and utopia, politics and the Reign of God, as well as those who have attended closely to the practical and theoretical questions of social science and the history of socialism. As much as possible I shall let these other thinkers speak for themselves, to give the reader the benefit of the eloquence and depth of thought that is already available on this subject. I also attempt to offer some clarifications about the present circumstances of the historical socialist movement and its possible future, to note some of the creative expressions of the socialist spirit today, to whet the appetite of readers to consult some of the substantial studies available, and to do their own thinking about their own social vision and hope.

I write this, then, in the conviction that the rich tradition of socialist thought and practice must not be abandoned. As a Christian, I say that socialism must again be rethought and revitalized, "for Christ's sake."

•

Besides Dr. Ken Ranney, mentioned above, there are a number of people whose kindness, knowledge, and wisdom have helped me to write this book. Of course all of my thinking has grown and developed from early years in conversation with my wife, Patricia Wells, whose contribution is the *cantus firmus* (the *canta firma?*) to all of my work. My esteemed friend Professor Gregory Baum, of McGill University, Montreal, read the original version of this manuscript and offered very helpful insights, corrections, and suggestions, as well as necessary encouragement in times of doubt. Professor Roger Hutchinson, of Emmanuel College, Toronto, also kindly and very swiftly read the first draft and delivered me from a number of errors. I have benefited from many theological conversations with my colleague in theology at Emmanuel College, Professor David Demson. From Professor Lee Cormie, my colleague of St. Michael's College, Toronto School of Theology, I have learned a great deal in the area of liberation theologies and social analysis. All of the colleagues mentioned above have helped by pointing to publications that have become important sources for this book. I am also particularly delighted to acknowledge that my son, Matthew Wells, now a graduate student in political science, has been a stimulating interlocutor and helpful guide to relevant literature in his field. Most emphatically, none of these worthy people should be held responsible in any way for any of the follies that may be discovered between these covers, since I have reason to believe that all of them would disagree heartily with at least some of what I say here!

Also indispensable to the appearance of this book has been the assistance of my friend Paul De Roo, of Burlington, Ontario, my original computer teacher and constant rescuer in the face of computer snags. Wanda Loc, of Emmanuel College, was gracious and generous with her time producing computer printouts. And, not least, publisher and editor of Trinity Press International, Dr. Harold Rast, has been the helpful and encouraging *sine qua non.*

H. G. W.

Toronto
Advent 1995

Part I

What Is Political Theology?

Chapter 1

Political Theology and Ideology

Can it be said that Christian faith points us in one political direction rather than another? Does the gospel inherently predispose Christians toward any particular political/ideological stance, or is the gospel of Christ simply neutral in political matters? In modern times Christian people in various circumstances have committed themselves courageously to quite specific political causes for the sake of the gospel: abolitionists against slavery, the German Confessing Church Christians against the Nazis, South African black Christians and their supporters around the world against apartheid, members of the peace movement against the arms race. Here I am particularly interested in the tradition of Christian socialism. Since early in the nineteenth century many Christians have opposed what they considered to be the unjust and inhumane socio-political/economic system known as capitalism and held up alternative visions of society as a truly solidaristic and cooperative "community of friends." They believed that the life of justice and love for the neighbor cannot be limited to the practice of personal charity, but also implies commitment to social structures and systems that embody these values. They not only saw visions; they also struggled to realize them by practical action. I wish to tell a little of that story and to reflect theologically about the great variety of concepts and practices that have come under the name "socialism." I shall defend the proposition (contrary to the apparent view of Hauerwas, Willimon, and others[1]) that the gospel is not at all neutral about such matters and that indeed Christian faith does point us in a socialist direction.

Christians, Socialism, and the Present Situation

"Socialism has reached the end of the line," someone said to me just after the Canadian election of 1993. Not only was the governing Conservative Party almost eliminated and more or less replaced as the voice of conservatism by a more right-wing party; the New Democratic Party, which pioneered and fought for universal medicare and pension plans, the main repository of the Canadian socialist tradition, was able to garner only 7 percent of the popular vote and lost its official party status in parliament.

The new federal Liberal government, which had campaigned on a platform of employment, economic stimulation, and commitment to social programs, once in office continued the Conservative Party focus on deficit and debt reduction and high real interest rates, with major cuts to funding for social welfare, health, and education. Meanwhile, Republicans of the far right have taken control of the U.S. Congress.

We have heard it often of late: "The experience of the Soviet Union and eastern Europe, and China and Cuba too, have proved that socialism simply does not work." We hear it said over and over again: "Socialists are in disarray in Latin America and Africa. Socialism hardly exists at all in the United States, and in Canada it is in full retreat." In Canada, in the province of Ontario, a social democratic government struggled to achieve deficit control and maintain its credit rating in what looked, to many of its own party members, like neo-conservative policies.

In 1995 this provincial government was replaced by an extreme right-wing Conservative government, which has begun to implement an unprecedented policy of drastic cuts to social assistance for the unemployed poor and to education and health care, together with major tax reductions for those who are prosperous and employed. The cornerstone of Canadian social democracy, universal "medicare," appears to be in danger, and the freedom and power of the labor movement has been seriously reduced.[2] Even in the so-called "Third World," elements of the left appear to be bowing down to "the market."

> In El Salvador, former Marxist ideologues, such as Ruben Zamora, are asking experts for lectures on free-market economics and urging that right-wing army officers not be barred from electoral politics.
>
> In Brazil, the hottest candidate to replace the recently impeached president, is Luiz Inacio (Lula) da Silva, a former metal workers' leader, whose rabble-rousing speeches are now tempered with calls for foreign investment and growth.[3]

In France, socialists in power began to behave like conservatives, only then to be outdone by the real conservatives in the elections of 1993 and 1995. In South Africa the African National Congress seldom speaks of socialism. The Reconstruction and Development Plan is now conceived in terms of investment in construction projects, and President Nelson Mandela seems mainly concerned about stability in order to attract investment.[4] This is not simply a moral lapse on the part of former socialists; it represents their honest effort to cope in practical ways with a powerful capitalist world-economy.

All of this should not be overstated. The Chinese colossus remains communist (though even this statement has to be qualified). Many democratic socialist policies have remained firmly in place in countries like Germany, the Scandinavian nations, and other parts of western Europe, even when socialist parties have been out of power, and in Sweden the previously rejected democratic socialists have recently been returned to office. Nevertheless, that socialism is in crisis is hardly in question, amid suggestions that the viable goals of socialists have already been realized in most western democracies and that, in view of the fate of Soviet communism, further developments would be destructive or unrealistic.[5]

For a long time, as I said above, "socialism" has been the political commitment of many Christian people. For more than 150 years a significant minority of Christians, including most theological leaders, have been critical of the inhumanity of capitalism and have seen socialism of one kind or another as the "ideology" or political philosophy that best coheres with their Christian faith and hope. Surely capitalism, they have felt, being centered as it is in private ownership, competition, and profit and driven by individual self-interest, must be replaced by a more cooperative social order that allows human beings to care for one another in a social and economic community. Can human beings really not organize economic production and political life in a way that gives priority to satisfying human needs and that respects and sustains the natural environment, rather than serving, above all, the enrichment of private individuals? Can we really not order ourselves in a way that gives priority to labor over capital and environment over profit, giving dignity and meaning to work, allowing human beings to serve God and not mammon? Surely something more than private profit can guide and determine our social and political priorities. These are the typical attitudes and concerns that have motivated many Christian people to turn toward socialism.

Christians were prominent among the originators of socialist thought in the first half of the nineteenth century, and their socialism was motivated by Christian conscience and hope. Christian socialists believed, as citizens of what they considered to be a "Christian society" or "Christendom," that the lordship of Jesus Christ should be manifest in human social structures, that economic and political life could not be left to itself as a kind of kingdom of the world. They saw that Christian life could not be a depoliticized or privatized affair that concerns itself only with personal righteousness and personal salvation, since the gospel is "good news" for the social order and the whole creation, and not only for individual human souls. The early Christian socialists climbed a steep hill indeed, suffering many defeats — I shall tell a little of that story in the pages that follow — but over the decades they have also achieved a great deal for the humanization of many societies.

In Canada the connection between Social Gospel theology and socialism and its achievements in creating a more equitable economic order are well documented, if often forgotten. Moreover, in our time the liberation theology of Latin America has generally identified itself as socialist, linking its understanding of the gospel of Jesus Christ to a socialist social analysis and agenda. Socialism has been the avowed political commitment of major Christian theologians in this century, from Walter Rauschenbusch to Karl Barth, to Gustavo Gutiérrez and Jürgen Moltmann.

In addition, the Christian feminist theological movement, and especially eco-feminism, calling for gentler, more cooperative, and non-hierarchical structures of human life rooted in a respect for the natural world, has a clear affinity to socialist thought. This is explicit, for example, in the thought of one of the most prominent of feminist theologians, Rosemary Radford Ruether, who believes that the liberation of women as a caste is impossible without the structural transformation of the whole of society along the lines of "communitarian socialism."[6] Canadian feminist/socialist Marsha Hewitt argues for the essential interdependence of feminism and socialism, for

> without a feminist consciousness, socialism is incapable of understanding or even seeing the specific oppression of women and the dynamics of sexist domination. At the same time, in the absence of a socialist consciousness and political praxis, feminism is endangered by turning in on itself in a kind of narcissistic,

revolutionary escapism that deludes itself into thinking women's liberation may be achieved without the transformation of the entire social structure.[7]

However respectable and essential socialism may be in the minds of theologians and feminists, socialism is in crisis and its future very much in doubt. This in itself is not new. It has always been the ideological underdog struggling against the gigantic dominance of capital. But today especially socialism is in confusion everywhere, and a major new factor is the decisive collapse of the great "socialist" experiment of the U.S.S.R. The Union of Soviet *Socialist* Republics (though regarded by many socialists as in fact not truly socialist at all) has renounced its socialism and aspires to be part of the capitalist world. The peoples of eastern Europe threw off "socialist dictatorship" at their very first opportunity, and China appears to be moving more and more toward a "free market" system. Even if the U.S.S.R. was not genuinely socialist, it did constitute a challenge to the dominant capitalism of the western/northern world, so that the south now appears to be more than ever at the mercy of international capital. Africa is languishing under the free market ideology of the International Monetary Fund; bold experiments in "African socialism" are no longer mentioned. The semisocialist experiment of Nicaragua was pummelled into the ground by American military support for the contras, and Cuba, facing continued economic hostility from the United States and without the backing of the U.S.S.R., appears to be next. Liberation theologians, daunted by events in Chile, Grenada, and Nicaragua, no longer dare to hope for socialist revolution in the face of the gargantuan power of international capital backed by the military and political might of the United States. It has become evident that localized socialisms will simply not be allowed in the western hemisphere — or anywhere else for very long. In Canada, despite our venerable democratic socialist tradition, politicians of the left have not dared, for a long time, to call themselves socialist in public, preferring the term "social democratic." After all, it is argued, communists, and even Nazis, have called themselves socialist, and in electoral politics in North America "Socialist!" is hurled at opponents as an accusation of political softheadedness. In the present technological/economic circumstances, social democratic parties, even when elected with a parliamentary majority (as in the province of Ontario) find themselves unable to expand, or even maintain, the network of social democratic measures that they fought for so long while in opposition. With the decline of the economic power of governments and the ascendancy of the power of international corporations through free trade agreements, the achievements of the welfare state appear to be in peril. In the United States, not only the word "socialist," but even the word "liberal" is virtually banned from respectable political discourse, as the right wing of the Republican Party controls the Congress. All of this is bad news for the historical socialist movement and, I daresay, for the democratic character of our western/ northern societies.

Should Christians, then, abandon socialist thought and simply resign ourselves politically to the triumph of the capitalist "new world order" and "globalization"? Should we admit that humanity is not capable of living generously and cooperatively in society and utilize the doctrine of sin, as so many others have (i.e., "human beings are just too selfish to live in a socialist society"), to justify alliance with destructive, essentially antihuman social and economic arrangements?

The questions are obviously rhetorical. My purpose here is to reflect on the present crisis of world socialism from a Christian theological perspective, i.e., in relation to "the gospel." I want to argue that genuine socialism is still the most faithful political option for Christians — now more than ever, for it is not only socialism that is in crisis, but the whole world economic system. Of course not all socialists are Christians, but this essay is a reflection on socialism specifically from within Christian faith. I also hope it will be a modest contribution to the present rethinking that is now going on among socialists in general.

Christian Socialism?

Perhaps an immediate clarification is called for: By using the term "Christian socialism" I do not suggest that by definition Christians are socialist. I recognize that conscientious, faithful Christian believers may take up another political stance. The failure and corruption of much that has been called "socialism" in history makes this understandable. Nor am I proposing a political party or movement called "Christian Socialism." Christians obviously have no monopoly on political wisdom or social righteousness, and in their political life Christians should be involved with others who are not Christian. Nor do socialists have a monopoly on political wisdom or social righteousness. Since many decent, rational human beings adopt, for what they consider to be good reasons, nonsocialist political stances, it is not my intention to suggest that other ideologies are simply evil. Nor is it my intention to condemn all capitalists and all capitalist institutions or ideas. No one today advocates total state ownership of the means of production or expects cooperativism to take over the economic world. Most of those who call themselves socialists today, while worried about the enormous power of great corporations, are supporters at least of small business and family farms. Many favor "mixed economy" within political democracy or cooperative, communitarian efforts within capitalist structures. This implies that some forms of "capitalism" (private ownership and control of the means of production) would continue, even if socialists had their way. Indeed, since no pure socialism or pure capitalism exist anywhere, nor probably will they ever, socialism and capitalism, as opposing ideologies, have to be seen as existing within a continuum. The opposite ends of this continuum are radically different from each other, yet never entirely discontinuous. It is not helpful or fair, then, to simply demonize the people who disagree with us. There is need, however, to clarify what socialism means, or can mean, in the decades ahead.

When I speak of "Christian socialism" I refer to an option for socialism among some Christian people for Christian reasons — a political philosophy that some Christians adopt because of the way they understand their faith. This study is, to some degree, an exercise in "comparative ideology."[8] This does not mean that I claim to be an objective or detached observer. While attempting to hear and heed negative critique of historical socialist ideas and practice and to be respectful of other stances, I shall argue here that socialism is the most appropriate kind of political/ideological stance for Christians.

But this is not to absolutize "tolerance." It is easy to think of twentieth-century political ideologies that do not warrant respectful, sympathetic understanding or dialogue (and this is often clearer with hindsight). Most of us now know that it is inappropriate to "dialogue" with Nazism, apartheid, or other forms of fascism, which offend so clearly and fundamentally against human dignity and well-being. Tolerance as a virtue has its limits. Some manifestations of capitalism, as well as some forms of "socialism," rightly evoke only our indignation and vigorous opposition. Unfortunately, it is not always obvious within the historical moment which ideologies call for dialogue and which deserve forthright condemnation. One of the functions of political theology is to clarify questions of this kind.

•

This book is an exercise in "political theology" — a term in common use today, but just what is meant by it? Political theology, as I choose to use the term here, is an attempt to think theologically about the political order.[9] This means bringing the light of the gospel to bear upon "the political." The term "political theology" is often used to refer to a particular genre of theology especially associated in Europe with the names of Metz, Moltmann, Soelle, and others, and also with Third World liberation theologians who attempt to understand the whole of Christian faith in a political way. This does not mean reducing theology to politics; it does mean making theology more conscious of and intentional about its political function, bringing out the political meaning and implications of every aspect of faith. The theology of Christ, and the theology of salvation and of the Spirit, of the church and its mission, of sacraments, and so on, are viewed with respect to their political implications and, in turn, with respect to the implications of political realities for them. The presupposition here is that ideas have power and that theological ideas have ripple effects upon political awareness and upon the political world. To be conscious and intentional about this is what Jürgen Moltmann calls a "political hermeneutic of the gospel"[10] — an interpretation of the gospel that brings out its political implications. Here I shall be constantly in debt to these theologians, and it will be essential to enter into discussions about Christ, salvation, sin, mission, etc., in any discussion of "Christian socialism." My primary purpose here, however, is not so much to articulate particular doctrines, but rather to reflect theologically upon that constellation of political options which has historically been called "socialist," as well as its ideological adversary, capitalism. This includes also, of course, reflection upon the political significance of key doctrines.

Both Christianity and socialism are, as others have suggested, "utopian" movements in the positive sense of that word, and the two have an important historical relationship. We cannot, I think, appreciate the historical significance of socialism nor think clearly about its future, if we do not recognize its utopian character, i.e., its drive toward u-topia, "no place" — that which has nowhere been achieved in human society. Christian faith too lives in hope for "no place" — that Reign (Kingdom) of God which has not yet been realized on the earth. Christian socialism brings together Christian hope for the world with visionary political goals and programs, and does so because of faith in the risen

Christ. By Christian socialism I also refer to a great tradition, a history, a vision, and a struggle within which I am proud to stand — especially its contribution to early democratic socialism in Britain, the Social Gospel socialist tradition in Canada, and more recently the socialist dimension of the liberation theologies of the Third World.

A word is called for concerning the method of this particular study. I do not approach the question of the relationship of socialism to the gospel in the style common to "Christian-Marxist dialogue" (as in the longstanding discussions of Christian theologians with Marxists such as Roger Garaudy, Ernst Bloch, Milan Machovec, or the work of John Bennett, Donald Evans, or Giulio Girardi).[11] This study does not purport to be an exercise in such dialogue; rather it is a Christian political/theological discussion of the relationship of Christian faith to a particular political/philosophical option. Its method is therefore christocentric, biblical, and contextual and, as the reader will see, owes much to the christologically oriented forms of liberation theology. It is not my intention to compare Christianity and Marxism on issues such as the nature of humanity, work, alienation, and hope. Although Marx is one of the greatest, and certainly the most influential, of socialist thinkers, this study is not by any means limited to Marxism, but is interested in socialism in a much broader sense. If there is a comparison occurring here, it is not between Christianity and socialism (apples and oranges) as though these two belonged somehow in the same category, but between socialism and capitalism, in light of Christian faith. Christianity is not an "ideology," nor is socialism a "faith." Here, as discussed later, I borrow from Segundo and Ricoeur.

While socialism is much more than Marxism, the thought of Karl Marx, especially his central insight known as "historical materialism," has in various degrees informed most serious socialist thought. The central idea of historical materialism is that history and human society are shaped and driven by the need to meet material needs, that the material "mode of production" and relations of production (the state of technology, as well as ownership and control of the means of production) powerfully determine the course of history. This view is, I think, remarkably congruent with biblical faith, which is so profoundly concerned with history, with the body, with land, and with political and economic power. I believe that, in view of the historical/political/materialist character of biblical faith, the insights of historical materialism, though not in an atheist or determinist form, are serviceable for Christian political theology.

A mere ethical rejection of capitalism, however, is not enough for political theology. *Denunciations* of capitalism are common among Christian theologians and ethicists, but (to borrow terms from the early work of Gustavo Gutiérrez[12]) *annunciation* is also called for. Denunciation of a system is all very well, but of little value without some suggestion as to what might replace it. If we are seriously critical of the dominant capitalism of the contemporary world and believe it requires more than minor repair, then presumably we support some form of socialism. If no credible alternative vision is set forth, our hearers may be forgiven for thinking that the socio-political status quo is somehow eternal and necessary and that, beyond minor tinkering with the workings of capitalism, we have nothing more to hope for in the political sphere. This does not mean that theologians and preachers as such, or political philosophers, should propose "five-year plans" (though they may be, as citizens, participants in such discussions about the details of public policy). Their specific task, beyond denunciation, is rather to clarify alternative social values and goals, to hold up possibilities, hopes and visions, bringing the gospel of hope into dialogue with the knowledge and wisdom provided by historians, social scientists, and politicians. Political theologians cannot do this "out of the blue." They must speak in an informed way about actual political realities and as "organic intellectuals" (borrowing the concept of Antonio Gramsci), i.e., out of genuine contact with the lives of working (and unemployed) people and participation in the political process. The history of socialism, including Christian socialism, is nothing if it is not the story of arduous efforts and struggles to find practical alternatives.

I have said that it is not theology's task to propose detailed political plans and policies, and that is why I speak cautiously about "Christian socialism." What, then, does theology have to contribute to social and political thought? Christian theology is the rational and coherent articulation of the content of Christian faith — faith seeking understanding. Yet such understanding is also in search of praxis and must be informed by and in constant interaction with practical action. It is obvious that Christians, for the sake of their own integrity and their own mission, need to think out the political implications of their faith in Jesus Christ, as well as the implications of their political experience for faith itself. If Christ is their Lord in every dimension of life, their political existence must be spun out of the gospel, and their understanding of the gospel informed by practical political discipleship.

But Christians also have an important contribution to make to general public discussion in this part of the world, if only because Christians still constitute the largest religious community in the western world and have played a major role in shaping the political values of our civilization. As much as secular thinkers may prefer to ignore Christian thought, it is clear that the church has had and, at least with some segments of the population, still has a profound impact on the political attitudes of people. That capitalism, as it developed out of feudalism, came to have the blessing of Christianity was not irrelevant to its triumph. Canadian New Democratic Party (former) leader Ed Broadbent has commented:

> In the evolution from medieval society, the making of profit shifted at a certain point from being a marginal and morally negative aspect of society to being pervasive. This transition was accompanied by a parallel development in Christian theology. When theologians ceased condemning the pursuit of profit as a sin and started to describe such market activity as a normal and, within limits, acceptable mode of behavior, capitalist economic activity and relations had finally triumphed.[13]

The churches still have a legitimizing power in society, even with many who no longer attend worship. No other institutions in society so consistently focus attention on social and ethical issues with large numbers of people, with the potential for challenging the reigning capitalist and consumer ideology. If a society is to move toward socialist structures, seeking greater equality in the distribution of goods and, even more, seeking a more authentically human and qualitative existence, it will need some normative notion of community, some shared conceptions of justice. It is hard to be persuaded that a postmodernist deconstructionism will effectively lead whole societies to the "liberal utopia."[14] The dominant social vision in the United States just now appears to be that of the "religious right." It is difficult to imagine, in fact, where alternative visions will come from in the western/northern world, if not from the Christian community.

Basic socialist ideas and attitudes have deep roots in the biblical and Christian tradition. Socialism, of course, is a modern phenomenon. It grew out of the technological conditions of the Industrial Revolution and also utilized the value concepts of the Enlightenment and the French Revolution. The essential equality of all human beings, for example, is a rock-bottom ethical commitment of most socialists.

Equality is a concept heralded by the Enlightenment of the eighteenth century that often faced the opposition of Christian authorities and institutions. In that eighteenth-century context "equality" was, however, primarily a bourgeois concept — an insistence on the part of the new middle class that they were "equal" to the old noble classes. Equality had to do with equal rights to own property and to exercise social power through property. The first socialists — and I shall discuss this in a later chapter — were those who became dissatisfied with the results of this liberal, "bourgeois" revolution, precisely because it did not go far enough toward the goal of true social equality. But the concept of equality in a deeper ethical sense had its source and justification in the Christian tradition of western European culture. George Grant, always a critic of modern liberal thought, made this point well many years ago:

> It must be insisted . . . that the idea of equality arose in the west within a particular set of religious and philosophical ideas. I cannot see why men should go on believing in the principle without some sharing in those ideas. The religious tradition was the biblical, in which each individual was counted as of absolute significance before God. . . . To state this historical fact is not to deny that many men have believed in equality outside this religious and philosophical tradition. The question is rather whether they have been thinking clearly when they have so believed. This religious basis for equality seems to me the only adequate one, because I cannot see why one should embark on the immensely difficult social practice of treating each person as important unless there is something intrinsically valuable about personality.[15]

A little further back the social historian Karl Polanyi made a similar point, arguing for the rootedness of socialism in Christianity. He noted that Christian leaders and institutions have often stood in opposition to socialist politics. However, in the fascist context of the 1930s, when both church and socialist parties were under attack, Polanyi declared: "No attack on Socialism can be permanently effective that fails to dig down to the religious and moral roots of the movement. But at these roots lies the Christian inheritance."[16]

To assert an ultimate foundation for political thought in faith and ethics, or what Grant calls "an explicit doctrine of human good," is part of theology's ongoing contribution to public discussion. This is political theology. Christians will ground their understanding of "human good" in their faith in Jesus Christ and will enter into dialogue with others in society out of their center in him.

The Lordship of Jesus Christ

The task of Christian political theology, as I am using the term here, is not to speak in vague abstractions and generalities about the political order. Rather, it is to clarify political options for Christians as followers of Jesus Christ. Of course one expects that many will disagree; any particular political theology is a contribution to a debate, not an official pronouncement. De facto, however, Christ will always be central to that debate, since he is clearly central for Christians' understanding of God, humanity, and the whole of life and central to the church's worship, mission, and ethics. Through the centuries and in every major Christian tradition, Jesus the Jew, crucified and risen, stands alone as Messiah of Israel, as Word and revelation of God, as embodiment of God's Reign, and as the ground of hope for the world. That is why political theology explores the congruence of various political options with the lordship of Christ. This is the meaning of "christocentrism" (Christ-centeredness): every doctrinal formulation, every liturgy and mission policy, every ethical stance, every cause and political option, is measured in terms of Jesus Christ, who, in his visible concreteness as flesh, is one with the Father and the Holy Spirit.

Political theology does not flow unambiguously, however, from the name of Jesus Christ. Those who name Christ as Lord may and do differ drastically about the political implications of his person and work. These differing political views often have their counterparts in differing views of Christ himself, i.e., our theologies and our politics mutually condition one another.

Here the concepts of Brazilian theologian Clodovis Boff are helpful when he distinguishes between "first" and "second theology." "First theology" articulates the content of Christian faith itself — the identity and work of Jesus Christ, the Holy Spirit, salvation and sin, mission and sacraments, etc. "Second theology" reflects theologically upon "nontheological" dimensions of life, such as politics, art, sexuality, science. Political theology in the sense that we are using it here is a type of second theology.[17] Theology cannot merely pontificate in an abstract manner about complex realities of which it knows nothing. To think theologically about physical science one must know something of physical science. To think theologically about sexuality, one must know something of sexual life, and what biologists, psychologists, sociologists, and so on can tell us about it. So also, to think theologically about "the political," one cannot simply read politics out of the Bible; one must know the political more than superficially, learning from social scientists, historians, and politicians, as well as the practical, lived reality of political existence. "First theology" clearly and rightly informs "second theology." Christology, for example, is fundamental to Christian political thought. But "second theology" must also contribute to and even modify "first theology," so that contextual, social/political analysis may modify christological understanding. For example, looking at Jesus through the eyes of marginalized and oppressed people, or through the eyes of women, will have a bearing upon what we see in him and hear from him.[18] Insight into the structures of domination in the world, whether the patriarchal domination of the male sex, or the dominion of capital in the economic world, will enable us to see the significance of Jesus and his mission differently than we otherwise would. Without the contribution of "second theologies" and their interaction with practical realities, "first theologies" will remain abstract and out of touch with real life.[19]

However, for those of us who continue to call ourselves Christian and who wish to be followers of Jesus, the lordship of Jesus Christ must be the primary determinant of our political theology. Is this a principle of domination, as some suggest? Though the English word "lord" originally meant a dominant male patriarchal figure, the word that it translates — Greek, *kurios* — when it was ascribed to Jesus by the early church was a liberating concept, proclaiming that not Caesar, but Jesus, the humble and crucified one, the servant who washes feet, is the one who carries true authority. That Jesus is "lord" means that Caesar most emphatically is not. I believe the lordship of Jesus is still liberating. Indeed, we call him "lord" precisely because we derive liberation from him — liberation from guilt and from the terror of death, from emptiness and meaninglessness, and from the authority of oppressive powers. Positively, the lordship of Jesus means liberation *from* self, *for* authentic loving service. In political terms, that Jesus is *kurios* means that neither the state, nor "the market," nor any old or new "ism" may have the last word over our lives.[20]

In light of the gospel the fundamental question arises for political theology: How are Christians to live faithfully in the political realm in light of the lordship of Jesus Christ? The question could be answered in very general terms simply by quoting scripture: We must "render unto Caesar the things that are Caesar's, and unto God the things that are God's" (Matt. 22:21). For biblical faith, everything belongs to God, and our worship, trust, and obedience belong to none other than the liberating God of Israel: "I am the Lord your God who brought you out of the land of Egypt, out of the house of slavery; you shall have no other gods before me" (Exod. 20:2). For Jews and for Christians, "God" is known fundamentally as the one who led enslaved Jews out of Egypt, out from the domination of the deified pharaoh. No system and no leader, therefore, can be idolized as divine; for Christians, the lordship of Jesus Christ, the Word of God made flesh, sets the direction for all of life, including political life.

The latter general point was eloquently stated by members of the Confessing Church in Germany at Barmen during the Nazi period:

> Jesus Christ, as he is attested for us in Holy Scripture, is the one Word of God which we have to hear and which we have to trust and obey in life and in death.

This means that Jesus Christ, in his oneness with God, stands alone as incomparable source of truth. Not "experience," nor "context," not "creation," nor "realism," nor even *theos* (God) abstractly understood, can become "bottom line" for Christians. Barmen went on:

> We reject the false doctrine, as though there were areas of our life in which we would not belong to Jesus Christ, but to other lords — areas in which we would not need justification and sanctification through him.[21]

After stating its recognition of the providential, "divinely appointed" role of the state, Barmen continued:

> We reject the false doctrine, as though the State, over and beyond its special commission, should and could become the single and totalitarian order of human life, thus fulfilling the church's vocation as well.[22]

It was precisely what had to be confessed at that time and place, and to do so in Germany in 1934 required great courage. Many members of the Confessing Church suffered terribly because of their faithfulness to Christ alone as Lord. Neither the national *führer*, nor the race or the nation itself, nor German "context," could become normative for them. Barmen articulates the essential and dangerous starting point for all political theology: the lordship of Jesus Christ. For our purposes here, this means that no emperor or führer can be *kurios*, not even a socialist one. Not even a faceless "system" or concept can be *kurios*. *Socialism* is not *kurios*. More to the point in the present turn-of-the-century world-economy: neither *capital* nor *the market* can be *kurios!*

Yet simply to affirm, as Barmen does, that only Jesus Christ is *kurios* gives too little guidance for political life. In later years, Karl Barth, one of the authors of Barmen, felt that it had concerned itself too narrowly with the question of the church's own integrity in face of the Nazi government's incursions and had not directed itself against "National Socialism" itself.[23] Christians will generally agree among themselves that political life should be guided by the lordship of Jesus Christ, yet go on to propose or support drastically different political parties, policies, and programs, and even quite different visions of the good society. When in political theology we speak of the lordship of Jesus Christ, we still have to ask, "Which Jesus Christ?" and a particular christology needs to be spelled out with particular political implications. If we simply say that Christ wills "justice," "compassion," and "liberty," all Christians (and most others as well) will agree that these are appropriate political goals or values. But they will go on to disagree about how these values are to be realized, and even about what they mean. In the United States, Falwell and Reagan, Buchanan and Robertson, would enthusiastically endorse the lordship and centrality of Jesus Christ, as well as justice, compassion, and liberty. So also, at the other end of the political spectrum, would Jim Wallis of *Sojourners*, black theologian James Cone, and feminist theologian Letty Russell. Similarly, people of widely divergent political views would endorse appeal to "Holy Scripture" (as in the case of Barmen). But political theology will have to read and hear scripture according to some particular, explicit political hermeneutic (i.e., a particular and intentional way of interpreting scripture) if it is to mediate among various possible political paths and choices. An allegedly apolitical or nonpolitical reading of scripture will be self-deceptive, since, as has often been pointed out, a so-called "apolitical" interpretation of the Bible, concentrating on personal salvation and individual morality, implies the theological irrelevance of politics, as well as the political irrelevance of theology. Such an individualistic version of Christianity merely lends support to the dominant ideology of individualism. Further, given the political ambiguity of the Bible, it will have to be read critically in light of its center, or (as Luther put it) its "lord and king," Jesus Christ.

Christians will appropriately authorize their political stances, then, by reference to a christology, even though their christologies may differ. As I have said, Jesus Christ is (de facto) "bottom line" among Christians for faith, worship, mission, ethics, and politics. Feminist theologian Rosemary Radford Ruether stated the matter nicely in one of her earlier books, *To Change the World:*

> The center of Christian theology is not an idea, but a person, a historical person, Jesus of Nazareth. . . .
> One's portrait of Jesus ultimately expresses one's own normative statement about the Christian message to the world today. If there is no connection between these two, then there is indeed no need to continue to speak of Jesus as the Christ or the gospels as scripture.[24]

Her logic is compelling. Yet particular christologies will require to be defended by reference to their scriptural base and their historical, ethical, and contextual credibility.

Now it is apparent that, if faith is to offer significant political guidance, it will have to go beyond bland generalities. In Nazi Germany (and it is easy to see this and say it in the safety of North America sixty years later) Christians needed to say more than that Jesus Christ is *kurios;* they needed to spell out more specifically just why, under the lordship of Christ, "National Socialism" had to be opposed, to denounce in no uncertain terms the anti-Jewish policy of the government, and to offer a more appropriate social vision.[25] An ardent supporter of Barmen, Robert Osborn, has criticized the declaration in this way:

> Even the Confessing Church . . . tended to address itself only to the question of the integrity and truth of the church and initially attempted to avoid political questions. Not coincidentally, therefore, did the Barmen Declaration fail to address the Jewish question; it ignored both the Aryan paragraph, which excluded Jewish Christians from service in the church, and the situation of German Jewry as such.[26]

The authors and supporters of Barmen were not entirely liberated from the Lutheran doctrine of the two Kingdoms, wherein politics as such is the separate concern of the state. Christ's kingship, in this view, pertains to the church and to the individual soul. Thus Christ's claim upon the political realm was, in the last analysis, surrendered to Hitler.

But if Christ is truly to be acknowledged as *kurios,* political realities must come under the judgment of Christ. To speak faithfully, political/theological discourse must be disciplined out of its christological center. This is a painstaking and arduous task for the church, for to do so, actual conditions and occurrences must also be investigated. Jesus does not call us to make vague, abstract, moralistic or religious pronouncements, but to "interpret the signs of the times" (Matt. 16:3). Like him, we are to name the names of those who "devour widows' houses" (Mark 10:40). Like him we are to discern which powerholder is truly a "fox" (Luke 13:32). Like him we are not to remain innocuously in the "religious" sphere, but to engage ourselves in the actual life-and-death conflicts of the world. To do this we have to utilize not only the Bible, but also factual information, social scientific data and analysis, historical experience, and so on.[27] Theologians and preachers, and Christians generally in their political life, must seek more than a superficial understanding of what is happening in the social and cultural world around them. As Douglas Hall has argued so persuasively, their theology must be "contextual," i.e., it must speak acutely to particular circumstances in particular places and to prevalent ways of thinking and acting.[28] To speak in vague generalities will not do. Nor is this task to be undertaken only by academics, though academics have an important role to play in the process; rather it must be undertaken above all by people deeply engaged in actual life struggles. Without pretending to detailed expertise in economics or politics, political theology will have to have something to say concretely about the signs of the times: Who is it that devours widows' houses in our time and place? Where does the power lie in the present world-system? Who controls industry and technology, and for whose benefit? Who determines the direction of investment and employment, and in whose interest? Which kinds of social systems are relatively more liberating and productive of social justice? Karl Barth's famous dictum has to be seriously implemented: If we are to do theology or to preach the gospel faithfully, we will have to do so with the Bible in the one hand and the newspaper in the other!

None of this, however — not the social analysis, nor the exegesis of scripture, nor the ethics, nor even the theology — will be entirely "objective," "pure," or value-free. People inevitably bring particular perceptions and commitments to the theological and political task. This is where political "ideologies" and ideology critique must come into play.

Ideology: A Positive Necessity

It is common for the term "ideology" to be used pejoratively, as though ideology could be avoided, as though only "those other people" have ideologies. Marx usually used the term negatively to refer to the "superstructure" of ideas that serves the interest of the ruling class, a false consciousness to be avoided,[29] and many theologians follow Marx in this usage of the term.[30] Some religious people especially imagine that faith is enough, and that ideologies are unnecessary or undesirable. "Ideology," comments Paul Ricoeur ironically, "is the thought of my adversary, the thought of the other. He does not know it, but I do."[31] Ricoeur sees that ideology is inescapable and far too important to be treated in a merely negative manner. Unfortunately, a purely pejorative use of the term encourages us to think that we can be ideology-free or even apolitical in our theology and discipleship.

Latin American theologian Juan Luis Segundo offers a helpful discussion of the relation of faith to ideology, clearly distinguishing the two, while relating them positively. Faith, he argues, is an indispensable component or dimension of every human life and has to do with the absolute source of meaning and values.[32] Christians, specifically, have faith in the God revealed in Jesus Christ, the God who is love. Faith in the love of God gives value structure to Christian life. Ideology, on the other hand, has to do with analyses and strategies for the realization of meaning and values. An ideology, as Segundo uses the term, is "the system of goals and means that serves as the necessary backdrop for any human option or line of action."[33] Ideology in this positive sense bridges the gap between faith and concrete options in history. It is a vision of things, a perception (from the Greek *idein,* to perceive), which is instrumental for the realization of values. While faith is certainly not an ideology, it serves as "the foundation stone" for ideologies. Faith provides the reason for having an ideology, but it also relativizes and critiques every ideology. Faith in Jesus as *kurios* forbids that we bow down to any political system or system of ideas; that is, no ideology, however enlightened (whether socialism, or feminism, or environmentalism), may be absolutized. None of the liberation struggles may absolutize itself by claiming Christ as unambiguously on its side. Rather, as another author puts it, "Christ...may well claim some of them and Christians for them."[34]

However, Segundo goes on, "Faith without works is dead. Faith without ideologies is equally dead."[35] A faith unconnected to any particular perception of the world or any particular line of action remains ineffectual, or even destructive. The question is not, then, whether Christians will or should have "ideologies," but whether their ideologies are founded upon and congruent with faith in the gospel.

We may take the Nazi vs. Barmen situation again as an example. While Barmen and many members of the Confessing Church spoke in very general terms about the lordship of Christ, one Confessing leader, Dietrich Bonhoeffer (and there were others like him), made a very specific, concrete political commitment against Hitler. Bonhoeffer knew what was happening to the Jews. He had analyzed, both politically and theologically, what he came to see as the idolatry of Nazism and had reached an "ideology" in the positive sense — an analysis and a strategy that serve the ends of "faith." For him this meant, concretely, a risky political venture, i.e., joining the anti-Nazi resistance and, specifically, participating in the conspiracy to assassinate Hitler. He saw that "the Jewish question," as a political question, was also a theological question, that the political and the theological could not be separated. His commitment to the Jews and to Christ meant a particular, practical political and "ideological" commitment, which, as we know, finally led to his execution. It is not possible for Christians, if they wish to be faithful to Christ, to keep their hands clean of ideology, to remain safely above the battle about actual issues of justice and peace in the world. They must take sides ideologically and practically amid all the ambiguities of the political realm. This may mean joining and working hard for and within a political party, or participating in social justice movements, despite the fact that all such human organizations will be flawed and ambiguous in their actual goals and methods.

This distinction between faith and ideology is extremely important if we are to think clearly about the relationship between socialism and the gospel. We are not here comparing two ideologies, nor two faiths. Christianity is not an ideology, though it is capable of being used or instrumentalized as such, often becoming the tool of a dominant class or a cultural attitude. This is always a distortion of Christian faith. Socialism, on the other hand, is not a faith, though (like capitalism) it is capable of becoming religious in character, and so of taking on the absolutist characteristics of faith, becoming totalitarian. This is a distortion of socialism.

Love, Equality, and Class Struggle

It is not difficult to see why a theology of the love of God, especially the doctrine of the incarnation of God in Jesus Christ, predisposes many Christians immediately toward socialist ideology. The gospel proclaims that "God so loved the world" (John 3:16) that God's Word became flesh in Jesus Christ (John 1:14). God identified so utterly with the human condition in agape love that God entered into the human condition, taking upon God's very self the pain and consequence of human sin. The first letter of John draws out the ethical implications:

> Beloved, let us love one another, because love is from God; everyone who loves is born of God and knows God. Whoever does not love does not know God, for God is love. God's love was revealed among us in this way: God sent [the] only Son into the world so that we might live through him. In this is love, not that we loved God but that [God] loved us and sent [the] Son to be the atoning sacrifice for our sins. Beloved, since God loved us so much, we also ought to love one another. No one has ever seen God; if we love one another, God lives in us, and [God's] love is perfected in us. (1 John 4:7–12)

The confession that "God is love" in God's very self, that love is the very nature of the eternal God, that indeed the triune God is an eternal *koinonia,* communion of love, is closely tied by some theologians to the doctrine of the Trinity. The feminist theologian Elizabeth Johnson, for example, rejecting "classical theism," believes that God cannot be thought of as self-enclosed absolute; rather God's holy mystery is an unimaginable, open communion in herself. Such a vision of God nourishes coequal humanity in community.[36] Other theologians too speak of "social Trinity," which in turn is rooted in the doctrine of the incarnation of God in Jesus Christ. The doctrine of the Trinity assists us, according to Jürgen Moltmann, to overcome individualism in anthropology by developing simultaneously "a social personalism and a personal socialism."[37]

That "God is love" implies that love is the meaning and end of all created things. The governing ethical precept for Christians is the command of Jesus: Love God with heart, soul, strength, and mind, and love your neighbor as yourself (Luke 10:27). "On these two commandments hang all the law and the prophets" (Matt. 22:40). That God loves every human being, that "even the hairs of your head are all counted" (Matt. 10:30) gives every human being infinite worth and implies the equal worth of all. Love and care for neighbors are not limited to "the deserving," since we are, all of us, loved and forgiven regardless of our merit. For Christians the political notion of equality can rest, ultimately, only on this gracious, equal love of God for all and the command to love all alike. It is natural, then, that Christians, when they come to think and to act in the political sphere, will wish to embody love for all alike in the structures of society. They will imagine human society as a sharing and cooperative community of friends. In our present pluralist and secular societies we can no longer speak of a "Christian social order" as our parents or grandparents did only a generation or two ago.[38] Moltmann states the matter succinctly:

> One can derive from [the lordship of Christ] directives for the political discipleship of Christians in political life but not a metaphysics of the state that is equally valid for Christians and non-Christians. Christocratic ethics can only be discipleship ethics. It is ethics for Christians but not Christian ethics for the state. It is political ethics of the Christian community but not Christian politics of the civil community.[39]

Nevertheless, as citizens, Christians will naturally put whatever political weight they have on the side of social structures and systems that express (relatively well) the love of neighbor and of all neighbors alike.

"Love" for all alike does not mean simply "the greatest good for the greatest number." Following the practice and teaching of Jesus, as this is passed on to us in the New Testament, love of neighbor is especially love for those who are most oppressed and most in need. Jesus persistently took the side of the oppressed, the poor, and the marginalized: tax collectors and rejected women, poor widows, the lame, lepers and the blind, children, women in general, strangers, those in prison. He "emptied himself of all position and power to stand with those who had neither position nor power."[40] He came as one laid in a manger, one of the poor, and died finally as one of the victims of the powerful, in confrontation with them as "king of the Jews." This has been the emphasis of both liberation and feminist theologies. The latter especially have pointed out the way in which Jesus rejected all hierarchical relationships, consistently taking the side of those on the underside of social hierarchies and undermining the prevailing structures of male, patriarchal domination. While the maleness of Jesus has often been a problem for feminists, Elizabeth Johnson points out that it actually has some positive significance, in that Jesus, a male, renounces the hierarchical privileges of his maleness. Johnson argues that

> a certain appropriateness accrues to the historical fact that he was a male human being. If in a patriarchal culture a woman had preached compassionate love and enacted a style of authority that serves, she would most certainly have been greeted with a colossal shrug. Is this not what women are supposed to do by nature? But from a social position of male privilege Jesus preached and acted this way, and herein lies the summons.
>
> ... The cross thus stands as a poignant symbol of the "kenosis of patriarchy," the self-emptying of male dominating power in favor of the new humanity of compassionate service and mutual empowerment. On this reading Jesus' maleness is prophecy announcing from within the end of patriarchy, at least as divinely ordained.[41]

Jesus himself was so totally engaged and "on side" not only with women, but generally with the marginalized, oppressed, and poor, that he made class enemies of the Pharisees and Sadducees, and so also of the imperial Romans, and was executed as a political enemy of the state. To follow him in this in political life clearly means what is commonly called in liberation theology "the preferential option for the poor."[42]

Taking sides with the poor usually means becoming involved in political conflict of one kind or another, even engaging in what many socialists have called "class struggle." Gutiérrez spoke very clearly about class struggle in his first major book (now a theological classic), *A Theology of Liberation*, pointing out that it is a fact that no one can deny.[43] There is no question of "promoting" class struggle, which obviously constitutes a problem for the universality of Christian love and the unity of the church. Yet,

> what the groups in power call "advocating" class struggle is really an expression of a will to abolish its causes, to abolish them, not cover them over, to eliminate the appropriation by a few of the wealth created by the work of the many and not to make lyrical calls to social harmony. It is a will to build a socialist society, more just, free, and human, and not a society of superficial and false reconciliation and equality.... To build

a just society today necessarily implies the active and conscious participation in the class struggle that is occurring before our eyes.[44]

There are those who argue that Gutiérrez has since backed off from his clear theological commitment to socialism, whether under the depressing political realities of the 1970s and 1980s or under pressures from Rome. By 1986 he was saying that "socialism" is not essential to liberation theology, that one can do liberation theology without espousing socialism.[45] However, what Gutiérrez meant by this is open to interpretation. What, after all, is "socialism"? Presumably by 1986 he no longer hoped for a vast Latin American political revolution, like that of China. After the experiences of Chile and Nicaragua, to name only two, it was now apparent that no such socialist option would be allowed in the foreseeable future.[46] Moreover, the statist style of "socialism" that held power in the U.S.S.R. and eastern Europe was certainly *not* something to be espoused by liberationists. It is impossible to believe that Gutiérrez is now reconciled to existing international capitalism. At any rate, the logic of his position as stated earlier was very persuasive: A Christian option for the poor and engagement in socialist class struggle precisely follows God's option for the poor made visible in Christ.

Ambiguity about the word "socialism" is evident also in recent statements of another major liberation theologian, Leonardo Boff. In an interview in 1994, Boff speaks of the "fall of socialism," by which he clearly means the fall of eastern Soviet bloc communism. He notes the absence of freedom and democracy in that system but points out that "socialism" in the minds of its founders was the real name of true democracy. He vigorously denies that the fall of "socialism" means the permanent triumph of capitalism or the market, as though these are now shown to be the true way. Boff goes on to argue that "democratic socialism" must be seen as the historical alternative for arriving at more dignified forms of work for everyone, and his opposition to capitalism is unrelenting.[47]

It is not only the theologians of liberation who have affirmed that the call to love the neighbor implies a political "option for the poor." Karl Barth (himself a democratic socialist in his political commitment) many years after Barmen but still predating liberation theology, testifies to God's own "option for the poor" in words that affirm God's participation in "class struggle":

God always takes His stand unconditionally and passionately on this side and on this side alone: against the lofty and on behalf of the lowly; against those who already enjoy right and privilege and on behalf of those who are denied it and deprived of it.[48]

The "lowly," it must be said, cannot be understood entirely in class terms, and this has been one of the limitations of much Marxist thought. It is not only workers as such, or the "proletariat" who have been in class conflict with owners and managers, but other marginalized or powerless groups as well require the solidarity of workers and of socialists generally: aboriginal peoples, women, the aged, the disabled, those who suffer because of race, ethnicity, or religion.[49] "Option for the poor" might better be expressed "option for the marginalized" or "for the oppressed." It is not that all the people who belong to these groups will wish to call themselves socialist, yet socialists, if they are committed to the community of friends, must be concerned with the well-being of all these people, and not only with "workers" or the poor as such.

It is evident that the ethic of love, founded in the love of God in Jesus Christ, is fundamental to a Christian socialist option. However, it is not obvious to all Christians that the ethic of love, or even the option for the poor, automatically implies a socialist political stance. The argument is not decided simply by citing the command to love, since people can disagree as to what really best serves the interests of neighbors and the poor. The Christian's choice of an "ideology" will certainly have to be informed by love but is not a simple case of applying the ethic of love to politics. Doctrines of sin and salvation will also be operative. Not only love, but faith and hope also inform the Christian's political options and commitments. Social analysis and historical experience will also come into play. The question is not only: How do we best love our neighbors in the political sphere? It is also: How much may we realistically hope for? What is the goal and end of social and political life in relation to the Reign of God?

Christian political theology, then, must seek to clarify the theological significance of particular political "ideologies" in view of their commitment to live in love for the neighbor, especially those oppressed, and in light of faith and hope in Jesus Christ. Part of its task is to throw light upon the theological/religious significance of various political options, attitudes, or commitments. It may do so about very particular political problems and issues, such as aboriginal self-government, the status of women, the financing of medicare or the welfare system, plans for urban development or taxation, gun control, or involvement in a particular war. In such matters theologians and preachers are wise not to claim special expertise on economic and sociological questions, nor to speak *ex cathedra,* yet they cannot escape bringing faith and love to bear upon these practical matters. If "war is too important to be left to the generals," then politics and economics are too important to be left to social scientists and politicians. Similarly, political theology must reflect upon broad political philosophies, systems, and ideologies, such as socialism and capitalism, and attempt to shed the light of faith upon them, providing not only criticism, but also vision and hope.

My aim here, then, is to think theologically about socialism, especially in face of the apparent world triumph of capitalism in the 1990s. For Christians, basic questions include: "How much do we dare hope for a social and political future that embodies and expresses love for the neighbor?" Or, "How should we relate utopian hopes to our hope for the Reign of God?" Or, "To what kind of social and economic life is the Spirit of God leading us?"

Chapter 2

Utopia and the Gospel of the Reign of God

Utopia

The Reign of God is the key utopian concept of the gospel. "U-topia" simply means "no place," or that which has not yet appeared on the earth. God's Reign (or, in the more familiar language, God's Kingdom) means God's Rule, God's will being done. The hope for "another place," for a different and better world, is foundational in the biblical tradition. What could be more basic to the Hebraic/biblical mind than the story of Abraham and his hope for a future blessed by God?

> Now the Lord said to Abram, "Go from your country and your kindred and your father's house to the land that I will show you. I will make of you a great nation, and I will bless you, and make your name great, so that you will be a blessing. I will bless those who bless you, and the one who curses you I will curse; and in you all the families of the earth shall be blessed. (Gen. 12:1–3)

The God of Abraham is the God of the promise, who reappears again and again in the life of the descendants of Abraham, in the time of Moses, in the time of the prophets, to promise a new and different future and to lead the people forward to the realization of the divine will. Beginning with Abraham the biblical story is a vision of universal history as a meaningful movement forward and of humanity and human beings as responsible actors within that divine movement. Through the Jews a truly revolutionary element was introduced into history — the notion that things can change, that this world is one in which it is legitimate to hope. The "ontocratic" structures (static structures of being) — of birth, growth, decay, death, and the eternal cycles of rebirth — are burst open. The liberating Lord of Israel is precisely the One who raised up Moses and set free the Hebrew slaves. The true

God was the One who "opted" for the Jews, an obscure and marginalized nation, to initiate a history that is leading the whole creation to a new and qualitatively different future. The exodus of the Jewish slaves from Egypt under the power and inspiration of their liberating God can be seen as the most fundamentally revolutionary event in the history of the ancient world, breaking through the pattern of divinized rulers and fixed class structures, demonstrating that "it is the force of possibility that rules the universe."[1] What we find later in the prophets of Israel is the confident hope that the God of the exodus has more in store for the people, and indeed for the whole of humanity and all creation. A. T. Van Leeuwen (and a good many other authors) have seen this biblical sense of history as having fueled the extraordinary historical dynamism of the Christian west and, later, the secularized, Enlightenment idea of progress, with all its far-reaching implications for science, technology, and political revolution.[2] Biblical prophetic hope, disseminated in the western world through Christianity, broke the bonds of fate and created an explosion of expectations for a new and different future in which

> every valley shall be filled, and every mountain and hill shall be made low, and the crooked shall be made straight, and the rough ways made smooth; and all flesh shall see the salvation of God. (Luke 3:5–6, from Isa. 40:3–5)

But today in our post-Holocaust world the idea of progress has long been in crisis, and vast numbers of "postmodern" people, having lost both their Christian faith and the modernist faith in progress, find no reason to work or hope for a meaningful future. Lesslie Newbigin writes with eloquence of the loss of hope among contemporary people:

> World history as it was taught in European schools for more than 1,000 years...was based on the biblical vision....Under the influence of the Enlightenment, this became secularized in the doctrine of inevitable progress, a doctrine which lasted perhaps up to the First World War....The doctrine survived in apocalyptic form in Marxism, which was strongly attractive to Europeans between the wars, but it also has lost its power as a key for explaining the whole human story.[3]

This loss of faith in the future leads to despair and resignation. Some retreat into their private lives, into privatistic, otherworldly forms of piety, or merely into hedonistic pursuits. Hopelessness about a credible, sustainable environment, about the possibilities of retaining, let alone expanding, the sphere of social justice, leads many to ethical and spiritual cynicism. After all, as Newbigin says,

> You cannot have hopeful and responsible action without some vision of a possible future. To put it another way, if there is no point in the story as a whole there is no point in my own action. If the story is meaningless, any action of mine is meaningless. The loss of a vision for the future necessarily produces the typical phenomenon of our society which the sociologists call anomie, a state in which publicly accepted norms and values have disappeared.[4]

If the history of the world has indeed any meaning or goal, this would presumably not be knowable until its end. Basic to Christian faith, of course, is the belief that the meaning of the human story has been disclosed in the midst of history, precisely and specifically within God's history with Israel, and in the Christ event. It is from within that tradition that Christians constantly pray for God's Reign: "Thy Kingdom come, thy will be done, on earth. . . . for thine is the Kingdom, and the power and the glory." This is an eschatological (end time) concept, expressing faith and hope that God's truth and righteousness will ultimately prevail. Moreover, according to the gospel, God's Reign has already decisively broken into the world in the life, death, and resurrection of Jesus Christ. That is, the goal and destiny of humanity and creation has been disclosed in the midst of history. This is what it means to confess that Jesus is the Christ (Messiah). Further, the Reign of God is a growing reality, and we have a part to play in its growth. Our human contribution toward God's Reign, our stewardship and responsibility for its growth in the world, can be closely associated with the political concept of utopia.

The concept was created by Thomas More, that bold and brave Catholic politician who was eventually beheaded by King Henry VIII. *Ou* (not), + *topos* (place), or no place: that which nowhere exists. Again (as in the case of "ideology") I choose to use the word "utopia" in a positive rather than in a pejorative sense. It has been common to use the term negatively to refer to a kind of impractical, unrealistic dream. Marx and Engels spoke sharply against "utopian socialism" and the "utopian dream" as a merely moralistic, sometimes religious aspiration lacking realism or rigor, devoid of serious analysis and strategy. Marx, who reserved some of his most cutting sarcasm for his so-called "utopian socialist" rivals, spoke of

> the robe of speculative cobwebs, embroidered with flowers and rhetoric, steeped in the dew of sickly sentiment...in which the German Socialists wrapped their sorry "eternal truths."[5]

The word "utopian" has been used pejoratively also by some Christians, especially neo-orthodox theologians. Paul Tillich, for example, having seen personally the horrors of the World War I battlefield and then watching the rise of Nazism, used the term to refer to a naive assumption that the Kingdom of God will be realized in history, as though "the ought" will inevitably be transmuted into the "is."[6] Tillich contrasted "utopian" socialism with the "religious socialism" that he and others attempted to establish in Germany prior to the victory of Nazism. Reinhold Niebuhr too, though a politically active socialist in his younger years, experienced with his generation the disillusionments of the great depression and two world wars. He also sadly watched the growing corruption and tyranny of communism in Russia and came to oppose "utopianism" to "Christian realism." The latter recognizes the all-pervasive reality of sin in human affairs and tends, therefore, to be pessimistic about what can be accomplished in the socio-political realm. Niebuhr wrote cogently of

> the brutal character of the behavior of all human collectives, and the power of self-interest and collective egoism in all inter-group relations. Failure to recognize the stubborn resistance of group egoism to all moral and inclusive social objectives inevitably involves...unrealistic and confused political thought.[7]

Niebuhr's critique of liberal Social Gospel socialism is reminiscent of Marx's attack on the "utopians" of his day:

> It is sentimental and romantic to assume that any education or example will ever completely destroy the inclination of human nature to seek special advantages at the expense of, or in indifference to, the needs and interests of others.[8]

Niebuhr thought that the "utopian illusions" of communism made it more dangerous than Nazism, masking the evil domination of an oligarchy behind lofty moral ideals.[9] His insight and warning are important, yet his "realism" has sometimes had the effect of discouraging struggles for justice and peace, convincing people that not very much can be accomplished for the melioration of human affairs. Despite Niebuhr's own life-long intelligent commitment to social justice, his theology of "Christian realism" has sometimes been used to encourage resignation rather than active hope for a better social order.

But the theology of hope (Moltmann) the other political theologies that appeared in the mid-1960s (J.-B. Metz, Dorothee Soelle, etc.), and the theologies of liberation, which began to appear about the end of the 1960s, have encouraged us again to be positive about "utopia" and once again to link our hopes for change in history to our stewardship of God's Reign. These theologies are not innocent of the tragedy and misery of human existence. Their authors have passed through the experience of the world wars, Auschwitz, Hiroshima, Vietnam, and are keenly aware of the gross oppression and poverty of the Third World. Moltmann, who experienced the World War II battlefield, endured three years in a prisoner of war camp and the disillusionment and despair of postwar Germany, could not be accused of naive optimism. His theology has been, from the first, a theology of the cross, renouncing the cheerful optimism of any *theologia gloriae*. His second major book, *The Crucified God*, makes this abundantly clear. Nevertheless, for him hope in God's future remains the central and distinctive character of Christian faith:

> Christianity is completely and entirely and utterly hope — a looking forward and a forward direction; hope is not just an appendix. So Christianity inevitably means a new setting forth and a transformation of the present. Eschatology ... is not just one of Christianity's many doctrines. It is quite simply the medium of the Christian faith, the keynote, the daybreak colors of a new expected day which bathe everything in their light. For the Christian faith lives from the raising of the crucified Christ and reaches out towards the promises of Christ's universal future. But that means that the hoping person can never come to terms with the laws and necessities of this world ... This is why whenever faith develops into hope it does not make people serene and placid; it makes them restless. It does not make them patient; it makes them impatient. Instead of being reconciled to existing reality they begin to suffer from it and to resist it.[10]

It was in much the same hopeful spirit that Gustavo Gutiérrez salvaged the concept of utopia in *A Theology of Liberation*. Utopia, he insisted, expresses aspirations for qualitatively different social relationships. Borrowing from Paulo Freire, Gutiérrez said that utopia always has two aspects: *annunciation* and *denunciation.*

> Utopia necessarily means a denunciation of the existing order. Its deficiencies are to a large extent the reason for the emergence of a utopia. The repudiation of a dehumanizing situation is an unavoidable aspect of utopia. It is a matter of a complete rejection which attempts to strike at the roots of the evil. That is why utopia is revolutionary and not reformist.[11]

But utopia cannot stop at mere denunciation. It must propose some alternative vision, which is implied precisely by the denunciation:

> Utopia is also an annunciation . . . of what is not yet, but will be; it is the forecast of a different order of things, a new society. It is the field of creative imagination which proposes the alternative values to those rejected. . . . Utopia moves forward; it is a pro-jection into the future, a dynamic and mobilizing factor in history. This is the prospective character of utopia.[12]

Gutiérrez also thinks that utopia must be accompanied by a praxis (practice or action that is informed by critical theory). Otherwise it remains within the realm of academic discussion and provides no practical dynamism for transformation. Further, the gospel "does not provide a utopia for us; this is a human work." The gospel is the foundation of meaning and hope, but it must be concretized in particular historical situations by human plans and projects.[13]

Such considerations prompt us to ask whether the alternative to positive utopian thought is not a faithless, despairing resignation to things as they are. Or is utopian thought essentially illusionary, as Niebuhr warned?

When Thomas More wrote his *Utopia* he coined the term to name his vision of the good society. More, rather humorously, depicted an egalitarian, communal society in his work of 1516, "Concerning the Best State of a Commonwealth and the New Island of Utopia."[14] As I have said, Utopia literally means "no place." Or, alternatively, *eu-topia* can mean "happy" or "fortunate place." And indeed there is no thoroughly happy place on earth where human beings actually live together entirely according to the will of God. Nevertheless, it is right for us to have utopian visions of the future. It is especially appropriate for Christians, for whom every status quo falls short of God's will — i.e., all human social and political arrangements fail to realize the Reign of God. When we pray "Thy Kingdom come, Thy will be done on earth," we are praying for the transformation of the world, that is, for the coming of God's Reign, and in so praying, we commit ourselves to participate in such transformation.

Christians have usually believed that God's will will be done in the world only at the end time (when God's Kingdom comes), i.e., when, in the fulfillment of history, time as we know it is taken up into the glory of God's eternity. Tragically, this belief has often functioned as a dampener for utopian visions. Christians easily become convinced that nothing truly new can be achieved and so tend, often, to accept what is, in the vague hope that one day God will make all things right. This is understandable, considering what a qualitatively different world the Bible promises. Recall some of the truly utopian (no place) visions that the Bible offers about God's future. It is a new creation indeed, where "the wolf shall dwell with the lamb, and the leopard shall lie down with the kid" (Isa. 11:6). It is a world without sickness: "Then the lame shall leap like a hart, and the tongue of the dumb sing for joy" (Isa. 35:6). It is a world of peace: "They shall beat their swords into ploughshares and their spears into pruning hooks" (Mic. 4:3). It is a world of economic prosperity, justice, and security: "they shall [all] sit everyone under their own vine and their own fig tree and none shall make them afraid" (Mic. 4:4). Luke expresses his understanding of the meaning of the coming of Christ in socially revolutionary terms: "He has brought down the powerful from their thrones, and lifted up the lowly; he has filled the hungry with good things and sent the rich empty away" (Luke 1:52–53). In "a new heaven and a new earth," God "will wipe away every tear from their eyes. Death will be no more; mourning and crying and pain will be no more, for the first things have passed away" (Rev. 21:4). So unknown are such things in the history of humanity, so far beyond the possibility of human achievement, that Christians may easily conclude that striving for greater justice, peace, and wholeness in the world is a kind of presumption. God's Reign is God's work and not human work, we have often been told, and utopia is nothing but a dream of humanity's hubris.

Resurrection, Salvation, and
Historical Materialism

It is central to the proclamation of the New Testament that the Messiah has come, that the Reign of God (i.e., salvation) has already dawned in the life, death, and resurrection of Jesus. Particularly it is the resurrection of Jesus that is foundational and determinative for Christian faith: "If Christ has not been raised, then our preaching is in vain and your faith is in vain" (1 Cor. 15:14). Not that cross or resurrection can be ranked, one more important than the other. The resurrection is the raising of the crucified Christ; the cross is seen in light of the resurrection as the cross of the risen one (Moltmann). Yet the resurrection was the *sine qua non* for the apostles' recognition of Jesus as Lord and Christ. While the cross was a public event and part of the violence of this world, the resurrection was an eschatological event, vindicating Jesus as the Christ of God, revealing the salvific meaning of his death, and inaugurating the new creation of humanity and of heaven and earth. Leonardo Boff interprets the resurrection of Jesus as a preappearance, or preview, of utopia — the victory of the innocent victim over the unjust oppressor and the conquest of life over death.[15] Similarly, Moltmann sees the resurrection as an apocalyptic event — truly an event in history, truly something that happened to Jesus himself and not only subjectively to the apostles — yet a qualitatively unique event in which

> God unveils something ahead of time which is still hidden and inaccessible to the cognition of the present aeon, or world time. Under the present conditions of knowledge, the secrets of the end-time and God's future new world are still veiled and unknowable, for the present world of sin and violence cannot sustain the new world of God's righteousness and justice. That is why this righteousness of God's is going to create a new world, and will be manifested only at the end of the time of this world, and in the daybreak of the new creation. Only then will "the glory of the Lord appear." But even in the history of this world there are already revelations of the new world to come, revelations ahead of time.... The christophanies [appearances of the risen Jesus] were viewed as radiance thrown ahead of itself, the radiance of God's coming glory on the first day of the new world's creation.[16]

In the resurrection of Jesus God's saving intention and destiny for the world is disclosed "proleptically" (*pro-lepsis* — a preview, or pre-appearance). God is the one who "makes all things new" (Rev. 21:5). In the resurrection of Jesus, God is revealed as the One who "has brought down the powerful from their thrones, and lifted up the lowly" (Luke 1:52). This event is not simply about the salvation of souls, nor is this event a merely spiritual one. The New Testament witnesses go out of their way to stress the bodily nature of this resurrection. Although no one knows exactly what happened in Jesus' resurrection and no one can say precisely what was the nature of his risen "body," it is emphatically clear in the New Testament that the risen Jesus is no mere ghost. It is, by the power of God, flesh and blood that overcomes the power of death. It is this physical, fleshly order, which humans share with animals, plants, and inorganic matter, that is given in the resurrection of Jesus the promise of new creation and a share in the future of Christ:

> For the creation waits with eager longing for the revealing of the children of God; for the creation was subjected to futility, not of its own will but by the will of the one who subjected it, in hope that the creation itself will be set free from its bondage to decay and will obtain the freedom of the glory of the children of God. We know that the whole creation has been groaning in labor pains until now. (Rom. 8:19–22)

Moltmann declares, "The raised body of Christ therefore acts as an embodied promise for the whole creation." The resurrection has become the universal law of creation, "not merely for human beings, but for animals, plants, stones, and all cosmic life systems as well."[17] All of this implies, for personal life, a "spirituality of the body and the spirituality of the earth,"[18] a true spiritual rejoicing in bodily life and in the beauty and dynamism of the material universe.

But if we proclaim that Jesus is indeed risen, what does this imply politically? Certainly that God's salvation, disclosed in cross and resurrection, is not the salvation of souls for another world, but the salvation of this world. The resurrection of the bodily Jesus means that "bodily life is eternal" (Franz Hinkelammert[19]). This is the truly radical and scandalous claim of the first Christians — not that the body of Jesus was resuscitated to mortal existence, but transformed, or glorified: "We know that Christ, being raised from the dead, will never die again; death no longer has dominion over him" (Rom. 6:9). This was fundamental to the early church. What a bloodless and abstract thing Christianity is without it! Politically, it means that the needs and dignity of bodily life cannot be despised or spiritualized away. To spiritualize is to dehistoricize and to depoliticize. The reduction of salvation to the salvation of the soul, or to authentic existence, says Moltmann, "unconsciously abandoned nature to its disastrous exploitation by human beings."[20] Elizabeth Johnson too sees that because of Jesus' bodily resurrection,

> There can be no dichotomy between matter and spirit or prizing of one over the other, but matter itself is a treasure related to God. Resurrection announces that this will always be so, for the body itself is glorified in the power of Wisdom's spirit, not discarded. Furthermore, it is the tortured and executed body of Jesus that is raised. This grounds Christian hope for a future for all the dead and explicitly for all those who are raped, tortured, and unjustly destroyed in the continuing torment of history.[21]

Bodily life and this fleshly, material world that God has redeemed and for which God intends an eternal future in "a new heaven and new earth" (Rev. 21:1) must be respected and cherished. Love of bodily and material life implies a politics of hope for the future of this world. For Christians, the foundation of that hope is precisely the bodily resurrection of Jesus.

Here the congruity of biblical faith with some aspects of Marx's historical materialism becomes visible. By historical materialism (as indicated briefly in the previous chapter) I refer to Marx's brilliant debunking of "idealist" notions of humanity and of history that did not take into account the fundamental need of human beings to meet their material needs. He believed that the need of all human beings to provide food and shelter has always, of necessity, been the prime determinant of human activity and history making. This was not a kind of cynicism on his part; Marx was far too utopian to be cynical. He simply recognized the neediness of human beings. He knew it was impossible to understand the struggles of history or the structure of societies without reference to the "mode of production," that is, the means the people use to meet their basic physical requirements, and the "relations of production," that is, the human power relationships according to which material goods are produced. To speak of the "congruity" of historical materialism with biblical faith is not to suggest that Christians can accept a wholly deterministic, materialist, or atheistic philosophy (which was not of any great interest to Marx at any rate). The biblical history certainly testifies to divine and human agency in the making of history. Yet this history has to do with social and economic relationships. It has to do with finding new land (Abraham), with emancipation from slavery (Moses), with international war and struggles for hegemony (Jeremiah), with class struggles between the rich and powerful, and the poor and the weak (Amos). Christians, in light of Exodus and Resurrection, could never accept a theory of closed historical/economic determinism or a notion of the "iron laws of history" (and it is debatable among scholars of Marx to what extent he was really an economic determinist in his interpretation of history). Yet the necessity to sustain bodily life and struggles for power over land and labor are basic both to Marx's vision of history and to the biblical story. Nothing could be more earthy or "material" than the story of the relationship between the Spirit (the Wind) of Yahweh and the people of Israel. Nothing could be more fleshly than the story of the incarnation of God in the human Jesus, his eating and drinking with marginalized folk, his engagement in the social struggles of his time and place, his bloody execution by crucifixion, and his bodily resurrection to life. The biblical story of God's engagement with human history is a story of flesh and blood, of history and political struggle. I am not suggesting that Marx's central theory is already found in the Bible. I am suggesting that believers in Exodus and Exile, Incarnation, Cross, and Resurrection, should not find anything particularly shocking or surprising about Marx's suggestion that history and society must be understood in material/economic terms. Nor should Christians be shocked by theories of class and social conflict, following, as they do, one who was ignominiously executed as the loser in just such a struggle, yet raised to life as the sign of the victory of the victims of history.

Stewardship/Mission

Key biblical and theological concepts of great importance for political theology are stewardship and mission. The decisive inbreaking of God's Reign in Jesus Christ and his resurrection, and the assured hope of its ultimate victory, is basic to Christian faith. But do human beings have any responsibility for the coming of God's Reign? Is participation in historical process part of the Christian mission? There is much in the New Testament about the call to "enter the Kingdom" and to serve and nurture it. The "Reign" is a growing reality, like mustard seed or yeast (Luke 13:17–20), and human beings are called to the stewardship of God's Reign.[22] According to the parables of stewardship, those who are given responsibility for their master's kingdom are to extend his realm with the "talents" that are given to them (Luke 19:12–27, Matt. 25:14–30). God's Reign is precisely the reign of justice, love, peace, and wholeness, which we are called to serve in the power of the Holy Spirit. In Matthew, the parable of stewardship is followed immediately by the parable of the sheep and the goats (Matt. 25:31–46), which enjoins upon the nations the care of the hungry and thirsty, the stranger, the naked, the sick, and the imprisoned. The fact that, according to this parable, it is "all the nations" that are gathered for judgment, implies that it is not only individual, but social righteousness that is called for. Those in need cannot be adequately cared for on the basis of individual charity, but as members of human communities that must be ordered and structured in ways that serve the needs of all.

The theme of mission is also relevant to political theology. The mission is that which we are *sent* to do: "As the Father has sent me, so I send you. When he had said this he breathed on them and said to them, 'Receive the Holy Spirit' " (John 20:21). Christians are sent into the world to participate in the continuing mission of Jesus Christ. The Spirit that was in and upon him empowers his followers to continue his work in the service of God's Reign. It is clear in many New Testament passages that the mission of Jesus Christ has a political character. Of course, to say that Jesus was *political* is not to say that he was a politician, seeking office or political power. It does mean that his mission had to do with power in human relationships.

> The Spirit of the Lord is upon me, because he has anointed me to bring good news to the poor. He has sent me to proclaim release to the captives and recovery of sight to the blind, to let the oppressed go free. (Luke 4:18)

In the Song of Mary the significance of the birth of Jesus to a lowly and humble woman is seen in political terms:

> He has brought down the powerful from their thrones, and lifted up the lowly; he has filled the hungry with good things, and sent the rich away empty. (Luke 1:52–53)

The story of the flight of Jesus' parents with their newborn infant into Egypt to escape the wrath of King Herod (Matt. 2:13–18) signifies that Jesus is dangerous to the privileged and powerful, who will stop at nothing to be rid of him. All the powerful forces of Israel and Rome, we are told, came together to eradicate from their midst the one who undermined their power and exposed their corruption. This is the one who would say, "All authority in heaven and on earth is given to me" (Matt. 28:18). Rulers and systems can be defied, because "at the name of Jesus every knee should bend, in heaven and on earth and under the earth, and every tongue confess that Jesus Christ is Lord" (Phil. 2:10). Yet this authority is entirely that of the footwasher, the crucified one, the gentle authority of one who liberates:

> I will put my Spirit upon him, and he will proclaim justice to the Gentiles.... He will not break a bruised reed or quench a smoldering wick until he brings justice to victory. And in his name the Gentiles will hope. (Matt. 12:18–21)

It is difficult not to get the message that Christ's mission is the transformation of human relations in this world, specifically for the lifting up of the oppressed and poor, and that the mission of Christians is to proclaim and participate in this continuing mission of the risen Christ.

This implies, I believe, that we are to be a people who strive after utopia, a people who live in anticipation, who "dream dreams" and "see visions" (Joel 2:28) We are called to dream about a quality of human life and society that has never been known before, and not only to dream, but to strive for the realization of dreams. Or, to put it another way, we are called to "salvific activity."

Engagement in such dreaming and practical action toward the realization of dreams must be understood in terms of salvation. This very basic biblical concept has to do not simply with the forgiveness of sins and eternal life beyond death. These are indeed basic to the gospel, but they are not the whole of the gospel. Salvation is for this world and for historical time. This has been a fundamental emphasis of liberation theology, expressed so clearly by Gutiérrez:

> Salvation is not something otherworldly, in regard to which the present life is merely a test. Salvation — the communion of men with God and the communion of men among themselves —

is something which embraces all human reality, transforms it, and leads it to its fullness in Christ: "Thus the center of God's salvific design is Jesus Christ, who by his death and resurrection transforms the universe and makes it possible for man to reach fulfillment as a human being. This fulfillment embraces every aspect of humanity: body and soul, spirit, individual and society, person and cosmos, time and eternity" [citing a document of the Latin American bishops].[23]

Although salvation is entirely God's work (*sola gratia*), human beings are nevertheless called to salvific activity in the service of God's Reign. All struggle against injustice, all practical striving toward peace, is taken up and used by the Holy Spirit for the growth of God's Reign. This does not mean that by our human efforts, by social action, or by new political arrangements we will complete the end-time new creation of all things. We cannot create, through politics, science, or education, "the new heaven and new earth," nor raise the dead to eternal life, nor abolish sin from the earth. Nevertheless (borrowing words from Gutiérrez): "the historical, political liberating event is the growth of the Kingdom and is a salvific event; but it is not the coming of the Kingdom, not all of salvation."[24]

It is a sign of hope for us, a sign of the presence and growth of the Kingdom, that generations before us have engaged in just such "salvific" and indeed utopian activity. American abolitionists dreamed of a society without slavery, and this was thought to be unrealistic idealism. Social Gospel Christians in Canada — socialists like J. S. Woodsworth and Tommy Douglas — dreamed of a society where medical care would be available to all alike, and this was dismissed as impracticable. Suffragettes and early feminists like Nellie McClung dreamed of the vote for women and of a time when women would be educated and share with men in all the professions and in political life, and this was thought to be laughable. More recently, the enemies of apartheid in South Africa dreamed of a nonracial democratic society, and few expected that it could happen in this century. Dreams have been realized. "Utopias," utterly new, positive, and constructive things, never seen before, have actually appeared in history. No doubt (to borrow insight from Marx) material conditions made the world ripe for these developments; yet they were also the fruit of determined human struggle. People of faith find the Spirit of God at work in the realization of such dreams.

Sin and the Limits of Utopia

We have said that the full realization of God's will for the world awaits the end and fulfillment of history in God's eternal Reign. In Christian thought this is essentially because of human sin. "Sin" in the Bible is, first of all, the alienation of humanity from God, the blind and deaf refusal of human beings to trust God. Sin places trust in the nondivine instead of in God, turning the nondivine into an idol. The idol that Jesus himself identifies is mammon, or money:

> No one can serve two masters; for a slave will either hate the one and love the other, or be devoted to the one and despise the other. You cannot serve God and wealth. (Matt. 6:24)

Human creatures, resenting and evading the authority of God, seek to be "like God, knowing good and evil" (Gen. 3:5), finding wisdom and truth for themselves. The result of this is not freedom, but alienation from God, from neighbor, from oneself, and from the natural order. In the poetry of Genesis 3, the humans hide themselves from God and from each other. When accused, the man accuses the woman, who in turn accuses the serpent. The man and woman no longer see each other as gift. The neighbor is no longer one to be loved and cherished as co-worker in the human task of overcoming the chaos and cultivating the garden of the earth. They now see one another as rivals, to be outdone, to be accused. Having rejected the authority of God, they are no longer free to be "for the neighbor," but are bound in subjection to self. The poet goes on to depict the condition of bitter estrangement that grips the woman and man in their relationship and in their relationship to the animal realm and the earth (Gen. 3:14–19).

The mythical poetry of Genesis speaks to us profoundly of the tragedy of human sin as a trap or prison into which human beings have fallen. The New Testament sees sin in light of the cross of Christ and his resurrection, which disclose the utter lostness of human beings without God's grace. The doctrine of *sola gratia* (salvation by grace alone) implies that human sin is so profound and all-pervasive that there is nothing in human beings by which we can pull ourselves out of the trap into which we have fallen. Traditional doctrines of "original sin" are attempts to understand the predictable, inevitable, and systemic character of the sinful human condition.[25] As soon as we are able to reflect upon our lives we find that we are already sinners. We have not consciously decided to become sinful; we find ourselves already estranged from God and neighbor. This is true, in that human beings are born into an alienated race and into societies marked by selfishness and greed, in which people are against each other rather than for each other. The theologies of this century, whether Social Gospel, neo-orthodox, liberationist, or feminist, as different as they are from each other, have all taught us to see sin as not only individual, but social and systemic. The alienation that marks the condition of the individual is evident in the way in which our societies are organized. Christian socialists especially have emphasized this social and systemic dimension of sin and its embodiment in capitalism. Unfortunately we now know all too well that sin is embodied also in every kind of social system, including socialist ones.

It is especially important for us here to reflect upon this social or systemic nature of human sin. Jon Sobrino, Salvadoran liberation theologian, is particularly acute in this regard. He points out that for the Jesus of the New Testament, sin is essentially sin against the Kingdom. Like the prophets before him, he denounced especially the public, social, and structural aspect of sin. The social dimension of sin is the failure to anticipate the coming Reign of God in our life together here and now. Jesus particularly attacks the hypocrisy of those who have wealth and power. He hurls anathemas at the Pharisees because they pay no attention to justice, at the rich who will not share their wealth and power with the poor. These anathemas, Sobrino points out, are aimed not at individuals but at groups, and at the abuse of economic, religious, and intellectual power by privileged groups or parties against less privileged groups.[26] The point is a common but very important one, articulated well by Radford Ruether:

> This means the church has to speak, not simply of personal sin, but of social sin, of sin as collective and institutionalized violence and greed. Social sin is not just the sum of the sins of individual sinners. It becomes a world that we inherit and that biases our opportunities, either as oppressed people or as privileged people, even before we have been able to make personal choices. This means that even people of good will do evil and profit by evil because of their privileged location in this system. This sense of social sin gives liberation theology a new understanding of the Christian doctrine of inherited sin, not as sin inherited through biology, but through society.[27]

Niebuhr and others who have warned against unrealistic dreams for history are right to this extent: Because of human sin history is not some inevitable onward and upward progress from ignorance to enlightenment, from evil to good. Nevertheless, we may not take sin more seriously than the possibilities of God's grace. The hope for the coming Reign of God, founded in the victory of the resurrection, can and should, despite the reality of sin, serve as an encouraging and beckoning horizon for all our human efforts to approximate God's Reign in our life here and now. The resurrection discloses to the eyes of faith that the world is not a closed system of material and economic necessity. We live in God's world, which is a world of open possibilities. The God who raises the dead shows us that, despite appearances, we are not simply trapped in a hopeless world. We are not here for nothing; what we do in history matters in God's eternal design. We know in faith that our strivings for humanization are not futile, but assured of ultimate fruition, and that, while we will not "build the Kingdom of God on earth" (as our admirable Social Gospel forebears sometimes thought), history is nevertheless a meaningful process in which the God of Israel is at work. Those who live within the tradition of Exodus, Resurrection, and Pentecost cannot then be hopeless about history, as though God's presence and activity in history terminated with the Christ event. Segundo states the alternatives nicely:

> It is incorrect to view history as a process which, after the occurrence of its culminating event in Christ's thirty-three years on earth, has degenerated into the succeeding passage of individual lives until all have passed before the divine Judge.[28]

It is not that humanity is "progressing" morally, as Enlightenment and liberal thinkers have believed. It is not that the condition of human sin will diminish, nor that, through progressive growth in righteousness, humanity will exceed the need for God's grace. History is nevertheless a process of construction because of the continuing activity of God and the faithful responding obedience and struggle of human beings. Segundo explains,

> What accumulates in history is not [humanity's] goodness or badness. The human species does not become more moral with its progress, but it is progress nonetheless. What we can and ought to transmit are the conditioning factors that will allow

love, which will ever continue to be the object of free choice and intense struggle, to unfold in all its possible dimensions.[29]

Hope — active hope — and not despair or resignation, must be basic to any Christian political theology.

Still, as the history of this century has taught us well, there is no guarantee or inevitability that the conditions of human life will improve from generation to generation. The dangers of tyranny and disaster always lurk just around the corner, and vigilance for justice, freedom, and peace will always be required in the circumstances of human history. And there are limits to what can be achieved in history. The biblical visions of the future, so beyond our reach, warn us that our dreaming for the future must take account of the incompleteness of God's creation and of human nature, and of the reality of sin. Even Thomas More in his utopia foresaw the need to ward off the danger of tyranny by structural and, if you like, constitutional safeguards; i.e., More's utopia involved the rule of law, magistrates and police, and checks and balances against the abuse of power. Despite its egalitarianism it was very hierarchical, and human freedom was considerably constrained. Why would he create an imaginary utopia, yet ironically depict it as flawed and in some respects undesirable? Presumably as a Christian More possessed a doctrine of sin and knew that no human society in history can be wholly good.[30] If we are to dream of utopia our dream must have some semblance of practical credibility. If we are to envisage a socialist society, we cannot assume an end to the history of sin. Our vision must relate to the real world and to real people and take account of actual historical experience. In this, surely, Reinhold Niebuhr was right.

It does not follow, however, that the doctrine of sin leads us away from socialism. In so many discussions of the relation of sin and socialism it is assumed that capitalism is "realistic," while socialism is naively optimistic about human nature, overlooking human selfishness and the need for incentives to work, save, and invest. No doubt this has sometimes been true. But there is another way to look at it. If human beings are indeed as sinful as the gospel implies, it is urgent that great power over others should not fall into the hands of a few individuals. The evolution of political democracy, placing limits on the tyranny of rulers over people, has been perhaps the great social achievement of the modern era. Those who govern must be answerable, precisely because no human being is wise enough or good enough to be entrusted with absolute power over others. Yet capitalism, increasingly in the late twentieth century, allows enormous economic power, and therefore social and political power, to fall into the hands of the few. George Grant, writing in 1960, stated the point well:

> The conditions under which men are able to exercise their self-interest have radically changed since the early days of market capitalism. Power is increasingly concentrated, so that most people have to pursue their individual gain within conditions set by the corporations, while the few who set the conditions operate the calculus of greed, ambition and self-interest to their own ends.[31]

If we are to speak of sin in relation to the present social-economic situation of multinational corporations, where national democratic structures are increasingly powerless to control the mobility and utilization of capital, it is not so much the "laziness" of unemployed workers as the ambition and greed of powerful capitalists that must concern us, as well as the need to distribute economic power as widely as possible, subjecting it to democratic control. Socialists, unlike capitalists, do not trust the benevolence of those private individuals who control capital. They would rather trust democratically elected government, not because people in government are necessarily more benevolent than those in private business, but because democratic government at least requires the periodic consent of large numbers of people and in that sense disperses power widely.

In view of the doctrine of sin and with the bitter history of the twentieth century behind us, our Christian hope for human history must be a sober utopianism. Christian socialists will not live out of naive, optimistic illusions about the goodness of humanity. But they will be hopeful nevertheless. Rosemary Radford Ruether wrote with cautious hopefulness in her book *To Change the World:*

> There are some situations that are "closer" to the kingdom than others, not in an evolutionary progressive way, but in the sense of signs and mediations of the kingdom which better disclose what God's intention is for humanity; ... some systems allow for greater justice and mutuality.
>
> This does not mean that closeness to the kingdom is an assured possession of any particular system. A liberating situation can degenerate into an oppressive one. ...

Nevertheless it is possible, in the midst of the limits and transitoriness of human existence, to make societies which are more liberating and less oppressive, and hence closer to the kingdom. To deny this is to deny all efficacy to God in history, to make the world solely the kingdom of Satan.[32]

Or to borrow a term from Dietrich Bonhoeffer, Christian hope for history is only for the pen-ultimate.[33] It aims at particular, concrete pen-ultimates. Nevertheless, I contend, it continues even under the conditions of history to be hope for "no place" — for the appearance of pen-ultimates that have never yet appeared in human history — analogies, then, or parables or signs of God's Reign in the here and now. In this sense, Christian political theology is rightly utopian in character.

Socialism too, I shall suggest, is essentially utopian, but socialists generally, whether Christian or secular, have not been particularly optimistic about human nature. It is true that the word "socialist" derives from the Latin *socius,* friend. In English, to be "sociable" is to be friendly. Socialism is a hopeful vision of human society as a community of friends.[34] But Christian socialists have always known that, in view of the reality of sin, society can be "friendly" only if the inclinations to self-seeking and competition are limited and the rule of law extended into the economic sphere. However precisely we may define it, socialism can be characterized as having to do with visions and hopes for a more "friendly," cooperative social order: it hopes for the end of poverty and for greater economic justice and equality. More than that, it looks for an end to classes and to the exploitation of labor that alienates human beings from the process and product of their own work. But socialists have realized that none of this will come about spontaneously by the "free" operation of the market system, which in itself is simply the "free" reign of greed and self-interest. It is the essence of socialism to empower all those who work and to distribute economic power among all the people in order that economic oppression may have no chance. From within a Christian perspective on sin, then, socialism is an appropriate "pen-ultimate" goal, or rather, a constellation and spectrum of concrete social goals for human society.

An inevitable question arises, however, concerning the practicability of socialism. If historical and actual existing forms of socialism simply *do not work* (as many are saying today), i.e., if the implementation of socialist ideas leads to poverty, to loss of freedom, and to the general diminution of the quality of human life, while capitalist systems clearly enhance human life, then socialism cannot be supported ethically or theologically. Theological reflection upon social systems and political ideologies may not remain at an abstract, ethereal level. It must take account of and interact with the empirical realities that are described and analyzed by historians and social scientists. That is why our theological reflections must now move in the direction of socio-analytic and, especially, historical considerations.

Part II

The Triumph of Capitalism?

Chapter 3

Soviet Communism: The Tragedy of Utopia

Though we have not yet defined socialism, communism, or capitalism in a precise manner, we all know that *capitalism* can be characterized as the relatively "free market" system of private ownership and control of capital as we find it in the west, and *communism* the form (or forms) of self-professed state socialism that, until recently, prevailed in the Soviet bloc and still does in China, i.e., a state monopoly of economic power and resources.[1] The extension of these two systems in their respective empires can be found also in the nations of the Third World, though, clearly enough, the communist empire has collapsed. *Socialism,* however, is a vast and extremely varied and ambiguous phenomenon, certainly not limited to historical communism, and much more difficult to characterize and define. Suffice it to say, at this point, that socialists are those who envisage and strive toward social cooperation, preferring a wide, public diffusion of economic, as well as political power. As I have said, the two ideologies, in reality, overlap very considerably, since no "pure" forms either of capitalism or socialism exist. Those who espouse one ideology or system rather than another, though they may differ from each other radically, wish to move their societies in one direction rather than another along a continuum. It could be said that the *extreme* ends of the continuum, i.e., the extreme right and the extreme left — communism and fascism — tend to resemble one another in practice.

We need now to turn to the chief example of one end of that continuum, the state "communism" of the Soviet Union, which began with the first great "socialist" victory, the coming to power of Lenin and the Bolsheviks in 1917 — an event that has had unparalleled impact on the history of the twentieth century.

Lenin

Communism came to power in Russia in 1917 under the leadership of Vladimir Ilyich Ulyanov Lenin (1870–1924). Lenin was part of the Russian Social Democratic Labor Party (RSDLP), which had been formed at Minsk in 1898, building upon the work of the pioneer Russian socialist Georgii Plekhanov. A major split had occurred in 1903 between Bolsheviks (*majority*, led by Lenin) and Mensheviks (*minority*, led by Yuli Martov). While the Mensheviks believed in bottom-up socialist revolution of a more gradual kind, the Bolsheviks believed in a top-down seizure of power by a disciplined group of revolutionaries who would lead the working class to power. The arrival of socialism in Russia, a relatively backward nation, was not to be expected according to Marx's theory, which would have seen the revolution occur first in highly industrialized Britain, or at least in Germany, with their large proletariat populations. The seizure of power in 1917 was possible only because of the weakened state of the Russian monarchy during the war with Germany. The Bolsheviks moved violently into that power vacuum and managed to hold on and, over the next few years, solidify their position as rulers of Russia. Lenin had developed a theory of international capitalist imperialism, which saw the advanced industrial nations as the new international capitalists and the poor countries as the new proletariat. "Russia stood to Britain as proletariat did to capitalist."[2] Utilizing this theory, which became part of what is called "Marxism-Leninism," Lenin justified the seizure of power and "revolution" in an underdeveloped country. It has been argued that in fact Russia, as the weakest and least developed of the "core" capitalist nations and the strongest of the "peripheral" or underdeveloped nations (as in fact a kind of "semiperipheral" nation), was ripe for such a takeover.[3]

Many of Lenin's enemies in the Second International (the European international socialist organization formed in 1889[4]) were not pleased by the coup in Moscow. But the event was cause for great rejoicing and hope among most people of the various socialist parties and movements that had formed since early in the nineteenth century and that had spread also into North America. We hear the euphoria of international socialism as late as 1936 in the words of the Christian socialist economist (as he was then) Eugene Forsey, who was still very excited about the prospects for a socialist world taking shape in Russia under the auspices of Marxism. Forsey declared,

The devil of social injustice goeth not out but by grappling with the fundamental issues. This generation seeketh after a sign, and there shall be no sign given it but the sign of the prophet Marx. Until Christians learn to understand and apply the lessons of Marxism they cannot enter into the Kingdom of Heaven.[5]

Not long afterward Forsey was embarrassed by these words. (He later became a member of the Liberal Party of Canada and was appointed to the Senate.) But in the midst of the great depression of the 1930s the Marxist-Leninist revolution in Russia still appeared to many as the great sign of hope for humanity. Marx's dream of the classless society via the dictatorship of the proletariat had apparently come to power under Lenin. A nation ruled by the working class was taking shape, soon to realize Marx's truly utopian vision for society:

In a higher phase of communist society, after ... all the springs of cooperative wealth flow more abundantly — only then can the narrow horizon of bourgeois right be crossed in its entirety and society inscribe on its banner: From each according to his ability, to each according to his needs.[6]

Lenin (taking his lead from Marx's concept of a preliminary "dictatorship of the proletariat" led by a revolutionary vanguard) believed that, if the high aspirations that Marx had set forth for society were ever to be realized, a revolutionary intelligentsia, equipped with socialist theory and committed to gaining power for the people, would have to lead the way. Lenin saw no potential in the proletariat itself to analyze its situation or to launch a successful seizure of political and economic power. In *What Is to Be Done?* (1902) Lenin declared that "there can be no revolutionary movement without a revolutionary theory" and that "the role of the vanguard fighter can be fulfilled only by a party that is guided by advanced theory."[7] Leadership, initiative, theory, and planning would have to come from outside the ranks of the proletariat, for "the history of all countries shows that the working class, solely by its own forces, is able to work out merely trade-union consciousness."[8] He was contemptuous of all gradualist versions of socialism, as represented by the German socialist leader Eduard Bernstein,[9] and became common in the German Social Democratic Party and in the British Fabian and labor movements. Many democratic socialists in western Europe (including, for example, Beatrice and Sidney Webb in England, whose work he had translated) believed that evolution toward socialism was inevitable and had only to be assisted by socialist theorists and activists. Lenin was sure that such "economist" and "inevitabilist" views were naive; there was nothing inevitable about the victory of socialism, nor were the proletariat economically "determined" to come to power.[10] Indeed socialism would never prevail without a disciplined party, intent on seizing power, and of necessity this would have to be achieved through violent revolution.[11] Lenin's hard line on this matter is understandable. It was the disappointing, bitter experiences of the earlier history of socialism, his awareness of the vulnerability of the working class to bourgeois ideology, and the overwhelming power of the capitalist class, as in the experience of the defeat of the Paris commune in 1871, that convinced him of this.[12] Gradual melioration of working and living conditions for the working people through legislation or unionism were, he believed, nothing but adjustments within capitalism, designed to co-opt the working class. Lenin expressed awareness of the danger of party elitism and insisted that members must have both the right and responsibility to act and to speak: "any distinction between workers and intellectuals must be completely obliterated."[13] Yet, once a decision had been made, party discipline and unity were also essential.

As a social theorist Lenin was not a rigid dogmatist where Marx's teaching was concerned, believing that Marx's ideas would have to be modified, developed, and applied differently in many different circumstances. As we have already seen, Lenin's seizure of power in Russia was justified by an adjustment to Marx's own theory that the socialist revolution would have to arise out of a fairly advanced stage of industrial capitalism. Lenin led his revolution in one of the most backward regions of Europe, possessing only a very small proletariat class (about 2 percent of the population).[14] Thus Lenin believed that Russia required a broad "dictatorship" of proletariat and peasants, under Bolshevik leadership.[15] Faced with an underdeveloped country economically devastated by war and a hostile western capitalist world, Lenin attempted in the early years of his rule to set Russia quickly on its feet by the introduction of certain "capitalist" measures. In 1921, he declared:

> We must be bolder in widely applying a variety of methods and taking different approaches, giving reign to capital and private trade in varying degree, without being afraid to implant some

capitalism, as long as we succeed in stimulating exchange at once and thereby revive agriculture and industry.[16]

For Lenin, what was important, as G. van Houten argues, was not total nationalization and state ownership, but rather, which class held power and in whose interest power was exercised.[17] The build-up of productive forces could occur, he thought, through temporary and partial private ownership and control of capital and the profit motive.

As we have seen, Lenin was not unaware of the danger of bureaucracy and warned about the dangers of oligarchy and elitism.

The Warning of Rosa Luxemburg

Some of his socialist critics, however, were sharply critical of Lenin's own inclinations to tyranny soon after his seizure of power. One of the most acute of these was the great Polish/German revolutionary socialist leader Rosa Luxemburg (1870–1919). She had effectively encouraged worker agitation, organized insurrections and strikes, and tried to start a peasant uprising. She spent many years in a German prison during the first war and was eventually murdered. Not a "revisionist" and highly critical of the likes of Bernstein, she was also sharply critical of Lenin.[18] She is now, quite rightly, a heroine of democratic socialism, in part because of her protests against the corruption of the Russian revolution. For her, socialism and democracy were absolutely inseparable, and she had great confidence in the masses of the people to rule themselves. She had a high sense of the need for the preparation and readiness of the working class and of their full democratic involvement in revolution. As early as 1904 she had warned of the danger of elitist, centralist bureaucratic rule implicit in Lenin's revolutionary theory:

> Now the two principles on which Lenin's centralism rests are precisely these: 1. The blind subordination, in the smallest detail, of all party organs, to the party center, which alone thinks, guides, and decides for all. 2. The rigorous separation of the organized nucleus of revolutionaries from its social-revolutionary surroundings.[19]

In prison very soon after the revolution of 1917, Rosa Luxemburg wrote a pamphlet highly critical of Lenin's theoretical centralism and

practical elitism (a pamphlet that was long suppressed by her revolutionary colleagues). Her words of warning seem prophetic today:

> But with the repression of political life in the land as a whole, life
> in the soviets must also become more and more crippled. With-
> out general elections, without unrestricted freedom of press and
> assembly, without a free struggle of opinion, life dies out in every
> public institution, becomes a mere semblance of life, in which
> only the bureaucracy remains as the active element. Public life
> gradually falls asleep, a few dozen party leaders of inexhaustible
> energy and boundless experience direct and rule. Among them,
> in reality only a dozen outstanding heads do the leading and an
> elite of the working class is invited from time to time to meet-
> ings where they are to applaud the speeches of the leaders, and
> to approve proposed resolutions unanimously — at bottom, then,
> a clique affair — a dictatorship, to be sure, but not the dictator-
> ship of the proletariat, but only the dictatorship of a handful of
> politicians.[20]

Whatever might have been the frustrations, temptations, and enormous pressures upon Lenin and his colleagues after 1917, including
the hostility of the western capitalist world (no doubt they were great)
and whatever the flaws in Lenin's own revolutionary theory, Rosa
Luxemburg's warnings and predictions about centralism and elitism
proved all too accurate in the years that followed.

Stalinism

When Lenin died it was Joseph Stalin (1879–1953) who won the
struggle for power, outmaneuvering his chief rival, Lenin's colleague
Leon Trotsky. Having seized power and having eliminated all opposition, it was he who introduced an uncompromising state-owned
and state-controlled communism, eliminating all private and cooperative ventures. Stalin forced the total collectivization of agriculture as
well as industry into what is now commonly called the "command-
administrative" model, a highly centralized version of the so-called
"dictatorship of the proletariat," supposedly leading the people from
the preliminary stage of socialism to the more advanced stage of
communism. Stalin's rule really reactivated ancient Russian czarist authoritarianism, exploited the subordinationist, feudal mentality of the

peasant class, and built what is now universally recognized as an oppressive, bureaucratic elitism. This was utterly the opposite of what
either Marx or Lenin had hoped for, though it must be said that
Lenin's theory and deeds had paved the way. By 1934, 250,000 collective farms were created, a process that carried the horrendous cost
of the death of about ten million peasants through famine or slaugh-
ter! In the later 1930s some seven million people were arrested, many
of whom died in custody or were executed.[21] That Stalin was able so
to distort Lenin's revolution perhaps underlines the fact that the latter was in reality a "revolution from above," which had been built
upon the theory and dedication of a revolutionary vanguard but did
not enjoy the necessary understanding and support of the mass of the
people. Not long afterward, at least by the time of Stalin's pact with
Hitler in 1939, most of the world saw the Union of Soviet Socialist
Republics as a dreadful tyranny. In the postwar era the example of
undemocratic communism in the U.S.S.R. functioned in the west as
a warning about the danger of socialist collectivism to personal and
political freedom, and later to economic productivity as well. The utopian dream of Marxist-Leninist theorists had gone sour, to say the
least, in what has to be described as one of the great tragedies of modern history. However much we may deplore the methods and the cost,
we must recognize the extraordinary economic achievements in the Soviet Union, indeed, under the rule of Stalin. Russia and neighboring
east/central European nations had been part of an economic periphery
(or semiperiphery) in relation to the north/west European core of capitalist development since the sixteenth century.[22] Stalin's regime swiftly
set about to change this. During the period of the first five-year plan,
1928–37, the output of heavy industry increased three-fold, and elec-
trical power supplies increased twenty-fold. By the 1970s the Soviet
Union was the world's second largest economy, with a manufacturing capacity exceeded only by that of the United States.[23] Important
social achievements included political stability, near universal employment, education and medical care, a reasonable approximation to
widespread economic equality (despite the existence of a tiny privileged elite), and the fairly peaceful coexistence of many hitherto hostile
peoples. By North American middle-class standards people were relatively poor, but (with some notable and horrifying exceptions, such as
the Ukraine in the 1930s) they were not hungry or destitute as in many
parts of the capitalist Third World. The "failed" economies of the Soviet Union and eastern Europe actually had per capita incomes two to

five times higher than the average per capita income of Latin American nations within the capitalist orbit.[24] What had been a very backward region of eastern Europe rapidly became a superpower challenging the United States for world hegemony.

Similar achievements, varying a good deal from one country to another, occurred in other east European nations under more or less "Stalinist" regimes. China too would later demonstrate the power of a communist system to lift a Third World population out of poverty and illiteracy, and far outshine "development" in capitalist places like Latin America and most of Africa.[25] We must take care not to adopt wholeheartedly the negative propaganda of the capitalist west. It is by no means obvious yet that the Russians, Ukrainians, Armenians, etc., or the east Europeans are going to be better off under whatever kind of "capitalism" may develop there. Democratic elections in eastern Europe have already sometimes produced victories for people calling themselves socialists, even former communists. However, the Russian elections of December 1993, producing a parliamentary plurality for the right-wing nationalist leader Vladimir Zhirinovsky, showed us clearly that "socialism" in Russia was never more than skin deep, that Russian anti-Semitic fascism and imperialism, with their deep roots in czarist history, are all too much alive.[26] Can we hope to see a democratically governed socialist/capitalist mixed economy develop in Russia, or must we fear a Latin American style dependent capitalism combined with fascism?

It is true that at least by 1980 the U.S.S.R., under communist rule, was falling permanently behind the west in advanced technology and consumer goods.[27] Progress toward Marx's vision of a classless society as a free association of workers had long since ceased. It is now apparent that the great majority of the people knew themselves excluded from significant decision-making about their lives and their country and were profoundly alienated from their rulers and in their economic life. A Communist Party elite had long since co-opted Lenin's socialist revolution, as Rosa Luxemburg had predicted. Soviet and east European communism has long been exposed as cruel, tyrannical, and corrupt. Gross judicial injustice was common, even long after the death of Stalin. Arbitrary imprisonment, execution, mass killings, elimination of those politically out of favor, selective mass starvation, have all discredited Soviet communism, and in the minds of many, socialism as such. Environmental destruction appears to have been even worse in the communist east than in the capitalist west. Moreover, the relative social virtues that may have existed in the Soviet Union apparently did not count for much in the face of the ferocious arms race waged by President Ronald Reagan in his attempt to "roll back" communism.[28] The consequent economic pressure on the Soviets to develop militarily and the failure to advance in the production of consumer goods meant increasing public dissatisfaction with the results of Gorbachev's *glasnost*. Popular desire for consumer goods and political freedom was such that the peoples of the communist bloc, including the Russians themselves, took to the streets in their tens of thousands, eager to be rid of the communist system as quickly as possible. As everyone knows, the events of 1989–92 saw the dramatic collapse of eastern European and Soviet communism as a political and economic system and the end of the so-called "Cold War." It was no surprise that this debacle has been hailed in the west as the triumph of capitalism by such antisocialist champions as Margaret Thatcher and George Bush. They spoke unabashedly of the "total victory of our system" and equated democracy, freedom, and virtue with the capitalist economic system.

A Story of Failure

The apparent victory of capitalism and failure of communism is seen in the fact that refugees from the Third World and indeed from the former Soviet bloc itself scramble to get into the democratic, capitalist west and north. No one would choose to move from the U.S.A. to Russia in the aftermath of seventy years of "socialist dictatorship." People do not flee from Hong Kong into China, or from South Korea into North Korea. We have to say (with some qualifications) especially in the case of the Soviet Union, that seven decades of communism have been a failure. This was the nation that abolished private ownership of the means of production; this was the part of the world that, together with its satellite captive nations, called itself "socialist." What of China? China too, despite its enormous social and economic achievements, is apparently moving in a capitalist direction and would have moved there more rapidly except for the treacherous massacre of Tiananmen Square and the continuing political tyranny that followed. On what possible basis, then, could one propose socialism as an alternative to capitalism?

Here, unavoidably, we come to the difficult question, "What is socialism?" Was Soviet communism indeed a genuine form of socialism? Undeniably the Soviets implemented one common, historical socialist concept, namely, the abolition of the private ownership of the means of production. Soviet communism was in one sense "postcapitalist," in that there was no longer a capitalist class. But this in itself does not constitute genuine socialism. Immanuel Wallerstein has long argued that "establishing a system of state ownership within a capitalist world economy does not mean establishing a socialist economy."[29] Political scientist Paul Browne makes the point lucidly:

> Although ownership is centralised in the state, so that no individual person (in principle) owns means of production, there is, in the form of the state, one all-encompassing private owner expropriating all of society. Alienation persists not only in the form of expropriation but also in that of the fundamental divisions of labor which are at the origin of all class societies.... Under "really existing socialism" the state embodies the power of capital, owning all means of production, and subjecting to itself all labor power.[30]

As other critics of Soviet communism have often pointed out, the state had become one giant monopoly controlled by a party elite. The remote, bureaucratic character of this elite helped to assure that the economic system would not function efficiently. Without democratic political rights, without competing loci of economic power (i.e., other companies), and without an efficiently functioning market system, the worker/consumer was drastically stripped of social power. This state monopoly of capital, as well as of political power, created a totalitarian situation, which is as far from genuine socialism as one can imagine. Such a situation cannot be described as "socialist" because it is directly opposed to historical socialism's primary objective, which, as we have seen, is precisely the empowerment of the worker.[31] Indeed Soviet communism came to be another extremely lethal form of the rule of capital.

A Note on Gramsci

An important socialist thinker and political activist whose ideas are relevant to our discussion was Antonio Gramsci (1891–1937) — the dedicated Italian communist leader who spent eleven years of his short life in prison during the time of the Mussolini regime. This martyr of socialism was a Marxist and admirer of Lenin's revolution in Russia. However, like Rosa Luxemburg, he became sharply critical of what grew to be a gross distortion of true socialism.

Gramsci insisted that revolution, in the sense of genuine social transformation, must be understood as a process that begins within the old society and continues after moments of dramatic change. As a Marxist he was critical of a narrow "economistic" or strictly deterministic historical materialism in that he highlighted the power of ideas, which can become akin to material forces. Ideas shape preferences and perceptions of what is possible.[32] Gramsci had a strong sense of the deep influence of cultural transformations, such as the Renaissance, and the profound, long-term impact of religious institutions, such as the Catholic Church in Italy. A socialist revolution, if it is to be truly a social transformation and not a mere coup, must be made by the mass of the population, not by a small elite, and its leaders must understand and take account of such cultural factors. Gramsci opposed what he called "statolatry" — state worship — the "religious" belief in the state's ability to bring about social transformation.[33] He was unusual also, as a Marxist, in that he paid attention to nations and nationalism, to the actual culture and folklore of the people, and saw the necessity for building up social consensus.[34] For Gramsci, the hallmark of socialism was the democratic control by the mass of society over economic and political decisions, in contrast to the capitalist social relations, wherein political and economic spheres are controlled by a few people and democratic control remains at a formal level. But this was impossible without a process of true "revolution" beginning within the heart of a capitalist society and continuing long after the establishment of a new state. Alternative institutions have to be painstakingly created, for "the old society will fall only if a new one is built."[35] In a letter from prison he speaks of the necessity of achieving "hegemony" (the rule of the people) through all the organs of civil society before as well as after taking over the structures of the state.[36] He foresaw a "long historical period" of achieving social consensus, rejecting the assumption that the building of socialism would only begin on the day that the proletariat and its party acceded to power, whether by revolution or by winning 51 percent of the votes.[37] The basic problem was not how revolutionaries come to power. It was how they come to be accepted as guides and leaders. Leaders, then, must have organic contact with the social reality they wish to transform, including nation and class, religion, morality, music, and folklore.

This does not mean, however, that Gramsci believed in mere reformism, a mere accumulation of reforms and changes within capitalism, a kind of buying off of the working class wherein the real power to determine the direction of society remains with a few owners and managers of capital. Radical transformation cannot be overnight; nor, we may surmise, is "gradualism" to be equated with reformism. Gramsci could already see in the 1930s that the communism of the Soviet Union, which had taken power suddenly, had become a remote pseudo-socialist bureaucracy, and not truly the "hegemony" of the people.

Chapter 4

North American Capitalism:
Just What Is Wrong?

Capitalism is the market-organized economy in which the great majority of the resources and the means of production are privately owned and controlled. Individuals or groups of individuals (companies or corporations) own and manage land, mines, and forests, as well as machinery, tools, technology, industrial plants, etc. Workers are employed to do the work and are paid wages for their time and talent. Capitalist enterprises provide goods and services to consumers and compete with one another on the open market for the consumers' business. Their objective in supplying goods and services is, of course, to earn profit. Profits are earned through the ownership of shares.

Modern capitalism is thought to have begun to develop in the late Middle Ages; its origin in western Europe in the fifteenth and sixteenth centuries arose out of improved agricultural technology, rising population, and the growth of an entrepreneurial middle class. The development of capitalism as we know it accelerated rapidly in the late eighteenth century during what is called the Industrial Revolution (something we shall discuss later in relation to socialism). Our particular interest in this chapter is the form that it has taken in the latter part of the twentieth century, especially in North America, though this cannot be understood apart from its connection to the whole capitalist world-economy.[1] From a socialist perspective I shall be offering a critical outlook on capitalism in general, but it would be unrealistic, first, not to note the great success and dynamism of this economic system, historically and even in our present time.

First, What Is Right with It?

Socialists are often very negative in their rhetoric about "profit," and although this may be justified in terms of utopia, it must be recognized that everyone in an imperfect society must earn money in one way or another (even academics, clergy, philosophers, and poets). Those who set themselves up in business, investing money, energy, organizational talent, and ideas, are providing an important service to society. It all seems very reasonable and natural. Even socialists who believe in planned, social democratic, or "mixed" economies, or in worker-owned cooperatives, understand the need for productivity, the discipline of the market (providing what people will actually buy), the necessity for incentives to work, save, and invest, and the value of competition. Because we do not live in a social order of pure altruism, the reality of self-interest must be acknowledged. In keeping with what we said about "sin" in chapter 2, any viable social/economic system has to take account of the element of self-seeking in all ordinary economic life, whether in working or investing, in buying or selling. Some measure of "capitalism" (the structural characteristics and mechanisms I have just mentioned) will surely always be part of any reasonably healthy social/economic order — at least as long as we live on this side of the Kingdom of Heaven. That is why it is unrealistic, as Niebuhr argued a generation ago, to envisage a purely cooperative, "socialist" society, in which human beings live together, selflessly seeking only the public good.

Moreover, if we compare market-organized to state-organized systems (not that the latter is to be simply identified with socialism), the former appear to have definite advantages. The western capitalist economies have exhibited a flexibility, dynamism, and creativity not found in the eastern communist ones. There is a certain demonstrable sluggishness about state-organized economies (if we compare the old East Germany with West Germany, or North Korea to South Korea, or the U.S.S.R. to the U.S.A.).[2] Capitalist systems, at least in relatively "developed" parts of the world, have seemed to excel in productivity, innovation, creativity, and generally in material prosperity. If we take material and bodily needs seriously, as we should, these things are not to be sniffed at.

Beyond these purely material/economic considerations, it may be argued with some plausibility that market-organized economies are associated with relatively more social, political, and personal freedom, because of "a broader choice of things to buy, of places to work, and of businesses to go into."[3] There are exceptions to this: South Africa, South Korea, and Taiwan have not been models of civil liberty (though now after many years major democratization appears to be occurring). The fact remains that people regularly sought to escape communist countries and flee to capitalist ones and, at the outset of our own decade, gladly rejected communist governments when they had the chance to do so.[4]

If socialists are going to think clearly about the meaning of socialism and its future, these realities must be faced. As I will argue at length later, it is historically false to identify socialism with centralized state-owned and state-controlled economy. Socialism has to do with the wider, more democratic distribution of economic ownership and control. Moreover, historical socialism would not exist if private ownership, private economic power, and the operation of the market had not failed, in and of itself, to meet human needs in an equitable manner.

Distortions within Capitalism: According to Galbraith

Defenders of capitalism will usually and quite rightly point out that, like socialism (or Christianity, or any good thing), capitalism can be distorted and abused. These distortions do not necessarily prove that the system is fundamentally wrong — only that it needs to be modified and corrected. The Harvard economist and social theorist John Kenneth Galbraith, perhaps the most significant left-liberal critic of existing western capitalism, thinks that capitalism as we know it in the late twentieth century, especially as it exists in the United States, needs to be, and can be, mended. In his most recently stated view, socialism, which he defines as state-owned and state-controlled economy, is simply too inflexible to respond to diverse consumer demand, especially in the realm of agriculture.[5] He and other left-liberal critics have high respect for the Roosevelt New Deal and the Keynesian economics that allowed capitalism to modify itself through government action and to pull out of the depression of the 1930s. They believe that market economies function more effectively and equitably with a healthy dose of government intervention and regulation. They also support generous provision for public health care, education, social security, environmental protection, even subsidized housing — something close to what in other places would be called "social democracy" or "socialist measures within capitalism." "Free enterprise," or laissez-faire capitalism, according to this view, should be modified by a democratically elected government in the interests of all the people. In other words American "liberal Democrats" such as Galbraith believe that, while the market should be the fundamental mechanism of the economic order, the market must be in some measure modified, planned, and regulated. It must be said: left-wing liberalism and moderate social democratic socialism tend to fade into one another on the spectrum and are sometimes hardly distinguishable. Existing capitalism in the United States, however, is probably further to the right side of the socialist/capitalist continuum than any other place in the world.

Ironically, Galbraith's "post-Keynesian"[6] criticism of existing capitalism (especially in the United States, but to a lesser extent elsewhere as well) is not that it adheres too closely to laissez-faire (allowing the market free rein), but that in fact the capitalist economic order is manipulated by the powerful in their own interests. The rhetoric of laissez-faire and the free market is utilized ideologically in societies (especially the United States) where communism has been considered the great evil. Too much government involvement in the economy is seen as a flirtation with the enemy. If governments intervene too much or too often to redistribute wealth or to rebuild crumbling public infrastructure or to protect the environment, they exhibit a lack of faith in "the invisible hand." Galbraith sees the theological character of the reigning capitalist ideology: "The quiet theology of laissez-faire," he comments, "holds that all will work out for the best in the end."[7] To believe in the market is a kind of faith. To "get the government off the backs of the people" has been one of the most popular bits of capitalist rhetoric, skillfully utilized especially by Ronald Reagan. But Galbraith points out that in the United States government becomes very active indeed in certain restricted ways, and with the full support of the capitalist right wing. In his earlier book, *The New Industrial State*, he had already analyzed the major role of U.S. government fiscal, monetary, and taxation policies, as well as its propagation of the renowned military-industrial complex. Modern technological society requires the precommitment of enormous financial investment in infrastructure. Huge financial operations demand careful and accurate planning and market research. Advertising, to create or shape needs and desires, is essential to the process. The proverbial capitalistic "risk" must be minimized, or eliminated, if possible; the support of a sympathetic state, then, is essential. It is not that the state directs the world of capital in accordance with democratically determined goals, but that the state must be on side in support of capital. It is not government but large capital, he argues, that sets the economic priorities of the nation. This is basic to post-Keynesian economic thought, of which Galbraith is the best-known representative:

> The forces inducing human effort have changed. This assaults the most majestic of all economic assumptions, namely that man in his economic activities is subject to the authority of the market. Instead, we have an economic system which, whatever its formal ideological billing, is in substantial part a planned economy. The initiative in deciding what is to be produced comes not from the sovereign consumer who, through the market, issues the instructions that bend the productive mechanism to his ultimate will. Rather it comes from the great producing organization which reaches forward to control the markets that it is presumed to serve and, beyond, to bend the customer to its needs. And, in so doing, it deeply influences his values and beliefs.[8]

While Galbraith is far from Marxism, his analysis has something of the ring of historical materialism about it. He sees that it is technology, the means of production, and the control of these that are decisive in shaping economic and social relationships, and belief systems as well. In our time the technological means of production are largely under the control of gargantuan multinational corporations. Capital reigns more decisively than ever. In his book of 1973, *Economics and the Public Purpose*, Galbraith spoke of a kind of de facto "socialism" already existing in the United States, by which he meant a major subsidizing, supportive, and regulative role of government, which generally serves the interest of capital.[9] Of course it is highly ironical to use the word socialism in this way — i.e., the utilization of democratic government to serve the interests not of the workers or of the people, but of capital.

Government as a tool of capital, rather than planner and director of capital, is basic to his analysis also in his most recent book, *The Culture of Contentment*. But the intimate connection of capital and the military is the specific circumstance that undermines the proper functioning of democratic government. He notes that less than half of the electorate usually vote in American elections, presumably because the potential electors at the bottom of the socio-economic ladder see no significant choice between those on the ballot. Governments are in fact elected by "the comfortable," who are deeply convinced of the need to defend their privilege militarily. The religious character of capitalist ideology is evident in his comments on "democracy" (and here a Marxian insight into the ideological character of religion and the state is evident). The power of the military is held to be under the power of democracy, but

> democracy is here, as elsewhere, the gracing note for a singularly independent and self-reinforcing exercise of authority. It is the rood screen, perhaps more precisely the altar, behind which the modern military-industrial complex enjoys its self-generated and self-serving autonomy.[10]

Galbraith points out again the enormous economic role of the state through the military. The ideological fear of communism has meant that expenditures on the military cannot be questioned by anyone who hopes to be successful in politics. To be "soft on defense" has meant to be "soft on communism" and has amounted to political suicide in the U.S. Moreover, a great many people benefit from the military expenditures of the government: "Weapons expenditure, unlike, e.g., spending for the urban poor, rewards a very comfortable constituency."[11] The combination of ideology, economic benefit, and the alleged need for national security and secrecy makes the military an almost untouchable autonomous power within the American system. Even the recent collapse of communism has not so far affected the military budget significantly; an event like the Gulf War, with a new enemy in Islam, helped convince Americans of the necessity to "remain strong." The military, then, is one area in which government is not considered a burden.

Certain minimal levels of social security, which support the middle class as well as the poor, are also accepted as the proper role of government. But, Galbraith points out, this function is regarded pejoratively as "bureaucratic," especially where it involves actual welfare or food stamps for the poor. Taxes must be kept artificially low, leading to huge government deficits and interest payments, because taxes represent "government bureaucracy on the backs of the people." Marginal rates on the very rich were reduced from "a partly nominal 70 per cent to 50 per cent in 1981; then with tax reform the rate on the richest fell to 28 per cent in 1986."[12] The military and its expenditures, however, are never "bureaucratic" in the ideological language of capitalism. Nor is it a "bureaucratic" function to rescue banks or other financial institutions from bankruptcy.

Such are the exceptions that the contented majority makes to its general condemnation of government as a burden. Social expenditure favorable to the fortunate, financial rescue, military spending, and of course, interest payments — these constitute in the aggregate by far the largest part of the federal budget.... What remains — expenditures for welfare, low-cost housing, health care for those otherwise unprotected, public education and the diverse needs of the great urban slums — is what is now viewed as the burden of government. It is uniquely that which serves the interests of those outside the contented electoral majority; it is, and inescapably, what serves the poor.[13]

An important aspect of Galbraith's analysis, both in earlier and later writings, is his identification of the decisive role of management in the contemporary large corporation. Stockholders being numerous and mostly absent, management has become extremely powerful. Maximization of profit for stockholders is not necessarily the goal of managers, who are often interested instead mainly in their own rewards. While this phenomenon is not new, the tendency for fantastic salaries and other perquisites for management has contributed to the ill health of American capitalism — stock options, retirement, expense accounts, aircraft. In 1980, Galbraith tells us, chief executive officers of the three hundred largest American companies had incomes twenty-nine times that of the average manufacturing worker; but by 1990 the incomes of the top executives were ninety-three times greater! And during those same years the income of the average employed American declined.[14] This was accompanied in the 1980s by widespread real estate speculation, with absurdly spiralling prices, spectacular corporate raids, and a spate of insider buyouts, forced sales, and junk bonds — all of this, he argues, a result in part of government deregulation. In the general recession that followed, government bailout of banks was required: "A preventive role by government was not allowed; eventual government rescue was highly acceptable."[15]

Galbraith thinks that enlightened and charismatic leadership could conceivably turn American capitalism around. The system is capable of dealing generously with the inner cities, caring for the poor, dealing with drug addiction, providing better-paid teachers, well-financed welfare services, public investment in housing, publicly supported health care, and so on. The fact that western European social democratic states, and to a lesser extent Canada, have long since taken this route indicates that Galbraith may be right (though the long-term sustainability of social democracy in these places is now in question). Yet he is pessimistic that any of this will happen and forecasts for the United States a future of increasing violence and social polarization.

Are the likes of Galbraith to be regarded as socialists? When asked on television whether he was a socialist, his response was whimsical — "O heavens, no!" Certainly there is something of the socialist spirit about Galbraith. In *Economics and the Public Purpose* he actually spoke of the "Socialist Imperative"[16] — calling for recognition of the actual major economic role of government and proposing that this role be less fearful of the concept of socialism, claiming the democratic propriety of government planning for the well-being of citizens rather than of capital. Certainly he consistently favors what might commonly be regarded as socialist measures within capitalism and active democratic/government participation in the economy. Yet in his latest book he speaks disparagingly of socialism, seeming to identify it with communism.[17] Galbraith indicates concern not about the power of private capital as such, but about the abuse of such power; he does not appear to deplore the powerlessness or alienation of workers as such under capitalism (though he is supportive of the rights of the labor movement). On the contrary, he wants to see owners (i.e., stockholders) regain their control from managers. For all his humanity, he does not enunciate utopian or socialist visions of a transformed society. The attitude of Galbraith and other liberal Democrats in the U.S. is that most of the current trouble with capitalism is a result of the neo-conservative policies of Republican Party governments. A tempered and humane capitalism, in their view, really requires no radical reorientation.

As helpful as Galbraith's analysis is, his thought appears to give rather too little attention to the capitalist world-system as a global whole. Are there not international forces at work that militate against any substantial or effective adjustments to American political economy? Richard Barnet and John Cavanagh, in their book *Global Dreams: Imperial Corporations and the New World Order*, point out that

> in an integrated world economy the line between public authority and private power has grown murkier. The decline of the political power and technical means of national governments to regulate the behavior of global corporations operating on their territo-

ries has helped to bring about an ideological shift that makes a virtue out of this reality.... Because traditional Keynesian strategies for tinkering with interest rates and taxes no longer enable politicians to deliver on campaign promises of full employment, governments have lost public confidence and a large measure of legitimacy.[18]

From a standpoint such as that of Galbraith, the question arises: If capitalism has proved to be relatively so durable and successful, and if its distortions are capable of correction, just what is so wrong with capitalism? Why should we not be content with it and work at improving it? It may be argued that early capitalism was plagued with misery and injustice, but capitalism has shown great capacity to adapt and survive and to offer a better combination of prosperity and political freedom than any other system in history.[19] However, neo-Keynesian strategies for adapting capitalism may no longer suffice. Is there reason to think that there is something fundamentally wrong with capitalism as such?

Economic Failure and Injustice

We may reflect on the present state of the capitalist order in North America with regard to its capacity to offer economic prosperity, basic social equity, and meaningful work for the people. How successfully does "democratic capitalism" produce and distribute economic goods and economic power? How well does capitalism serve the fullness of life in a holistic sense? Are the present problems merely temporary aberrations in what is essentially a good system? As a Canadian author, I shall speak here from a Canadian leftist perspective, which differs considerably from predominant American views on capitalism, freedom, and democracy. Canadian capitalism has been considerably more modified in a democratic socialist direction than has American capitalism. Moreover, Canadians often have a clear sense of living on the margins of empire, with a keen awareness of powerlessness in the face of great economic forces beyond their control. However, the relatively more raw form of capitalism as it exists in the United States and its vulnerability to the operations of global capitalism are of particular interest to our inquiry. It will also be necessary, however, to see North American capitalism as part of the global capitalist economy.

Canada

We begin with the assumption that economic power is socially important. The power to make decisions about the deployment of natural
resources and labor, to decide about the availability of housing and
the costs of food and transportation — this is power indeed. In Canada
over the last two decades or so wealth and economic power have been
accumulated more and more into fewer private hands. A few statistics serve to make the point. Eric Kierans and Walter Stewart (who
do not call themselves socialists, but defenders of small-business capitalism) argue that in Canada small capitalists are the prime source
of employment and the foundation of the economy. But in the mid-
1980s 88.9 percent of all companies (i.e., mainly the small ones)
earned only 13.1 percent of the book profits before taxes. Middle-sized
companies, with assets between $1 million and $25 million, earned
18 percent, while a small group of large companies, comprising less
than 1 percent of all business enterprises, earned 68 percent of all
book profits! Through cross-ownership and interlocking directorates,
effective control is held by about five hundred of these.[20] These top
companies were able to defer indefinitely and without interest $27.6
billion in taxes, while writing off large amounts of money for replacing human and technological resources.[21] Other authors too have
pointed out that the growing accumulation of wealth and capital in
the hands of the few is found, e.g., in the food industry, where five
volume-buying groups account for 85 percent of all food retail sales.[22]
In recent years "Close to 80 per cent of the companies listed in the
Toronto Stock Exchange were controlled by a single family and/or
group. And almost 50 per cent of the value of these companies was
controlled by just nine families."[23] The point is that enormous economic power resides in the hands of a few individuals and families
who have not been elected by the people to wield such power. I refer, as I did above, to the power to control vast amounts of money
and material goods, to direct and redirect capital, to deploy resources
and technology, to employ or not to employ people. Owners and managers of capital are perhaps neither more nor less self-seeking than
other human beings. It is not that they capriciously decide to hurt
people or to damage economies or environments; they are simply doing business in their own interest, playing the game, usually according
to the rules. It is unlikely, though, that such individuals will serve
the economic interests of all the people, or of the poorest people, or

of the environment, unless these happen to coincide with their own interests.

In recent decades (not only the years of hyper-capitalist neo-conservative governments in the U.S. and Canada) the economic well-being of North Americans has deteriorated seriously. An indicator of declining economic conditions in Canada can be found in home ownership statistics. In 1965 50 percent of Canadian families could afford to buy and own their own house. By the early 1980s that percentage had fallen to 30 percent in Canada, and by the late 1980s in the city of Toronto the figure was as low as 10 percent.[24] This is clearly part of the functioning of the capitalist "free market" system, which had a freer rein during the Reagan/Bush/Mulroney years than in the preceding decades. In the field of housing, for example, more money is to be made in the production of luxury condominiums than in modest family homes. The maximization of profit, rather than human need, determines what will be built. Jesuits Michael Czerny and Jamie Swift make the point cogently:

> The analysis has come up against one of the limits of a so-called "free market" in supplying housing. The primary reason housing is not being built, in short, is because developers and lending institutions have found other commodities more profitable to build and more secure to invest in....
>
> The treatment of shelter as a commodity puts housing beyond the reach of one Canadian family in five. It also renders millions more insecure and vulnerable to anonymous-sounding "free market forces." At the same time old people and single women supporting families end up paying large portions of their already inadequate income for shelter.[25]

Large-scale real unemployment (perhaps as high as 20 percent in Canada) appears to be increasingly structural and permanent. Unemployment statistics do not tell the whole story, since part of the picture is the shift from good jobs to poor jobs and from full time to part time.[26] In Canada the progress of social democratic measures within capitalism appears to have been halted, and universality in medical and social security programs is threatened or eroded.[27] This coincides with the disappearance of large numbers of well-paying jobs, especially since the Free Trade Agreement with the United States, which has seen many companies move south to maximize the benefits of the market.

Richard Barnet and John Cavanagh tell us:

In the four years after Canada concluded a bilateral free-trade agreement with the United States in 1988, manufacturing employment in Canada fell over 15 percent as hundreds of thousands of industrial jobs, particularly in the auto and food-processing industries, moved south to low-wage areas of the United States and Mexico.[28]

The agricultural sector has also been hit ferociously within the Canadian capitalist system. This is dramatically illustrated by Ben Smillie, writing from Saskatchewan about banks and farmers in western Canada:

Under the headline "Bank Profits Hit New High," a 1989 newspaper article stated that the Royal Bank had the largest earnings, with a 63 percent increase in the first six months of 1989 over the same period in 1988. Meanwhile, according to reports from the Federal Farm Debt Review Board, between August 1986 and June 1989, 7,200 farmers faced foreclosure in Saskatchewan. This figure represents 40 percent of the province's farmers, and includes those who had voluntarily given up because they could not meet payments on bank loans, those who had not been able to make their payments to the Farm Credit Corporation, and those who had been evicted by agents of the bank. Surely there is more involved here than bad weather, bad luck, and bad management![29]

An important additional consideration is the particular position of women in Canadian economic life. Marilyn Legge (another Saskatchewan theologian) points out the continuing marginalization of women, despite the apparent and highly visible advances of some women in professional and political life. Women, who are 51 percent of the population and constitute 41.2 percent of the labor force, earn on average only 60 percent of what men earn.[30] Legge protests against the habitual assumption of radical Christian ethics that the economic reality of class exists as an undifferentiated mass, pointing out and documenting the particularly difficult position of many working women, who usually work a "double day" between paid employment and domestic work. Radical political movements, like mainstream society, have tended to collude in the invisibility and marginalization of women, both in the work force and in political life itself. She insists that gender divisions are as fundamental as class and race divisions for an understanding of social injustice.[31]

In view of this catalogue of inequities, we may suspect that there is more wrong with our capitalist system than a mere temporary right-wing glitch. The increasing globalization and mobility of capital and commerce, i.e., large-scale foreign multinational ownership and control of resources, makes municipal, provincial, and federal governments, especially in a smaller nation such as Canada, less capable of exerting democratic economic influence. Given the freedom and ease with which commerce can carry on across borders, especially with the United States and Mexico, Canadians are more vulnerable than ever to the machinations of "the market."

United States

In the United States too, where the free rein of capital is more complete than in Canada, working people are getting poorer (see the discussion of American economic conditions above according to the view of Galbraith). Rapidly increasing official "poverty line" statistics in the U.S. tell the story. In 1989 12.8 percent of the population (about thirty million people, including unemployed people) lived below the poverty line. "Poverty lines" can be very arbitrary, but this poverty line was defined as $12,674 per year for a family of four — poverty indeed![32] Census data of 1990, one year later, show that 14 percent were below the official poverty line.[33] However, by 1993, 18 percent of the U.S. *work force* was working forty hours a week or more for wages that put them below the poverty line as defined by the federal government.[34] Over twenty million people suffer from malnutrition in this prosperous heartland of capitalism and freedom! The real hourly earnings of American workers have declined since 1973.[35] This is because good jobs are replaced by poor or part-time jobs. More people are now employed by McDonald's restaurants than in the entire basic steel industry in the U.S., rapidly creating what is commonly called the "hamburger economy"![36] The somewhat more interventionist (less purely procapital neo-conservative) government of President Clinton has had enormous difficulty implementing a more left-leaning agenda, even an elementary medical care system, and since the elections of November 1994 appears extremely vulnerable to triumphant right-wing Republicanism.[37] The Republican "Contract with America" calls for cuts to the capital gains tax, but also to welfare provisions such as Aid to Families with Dependent Children (AFDC), increases to the budgets for the military and prisons, and protection for the right to own guns!

What has been happening to the working class of the United States has to be understood in relation to the capitalist world-economy of which it is a part and within which it no longer holds hegemony. Sociologist Alvin So explains that the industrialization of east Asia, especially in high-tech electronics industries (to be discussed below), has meant a process of *deindustrialization* in the U.S. Widespread plant closings occurred in the 1980s, especially in the northeast and midwest, as a result of massive relocation of American manufacturing plants to some two hundred export processing zones in the so-called "Third World."[38] American-based transnational corporations made these shifts to avoid labor union pressures for better wage rates, job security, and other benefits. They wished to avoid U.S. government taxes, social security payments, antitrust laws, and minimum wage and hazard regulations. Third World workers would work for long hours at low wages, and Third World governments, desperate for investment, offered minimum wage-free and regulation-free conditions regarding health and safety standards, low taxation, cheap rent, and duty free import to the export processing zones.[39] Consequently, high-paying jobs in the large subsidiaries of transnational corporations disappeared and were replaced by low-paying ones in smaller independent firms, especially in the service sector, such as department stores and restaurants. Later in the 1980s, however, a process of *reindustrialization* was observed. Small firms involved either in high-tech (e.g., electronics) or labor-intensive industries (e.g., garments) provided insecure, low-skilled, and low-paying jobs with poor working conditions, offering no overtime pay or unemployment insurance. The high-tech industries require fewer workers, and firms much prefer, of course, to pay the low wages that allow them to compete with relatively lower wages in east Asia. Labor-intensive garment industries too wish to avoid high-cost unionized American workers. Consequently many of the workers are illegal immigrants from Mexico or Central America, a majority of them women.[40] With gradually improved working conditions and hostile attitudes in some parts of the Third World, especially east Asia, some transnational corporations have participated in the reindustrialization process, making use of the same illegal immigrants. According to Alvin So and studies that he cites, these very vulnerable people were recruited in the United States with the tacit consent and cooperation of government, interested in shoring up its international economic position for competition on the world market. The result of all this, not surprisingly, is a shrinking American work force, a weakened and declining labor movement, and a poorer and less secure working class.

> Labor is less mobile than capital (since labor is tied to a particular community or region), and can protest only within the boundaries of a nation-state. But capital is highly mobile because it can move from one nation to another in search of labor, raw materials, credit, and markets. Each move across national boundaries, therefore, strengthens transnational capital at the expense of the national labor unions, local communities, and the nation-state, leading to loss of jobs, decrease in tax revenues, and dislocation of the national economy.[41]

A remarkable reality facing the United States is the presence of foreign-owned firms operating within its borders, exercising enormous economic and political clout, while contributing little to the well-being of the country. In 1987, "59 percent of these non-U.S. companies reported no profit in the United States and paid no tax."[42] It is startling to realize that the American working class is actually now becoming a pool of cheap labor for foreign multinationals. Foreign manufacturers, mostly Japanese and European, have set up factories in the United States precisely to profit from cheap labor! "Wages in the United States were falling in real terms, and the decline of the dollar made it cheaper still for foreign companies to meet payrolls in America."[43] This is especially so in Tennessee, Kentucky, and South Carolina; the latter state is now home to 185 non-U.S. companies. "BMW is likely to pay around $12 an hour in South Carolina rather than the $28 it has to pay in Germany."[44] On the other hand, American wages are not yet so low that American-based companies do not find it cheaper to utilize labor forces elsewhere. For example, in 1990 Texas Instruments, a Dallas-based semiconductor firm, set up 41,500 computer terminals in its operations outside the U.S.A. Microchip design is done in the Philippines and in India, and even in Russia and the Ukraine, where engineering costs are far lower than in Texas. Even middle-class professionals, then, must compete with their opposite numbers in such places, who are able to transmit design specifications by computer.

Much more shocking is the rise of illegal child labor in the United States. Since child labor of ghastly proportions is to be found in various parts of the Third World, American employers feel that, to compete, they must follow suit at home.

> According to the U.S. Department of Labor, the number of minors illegally employed in sweatshops increased 128 percent in the second half of the 1980s. The United Farm Workers of America estimates that 800,000 children and teenagers are working as migrant laborers. According to the American Academy of Pediatrics, 100,000 children are injured on the job in the United States each year. The choice is clear. Either global standards will be raised to some decent minimum, or workers everywhere will be dragged down together by the forces of international competition.[45]

It would appear that in some respects the capitalist global economy, through the reign of the market, is returning to some of the most inhuman conditions of the early Industrial Revolution.

All of this leads to intense anger and frustration among working people, intensification of racial hatred, ethnic hostility toward immigrant workers, and increasing violence.

What is notable and ironical about all of this is that it has been happening in spite of, and in part because of, the dramatic new computerized technology, the so-called "hi-tech," which, one would have thought, should have enriched the quality of human life, not impoverished it. The "leisure society," which some people thought they glimpsed thirty years ago, has failed to materialize. Not only are many people poorer; people feel they are working harder. It appears that the conditions for the extension of social democratic measures within capitalism have disappeared, and in a knowledge-intensive and technology-intensive situation, labor has seen much of its bargaining power dissipated in transition toward a model of capitalism "inhospitable to social democratic reform and regulation, intent on dismantling the old political base of social democracy."[46] The point is that not only communism, but capitalist economies too are in crisis, in that, as I have been arguing, large numbers of working-class people in North America, whether working poor or unemployed, are getting poorer, and the prosperous middle class is shrinking.[47]

Is Capitalism Amoral?

Many authors have argued that the capitalist vision of society is essentially an amoral one. The "free market system" appears to be more and more what it always was, a mere jungle where "survival of the fittest" is the only law. Under capitalism a human being is a means to an end — profits, advantages, and power for those who own and control capital. Meeting the needs of people and of society as a whole is not what capitalism is about. Capitalism is about individual self-interest. Natural resources and the means of production do not exist within capitalism for the benefit of all, but for the private enrichment of the individuals who own and control them.

Not everyone agrees with this assessment of capitalism. American Lutheran ethicist Robert Benne, for example, deplores the tendency of theologians and ethicists to side with socialism, being almost solely concerned with issues of distribution and contemptuous of those concerned with productivity. Benne, building an ethical argument for "democratic capitalism" upon the theology of Reinhold Niebuhr, argues for the necessity of the decentralization of power and the virtues of the capitalistic separation of political and economic power. The issue of the distribution of power, of course, has always been central to the concern of socialists, many of whom are also very critical of the concentration of economic power in the hands of the state. Yet Benne demonstrates too little awareness of the dangers and injustice of the concentration of economic power in the hands of unelected owners and managers of capital. He thinks that social justice can be achieved very well within a capitalism that provides a social safety net.[48] His analysis has not yet seen the pitiful insufficiency of safety nets in the United States, the terrible plight of large numbers of working people, including children, or the decline of universal medical care and universally available higher education in Canada. Nor does he give sufficient credit to the achievements in productivity and prosperity found in relatively "socialist," social democratic nations such as Sweden, Germany, France, Belgium, and so on[49] (something we shall discuss again later).

Michael Novak, American Roman Catholic theologian, has also written a substantial theological/ethical defense of capitalism. Novak defines "democratic capitalism" as

> a predominantly market economy; a polity respectful of the rights of the individual to life, liberty, and the pursuit of happiness; and

a system of cultural institutions moved by ideals of liberty and justice for all.[50]

He speaks of the "ideal" of democratic capitalism as fundamentally an ethical phenomenon concerned with limiting the power of the state in defense against tyranny and stagnation, liberating the energies of individuals for economic enterprises that meet human needs. He celebrates the unparalleled success of capitalism in producing wealth, accompanied by political freedom. Novak scolds socialists, especially religious socialists, for failing to do their economics homework, for talking about complex economic problems as though they could be solved by mere moral/religious rhetoric. He sees the "nondoctrinaire" efforts of self-critical socialists as a form of retreat, now identifying socialism with mere "highmindedness."[51] Novak is aware of the human imperfections of capitalism, but thinks that all the alternatives are inferior, i.e., prone to both tyranny and economic inefficiency. His challenge deserves to be heard and heeded by socialists. It will not do for socialists to contrast their ideals with the worst realities of capitalism and to overlook the actual successes of capitalist systems.

One of the problems of Novak's analysis, however, is that he tends to define socialism as communism or statism and to cite all the worst examples of the latter to dismiss the value of socialism as a whole. He does not take account of the fact that the societies he regards as "socialist" (the communist ones) attempted to build socialism out of an economically peripheral position and without a previous democratic political tradition to build upon. Novak does not take seriously the damage to democratic/economic development of western/northern capitalism in the Third World and ignores the negative significance of the power of capital generally for a truly democratic order.

Defenders of capitalism, such as Novak, give little space to the mindlessness and heartlessness of capitalism and the free rein of markets that have become particularly evident through the 1980s and increasingly in the 1990s. If the conditions of "efficient" production happen to favor workers, giving them bargaining power (as was the case for two or three decades after World War II) workers may do fairly well. Capitalism, plus a minimal safety net of social security, may look good in such circumstances. But if the "mode of production" changes — if workers are less in demand, while new means of production are in the hands of a few owners and managers, the great majority of the people may become poorer. Not at all because society has less productive capacity, or less wealth is produced, or workers are inefficient, lazy, or unproductive: In the present situation the potentially humane value of highly efficient new technology benefits those who own and control it and increasingly impoverishes those who do not.

Increasingly, Novak's defense of "democratic capitalism" appears out of date and naive. In an integrated capitalist world-economy, where the power of elected governments is in rapid decline, it is not the tyranny of the state that constitutes the great problem; it is the anonymous and hidden tyranny of unelected controllers of capital whose power needs to be brought under democratic control.

The Limits of Social Democracy within Capitalism

The extent to which a fundamentally capitalist economy can combine with socialist objectives is an old and extensive debate (one to be considered again in a later chapter). A helpful analysis for our present purpose is offered by Michael Lebowitz in his article "The Limits and Possibilities of Social Democracy: A Marxian View."[52] He argues that the premise and presupposition of social democracy (i.e., left-wing parties aligned with labor unions that fight for better wages and conditions for workers within capitalism) is the "positive-sum state" wherein wages can rise and working conditions, hours, and benefits improve for workers while actually improving profits. This can be the case (as in Keynesian economics) when increased wages improve effective demand, and so stimulate capitalist job-creation, investment, and profit. Within this set of technological/economic circumstances the condition of working people can improve, not only through better wages but also government social security arrangements, rent controls, etc. Even in a situation of a "zero-sum state," where wage increases, direct or social, can occur without a reduction of profits, social democracy may accomplish much. However, he argues, in a situation of the "negative-sum state," technological conditions are such that employing large numbers of people at good wages and benefits results in falling profits. This inevitably results in a negative response by capital, i.e., employment cut backs, and/or capital flight or "capital strike."

This is particularly so in present conditions of free trade and multinational capital mobility. President Reagan, defending North American continental free trade, spoke of NAFTA as "an economic constitution for North America."[53] In fact a major reality of the North American Free Trade Agreement is that it prevents the three national governments of Canada, Mexico, and the U.S.A. from interfering with cross-border competition. The agreement essentially establishes hands-off rules for democratically elected governments with regard to investment and capital flows, state subsidies, regional distribution, the location of industries, levels of employment, etc. The agreement can be seen, then, as a direct transfer of power from elected representatives to executives of transnational corporations. Lebowitz sees free trade agreements linked to technological conditions in a way that vastly increases the power of capital and "the market."

> Improvements in communication and transport, the reduction of national policy discretion as the result of reduced trade barriers under GATT and regional free trade agreements, the relative decline in resource-intensive activities with the growing importance of knowledge and technology-intensive products — all contribute to the increase in capital mobility which makes the threat of a capital strike in any particular locality more credible.[54]

It would appear that in North America we find ourselves now in a negative-sum state, wherein the power of capital has high incentive for resistance to worker demands and citizen rights. The problem is not only how to improve workers' conditions, but how to avoid the erosion of existing social democratic gains. Profits must now not only be high; they must be higher than elsewhere if capital flight is to be avoided. In the present global economy, the competition of Third World labor, without minimum wages or benefits, and the great efficiency of the (planned) capitalist systems of Japan and the other newly industrialized countries of Asia also militate against not only the expansion, but even the retention of the well-being of First World working classes. "In short, the prospects for any challenges to the logic of capital (including its treatment of the natural environment as a mere means to profit) appear, under the present conditions, to be non-existent."[55]

All of this could simply lead to a very conservative economics: Give capital all that it wants and benefits will (or may?) trickle down to the masses; any taxation or controls placed upon capital will produce only negative results for the economy as a whole. But Lebowitz argues that this logic of conservative economics ("barbarism with a human face") holds only as long as wealth is believed to be the product of private capital exclusively. If the public sector enters into areas that capital threatens to abandon, the conservative logic no longer holds. Where living and working conditions, social benefits or environmental standards are threatened by the "logic of capital" (maximum profit) the response of social democratic governments should be to foster the development of public sector firms and cooperatives that will serve the interests of people and of the environment rather than the interests of those who possess property rights. Lebowitz sees the negative-sum state as an opportunity for socialism:

> The very gap between the logic of capital and the needs of people in a negative-sum state is an opportunity to convince people of the need to reject the logic of capital if they are to satisfy their needs. It is an opportunity to mobilise people in their own interests — a mobilisation without which no socialist government can hope to make sustained inroads upon capital. It is, in short, an opportunity to carry through that challenge to the logic of capital which has always been the raison d'etre of social democracy and socialism.[56]

Whether in the present climate any political party would dare to propose such bold "socialist" measures, i.e., major public ownership of the means of production, seems very improbable. Such socialist measures undertaken in any one nation are likely to come to grief, given the interdependence of the global capitalist economy. But if "social democratic" measures within capitalism continue to be eroded, and labor, employment, and environmental conditions continue to disintegrate in the capitalist world, the proposals of Lebowitz may, over time, become increasingly credible and attractive. May not democratic electorates in various parts of the world begin to cooperate to control the humanly destructive power of capital? At any rate, Lebowitz's analysis suggests that the burgeoning prosperity of North America in the thirty years following World War II and the high employment, the increasing wages, and the social democratic achievements for working people that accompanied it, may have been the exception rather than the rule for capitalist systems.

Chapter 5

Capitalism and the Third World

Even as the western/northern right wing exults in the collapse of communism and the victory of "free market capitalism" in the Cold War, people in the Third World, especially Africa, Latin America, and the Caribbean, are not so convinced that the triumph of capitalism is a step toward the Kingdom of God. According to U.N. data, forty million persons, half of them children, die every year from hunger and malnutrition. In Brazil, the world's eighth largest capitalist economy, four hundred thousand children under one year of age die every year — the equivalent of a Hiroshima atomic bomb every fifty days![1] It is not surprising that, under such conditions, repressive, tyrannical governments have been common throughout the capitalist Third World. To many thoughtful people in the Third World the collapse of communism is bad news indeed — not because they had a naive view of the righteousness of the Soviet bloc, but because capital is now virtually unopposed in the world. Franz Hinkelammert of Costa Rica writes,

> Capitalism believes it has won. The world which now appears is one in which there is now only one Lord and master and only one system. Now we have a world with only one empire, which reaches everywhere. The empire covers the entire planet.... It has absolute power and it knows this.... This means that for the first time the Third World is completely alone.[2]

Domination and Debt

The ongoing problem of Third World poverty and questions of "development" and "underdevelopment" are exceedingly complex, a veritable minefield of conflicting theory, in which highly sophisticated economists and political scientists cannot agree, either in their analysis or in their prescriptions. I shall not attempt, in this brief chapter, to expound or adjudicate among all of these theorists. On the other hand, we cannot allow our political and ethical thought to be paralyzed by the disagreement of the experts, since the disagreements among social scientists are almost as notorious as the disagreements among theologians and ethicists. Philosophers reflecting on the methods of social science have been teaching us for some time now that all social analysis is a work of interpretation.[3] One's selection and weighing of social data will always be impacted by our finite perspectives. While social science rightly seeks to avoid self-deception by the use of hard data and statistics, we recognize that the social sciences, though empirically based, cannot be well understood on the model of empirical natural sciences. Positivist or "value free" social science, modelled upon the apparent objectivity and precision of the physical sciences, is not possible.[4] We are naive, therefore, if we claim that our viewpoints on issues of Third World poverty are "ideology free." Further, our Christian and ethical/faith perspective here informs and predisposes us toward some social science outlooks rather than others. For example, our biblically based understanding of sin and oppression, our attachment, in faith, to a poor and crucified Lord, predisposes us to see poverty as sinful oppression, and exploitation. Merely functionalist theories of "underdevelopment" (associated with classical and neo-classical "liberal" economics[5]), wherein societies are seen on the analogy of functioning organisms striving for equilibrium, are inadequate, since they overlook the domination, oppression and class struggle that characterizes social change.[6] We are predisposed, then, toward "dialectical" theories that take seriously the reality of injustice, social conflict, and class struggle. Such a predisposition should not be entirely determinative of our thought about poverty in the Third World. Conflicting theories must be assessed in terms of their power to account for empirical realities and illuminate the situation in a persuasive manner.

A helpful exposition by sociologist Alvin So discusses development theory in terms of three types: modernization, dependency and world-systems theories.[7]

Modernization theory, which predominated in the 1950s, tends to be "liberal" and functionalist, assuming "progress" from underdeveloped to developed conditions in the Third World. A key theorist here is W. W. Rostow, who wrote of "the Take-Off into Self-Sustained Growth." This optimistic approach was widely discredited by the 1960s, especially by Third World social scientists, as "developmentalist" efforts through capital investment and foreign aid failed to lift up the masses of the poor in the Third World. "Development" often occurred, in the sense of increased industrial capacity and increased extraction of mineral and agricultural resources, but this was usually "capital" rather than "labor intensive." Only a local elite benefited, together with First World investors, who reaped resources and profits. Modernization theories have been refined in response to their critics and continue to be a major presence on the scene.[8]

In Latin America especially a school of *dependency theory* arose, rejecting modernization theory and operating with dialectical, Marxist-inspired concepts of class struggle, but applying this to the relations of the First and Third Worlds. The poorer nations cannot be expected simply to repeat the development history of the west through modernization. Key concepts here are metropolis/satellite, or center/periphery. The periphery nations and regions of the world provide raw resources for the center, or core, nations and regions. The periphery is forced to serve the interests of the center and is dependent upon and dominated by the center.[9] Key dependency theorists are, for example, A. G. Frank, F. H. Cardoso, E. Faletto. This theory has been criticized and modified but continues to inform many analysts.[10]

One of the perspectives from which dependency theory has been modified is *world-systems analysis,* which appeared in the 1970s. The key thinker here has been Immanuel Wallerstein.[11] He insisted on the interconnected or holistic character of the capitalist world-economy, which must be understood historically and culturally, as well as in terms of politics and economics. In many ways world-systems analysis resembles and borrows from dependency theory, but complexifies the analysis, speaking of core, semiphery, and periphery. This three tier analysis enables researchers to analyze, among other things, the transition of certain Asian economies from peripheral to semipheral or even core status. This kind of theory does not pretend to be value free, but seeks to inform transformation for humane purposes. It teaches that "class struggle movements must be waged at the world level in order to be effective in forcing the pace of the transformation of the capitalist world-economy."[12]

Liberation theology generally has operated with some kind of dependency theory as its socio-analytic mediation, and here too we are informed by the dependency (center/periphery) analysis, modified and refined by world-systems analysis. If we begin to be specific and concrete in our understanding of ongoing poverty in the Third World, we will recognize that the domination of the Third World by international capital occurs to a large degree through the work of the International Monetary Fund (I.M.F.) and the World Bank. These institutions, dominated politically by the United States and other large western/northern nations, ostensibly exist to stabilize and regulate the world-economy and, the World Bank especially, to assist the less developed countries with economic development. They operate according to a very clear "free market" ideology. Third World countries, already deeply in debt, if they wish to obtain loans or rescheduling of debt and avoid complete ostracism in the world-economy, must conform to the so-called "structural adjustment programs" (SAPs).[13] The SAPs consist of the application of free-market ideology prescribed across the board in a dogmatic and authoritarian manner. Debtor nations are required to remove government subsidies on imports for urban areas, allowing the market to allocate resources and prices. They must reduce the role, size, and cost of government by privatizing parastatals, privatize and/or reduce basic services to people, such as education and health care, and cut wages and salaries to civil servants. The welcoming of foreign investment on generous terms is encouraged, even required; export-oriented economic growth is prescribed, emphasizing the production and export of commodity items, and the process of production is to be on a purely competitive basis.[14] This has been the strategy that many Third World nations have been forced to implement through the 1980s. The whole process, however, has resulted in the further enrichment of the north at the expense of the south. Susan George, one author who provides information and analysis on Third World debt, tells us that during the 1980s the south has transferred to the north, through interest payments on debt, the equivalent of many Marshall Plans.

> It is in fact astonishing that third world countries would pay their commercial creditors an average of nearly $77 billion a year; more than $6.4 billion a month — yet find themselves as a group fully 28 per cent more in debt to these creditors than they were in 1982, in spite of a dearth of new lending.[15]

The debt of the African continent grew faster than that of any other region. In 1970 it was US $46 billion, but by 1992 it has reached $280 billion. John Mihevc cites the following U.N. statistics on increasing poverty in Africa:

Real wages have declined by 25 percent, employment has fallen by 16 percent. Over 30 million Africans are unemployed and an additional 95 million are underemployed. Per capita consumption in sub-Saharan Africa has fallen by one-fifth. Spending on health care has declined by 50 percent and on education by 25 percent over the last decade. As many as 10,000 African children are dying each day.[16]

A basic reality of the poorer countries is their bondage to export. Populations that once fed themselves off their own lands became dependent on export of agricultural products for the foreign exchange necessary for solvency in the world-economy. "Millions who went to bed hungry lived within sight of rich agricultural lands producing bumper crops for export."[17] Land has been used for coffee, sugar, tea, cocoa, beef, flowers, etc. There are many examples of this on the African continent, where almost all of the very poorest countries of the world are to be found, but for us in North America, our free trade partner Mexico is perhaps the most relevant example. Barnet and Cavanagh tell us that from 1940 to 1960 Mexico, guided by a nationalistic economic policy, was self-sufficient in food and the population reasonably well nourished. After 1960 an oil boom and a hopeful process of industrialization moved Mexico more and more into the world-economy. But market forces ended the oil boom and industrialization was stalled.

> Mexican farmers could get higher prices for animal feed for the livestock industry than for corn or beans, and so acres once devoted to these staples of most Mexicans went into sorghum and other higher-priced grains to feed the livestock that would eventually end up on the grills of affluent beef-eaters, mostly abroad....By 1990, 40 percent of the beans consumed by Mexicans was imported, as was 25 percent of the corn and 30 percent of the sugar.[18]

As a result, nutritional standards in the nation as a whole have fallen drastically, per capita consumption having fallen 28 percent. Almost half of the children in rural Mexico suffer from malnutrition. Meanwhile, large American food companies, such as Pepsico and Pillsbury, have moved operations into Mexico to profit from low wage levels, leaving unemployment in California. Food processing companies are also setting up alongside automobile and electronics production in the *maquiladoras*, the duty-free border areas of Mexico, free not only of export duties but also minimum wages, safety standards, or environmental laws.

Third World labor, as we have seen, helps to create massive unemployment in the First World, and this functions to bring down workers' wages in North America and elsewhere and to undermine unions and collective bargaining. Meanwhile U.S. retailers like Sears and K-mart are able to clothe the North American population with garments made in the sweat shops of Guatemala, Haiti, or the Philippines, where child labor is rampant:

> In the Philippines, according to a study of subcontracting in the garment industry in the town of Angono just south of Manila, 1,447 children are employed in sewing, stitching, or packing baby dresses. The typical work week is seventy-seven hours, 7:00 a.m. to 7:00 p.m. seven days a week.... Four-to-six-year-olds receive five pesos a day; an 11-year-old can earn as much as ten. The legal minimum wage in the area is sixty-nine pesos.[19]

Stories of this kind can be multiplied about the operation of the capitalist world-economy in the Third World. We have seen, in the last chapter, that labor conditions, including the expansion of child labor, have deteriorated in parts of the First World too, especially the United States. If we evaluate capitalist ideology and the operation of the global capitalist economy simply in terms of its ability to serve the material interests of human beings, the evidence of its effectiveness in capitalist-oriented Africa, Latin America, and other parts of the Third World is overwhelmingly negative. Nor is the capitalist Third World notable for its political democracy, freedom, or human rights. Yet free-market ideology continues to be promulgated as unquestionable dogma by those whose interests it serves.

In Contrast: China

The development achievements of China contrast dramatically with those of the capitalist Third World that we have just discussed. The communist revolution of 1949 frightened the core capitalist states, lest socialism spread throughout Asia. They did all they could to destroy the Chinese revolution, barring China from the U.N., imposing a trade embargo, and generally isolating China economically. This forced China to withdraw from the world-economy,[20] and because of its great size and immense resources, it was able to do so with success. The Maoist period (1949–79) saw rapid industrialization of an unparalleled kind. The gross value of industrial output increased thirty-eight-fold over the Mao period, and the growth of heavy industry alone was ninety-fold. This was the highest rate of growth of any country during any comparable period in world history.[21] China was not as successful in increasing agricultural production under its system of collective farms, which barely kept pace with the increase of population. However, the Chinese did not suffer the gross hunger, poverty, and malnutrition common in the capitalist Third World. China saw a vast expansion of literacy and of education generally, a near comprehensive medical care system, and a near doubling of average life expectancy (from thirty-five to sixty-five years).[22] This is not to say that the story of China is unambiguous. We know that the Chinese revolution was accomplished through widespread violence and repression. The lack of civil liberty in China (as in the capitalist developing nations) has become painfully evident to the world — not only in the Maoist period, but afterward as well.

Those who have studied China closely report that by 1979 the Chinese system was burdened by bureaucratic inefficiency, overstaffing, petty corruption and waste. Much of the socialist enthusiasm of the masses had been lost. This communist/socialist society had become, much like the Soviet Union, a state capitalist monopoly controlled by an oligarchy, confirming the view among many socialists and others that state ownership does not by any means guarantee the "self-government of producers." After Mao's death efforts were made to open up the economic system by decollectivization of most rural enterprises, and many de facto private ventures were permitted by pro-market type reforms.[23] The solid achievements of Mao's communism are being built upon by a China that is now reintegrating into the world-economy. The capitalist core states, by the early 1970s, began to see China as a valuable source of resources and markets. China needed reintegration, apparently, to overcome its own stagnation. A large middle class is rapidly developing in China, and class relations are developing more and more in the western style.[24]

These ambiguities notwithstanding, the Chinese experience proves at least this: another, more successful model of economic development for the material uplifting of the Third World poor exists outside the prescriptions of capitalist ideology. The Chinese story, resembling as it does the Soviet story, also raises questions about the long-term viability of state-owned monopoly "socialism."

Or does the Chinese success have something to do with Asian culture? The extraordinary success not only of socialism, but also of capitalism in some Asian nations, suggests that profound socio-cultural characteristics of Asian peoples may be an important factor favoring rapid economic development.

The Spectacle of East Asian Capitalism

If China has been a marvel of rapid Third World development under communism, other Asian nations, capitalist ones, appear to have out-shone China, at least in some respects. I refer of course to Japan and to the four smaller Asian capitalist nations that have made great de-velopmental leaps toward economic prosperity since the Second World War: Hong Kong, Singapore, South Korea, and Taiwan — sometimes called the "minidragons" or the "four tigers." I cannot begin to tell the complex stories of all these nations, nor adequately analyze the causes of their economic success. Nor do I suggest, by speaking of their phenomenal "success," that these are the most admirable, hu-mane, environmentally responsible, or compassionate societies in the world. For our purpose here it is important to note that capitalism, as private ownership of capital, has taken in these Asian nations a form quite different from what we find in the west and north.

The remarkable rise of Japan after World War II is well known. A defeated nation, driven to its knees by utter defeat in the war, operat-ing as late as 1949 with an enormous trading deficit, has become an economic giant with a huge trade surplus, competing well in automo-biles and other high-tech products with international competitors all over the world.[25] In the opinion of the world-systems analyst Waller-stein, Japan has effectively wrested world economic hegemony from the United States.[26] This judgment appears to be confirmed by facts and figures offered by Barnet and Cavanagh on the power of the Japa-nese banks in world financial markets: By 1992 eight of the world's top ten banks, ranked by assets, were Japanese. Between 1981 and 1989 Japanese banks increased their share of the assets of the world's top one hundred banks from 25 to 46 percent, while the share of U.S. banks fell from 15 percent to 6 percent. In 1989 Japanese banks provided 20 percent of all credit in California![27] Troubled by Japanese competition in automobiles, in the early 1980s the United States insisted that the Japanese build cars in the U.S., but the result of this was that the Japanese auto companies took over a still larger share of the U.S. market and extended control over the automobile parts and accessories business.[28] Moreover, the United States, because of the large government deficit incurred during the Reagan years, has become deeply dependent on foreign credit, and it has been Japanese capital that has bought up U.S. treasury bonds and other government securities.[29]

Whatever may be undesirable about Japanese society — rigid social hierarchy and authoritarianism, serious pollution, overcrowding, economic and racial/social injustice are often mentioned — the standard of living of most Japanese has risen rapidly indeed and is the envy of both First and Third World nations. This has amounted to a kind of late "industrial revolution" for Japan (and the four minidragons) — something that has not occurred in Africa or Latin America or other parts of Asia. Historians and economists who have studied Japan have debated endlessly about the factors that brought about this transformation. Most observers note a high degree of government economic interventionism, dubbed the "capitalist developmental state,"[30] quite the opposite of so-called "laissez-faire" capitalism. This amounts to a very close association of great corporations with government and a high degree of government authority in the management of the economy. As we have noted, government subsidization and cooperation with industry is common also in western capitalism (if we heed the analysis of Galbraith), but the Japanese have a much more powerful and authoritative state, which plans the whole economy in the national interest, not only in the interest of capital and upper management. Phillip Oppenheim, in his recent and highly enthusiastic book on Japan, *Japan without Blinkers*, points out that the difference between Japan and other capitalist nations lies not in government involvement or noninvolvement, but in the nature of that involvement, i.e., to help industry to "run with the grain of the market, rather than against it."[31] This means a highly efficient coherence between what industry produces and what people (the world over) actually want, useful goods of very high quality. It is in the nature of Japanese capitalism, for example, to practice a relative equality of earnings, and in this it differs remarkably, for example, from what we noted above about American capitalism:

Since the Second World War, the pay levels of the lower ranks of Japanese industry have been rising much more rapidly than have the pay levels of top executives, while the pretax compensation at the top levels of Japanese industry is still relatively low.[32]

Basic to the character of Japanese capitalism is its relatively solidaristic socio-economic arrangements, which in some ways resemble what we call "socialism" in the west. Students of Japanese history and society believe that much of Japan's (and generally east Asia's) recent economic success goes back to its neo-Confucian religious and cultural roots, which emphasize "the virtues of loyalty, filial piety, obedience to seniors, courage and self-sacrifice."[33] This broad Asian tradition, in its Japanese form combined with elements of Shinto and Japanese Buddhism, is particularly military in character, emphasizing loyalty to the emperor, but also to one's lord or one's immediate superior.[34] Thus the individualism and individualistic economic self-seeking that we associate with western/northern capitalism is much less present in Japan and its Asian neighbors. In old prewar, preindustrial Japan, a strict hierarchy of individuals and families operated within the village, which developed a kind of consensus democracy and spirit of mutual assistance. These deeply ingrained cultural attitudes, combining vertical and group ties, have been carried over into the operation of large modern corporations. J. Hunter, in her book on modern Japan, tells us that "the archetypal Japanese firm sets itself up as a paternalistic entity, caring for its employees in a way that breeds intense loyalty and hard work."[35] Oppenheim, an author who tends to play down the differences between Japan and western capitalism, agrees about this. The success of Japanese capitalism depends to a large extent on a hard-working, loyal, and enthusiastic work force:

> The word *uchi*, which means *home*, is also often used by workers to refer to their company. But this is loyalty which has been earned. Matsushita offers its employees pay and perks which would be the envy of most European workers. These include bonuses, low-cost homes, hospital care, travel loans and wedding grants. In return, the company is accorded almost total dedication. The Matsushita employee does not strike, is flexible in the work place, accepts low pay rises in lean years, declines to take all the holiday due and is prepared to adjust working hours to fit production schedules.[36]

What is described here is remarkably like Karl Marx's vision of unalienated labor and contrasts sharply with the attitudes of the profoundly alienated work forces that are to be found within western capitalism and, for that matter, eastern communism. The president of Kentucky Fried Chicken Japan describes the Japanese phenomenon as "more communist than the communist countries themselves."[37]

But it would be a mistake to carry the analogy too far. It must be said that many are excluded from the opulence of these large corporations: many Japanese work for smaller firms that cannot offer these benefits; the Korean minority in Japan and the longstanding underclass of *eta*, untouchable, "polluted ones," are among the victims of a society that is very far from "utopia."[38]

The pattern of capitalism in the other "four tigers," Hong Kong, Singapore, South Korea, and Taiwan, is remarkably similar to that of Japan (though to speak of all of them together is necessarily to overgeneralize). These nations, not long ago clearly part of the poor and oppressed Third World or periphery, must now be regarded, in the language of world-systems analysis, as "semiperipheral." The pattern of domination/dependence of center to periphery has been partially broken, not because of any benevolence on the part of the rich core nations, and not through a socialist revolution, but because of various historical and cultural factors that appear to be operative in these parts of Asia, as well as characteristics of the world-economy. As Wallerstein sees it, semiperipheral nations *seize the chance* of the weakened position of core countries and are able to do so because of aggressive state action.[39]

Steven Goldstein, in his study of "Minidragons," tells of the amazing industrialization and economic growth in these nations since approximately the end of the Korean war. The common thread, he notes, is the labor-intensive, export-oriented growth,[40] exhibiting many of the same characteristics found in Japanese society, including the interventionist, authoritarian state and a highly dedicated and loyal work force. Speaking of South Korea, political scientist Chong-Sik Lee informs us that

> the stimulus for economic change had to come from the state. In 1972 President Park launched the third five-year economic development plan (1972–76), an ambitious program which sought to redress the imbalance caused by the first two five-year plans (1962–71) by emphasizing the agricultural sector.[41]

Barnet and Cavanagh confirm this analysis, noting that the governments of the successful Asian "newly industrializing countries" (NICs) invited foreign investment into local factories, but took a heavy managerial role in economic development.[42]

But Chong-Sik Lee accounts for the possibility of this Korean phenomenon partly in terms of Confucian culture:

> The Confucian stress on human bonds and on duties and obligations has left both positive and negative legacies. Individual units (such as factories) and society as a whole can readily maintain cohesion and order because of the Koreans' ingrained sense of deference and mutual obligation.[43]

Yet, he goes on, this inheritance makes it easier for rulers and employers to exploit people for their own ends and can lead to nepotism and cronyism. Much of the recent economic success has occurred under highly authoritarian, oppressive rulers, in conditions that would be socially and culturally unacceptable to the west, which is both more committed to personal freedom and more individualistic. In South Korea, with a large Christian population, approximately 25 percent, and perhaps relatively more "westernized" than the others, a variety of liberation theology has arisen known as Minjung theology (theology of the crowd, or the oppressed masses), which has been an important part of the movement for democratic government. The fortunes of the Korean people generally have improved dramatically since the end of the Korean War. As recently as 1961, eight years after the war, South Korea was still a poverty-stricken nation with an average per capita income of less than $100 per year. By the time of the Seoul Olympics in 1988 it was up to $12,000 per year,[44] and after a great deal of social struggle and suffering, democracy in government and certain social democratic measures have emerged.

What do we conclude from this glimpse into the world of east Asian capitalism? First, that this capitalism is quite a different creature from western capitalism, and the validity and sustainability of the latter cannot be defended by reference to Japan or South Korea. The religious, cultural, and political history of that region is so profoundly different from that of the west that it is irresponsible to draw conclusions from the one for the other. Since Asian capitalism in some respects resembles socialism, the debate between capitalism and socialism in the west can no more be foreclosed by reference to the Asian economic miracle than to the failure of Soviet and eastern European communism. It confirms us in the presupposition of this discussion, i.e., that no "pure" capitalism or socialism exists anywhere in the world, that in fact these are opposing ideologies that nevertheless exist at opposite ends of a single continuum.

The Idolatry of Capital

We have noted the religio-cultural roots of Asian capitalism. Communism has often been accused of having *become* a religion or quasi-religion, or of being in fact a "faith," including a total world view, a way of life, a source of meaning and hope, a way of salvation, and so on.[45] And the case has been well made that totalitarian communism, like Nazism and other totalitarian systems, is clearly idolatrous. Capitalism, usually coexisting quite comfortably with various forms of religion, even supporting and financing various forms of Christianity, has appeared to be exempt from this accusation. But capitalism too can be analyzed as religious in character, and the idolatry of capital becomes dramatically visible in the Third World. That is, capitalism too, and today especially capitalism and its god, *the market,* vaunts itself as the true emperor and empire, the true *kurios.*

The characterization of capitalism as "religious" and of the market as potential "lord" goes back to Karl Marx's concept of commodity fetishism. A "fetish" is an object of unreasoned worship or devotion, or a fascination and fixation upon something that comes to dominate the human being. Human relations with commodities become a kind of fetishism partly because of the need and dependence of human beings upon things, but particularly because human beings lack control over these things. As Marx sees it, private ownership in the production process alienates people from the products of their labor. The proletariat producer has no control over the product, how it will be used, or how he or she will share in its value. But even the capitalist owner cannot control commodities, which become commodity-subjects, or as Marx calls them, "physical-metaphysical objects" with lives and behaviors of their own. In volume 1 of *Capital,* Marx explains:

> The form of wood, for instance, is altered if a table is made out of it. Nevertheless the table continues to be wood, an ordinary, sensuous thing. But as soon as it emerges as a commodity, it changes into a physical-metaphysical object. It not only stands with its feet on the ground, but, in relation to all other commodities, it

stands on its head, and evolves out of its wooden brain grotesque ideas, far more wonderful than if it were to begin dancing of its own free will.[46]

Franz Hinkelammert amplifies this quotation from Marx:

Commodities now set up social relationships among themselves. . . . Oil fights with coal, and wood with plastic. Coffee dances on world markets and iron and steel get married. . . .

The commodity producer comes to be dominated by the social relationships that commodities establish among themselves. . . . There emerges a bewitched and topsy-turvy world.[47]

The world is topsy-turvy precisely because the process of production has mastery over human beings; humans must adjust themselves to the market. They must become obedient to the will of the market, and only conformity to the will of the market will "save" them. Thus the market is *kurios*. Money becomes the focus of commodity fetishism, in that it expresses and mediates the value of all other commodities, and money becomes omnipotent:

With the possibility of keeping hold of the commodity as exchange-value, or exchange-value as a commodity, the lust for gold awakens. With the extension of commodity circulation there is an increase in the power of money, that absolute social form of wealth which is always ready to be used. "Gold is a wonderful thing! Its owner is master of all he desires. Gold can even enable souls to enter Paradise" (Columbus, in his letter from Jamaica, 1503).[48]

Marx continually uses biblical allusions to explicate the fetishistic relationship of human beings to money. He quotes Revelation 17:13: "They will come to agreement and bestow their power and authority on the beast," and Revelation 13:17: "Moreover it did not allow a man to buy or sell anything unless he was first marked with the name of the beast or with the number that stood for its name."[49] Though for John of Patmos the beast was Rome, for Marx the beast in modern times is capital, the power of stored-up human labor, which now, in the form of private property, rises up to dominate human beings: "As the chosen people bore in the features the sign that they were the property of Jehovah, so the division of labor brands the manufacturing worker as the property of capital."[50] The proletarians, of course, become themselves commodities, saleable for money in the labor market. But the owners of capital and hoarders of money also chase after "the eternal which can be touched neither by moths nor by rust, and which is wholly celestial and wholly mundane."[51]

Marx thought that private ownership of productive property was the problem leading to commodity fetishism, or what Christians might call idolatry — the worship of mammon. He believed that a reordering of economic relationships by socializing private property and a "free association of workers" would eliminate the distortion of commodity control of human beings. While we may agree that public or worker ownership and control would be salutary for human beings, we have good historical reasons to doubt whether these socialist measures can be as salvific as Marx thought they would be. We may doubt whether socialism, or any other socio-economic political arrangements, will cure humanity of the idolatry of mammon.

Nevertheless, Marx's analysis of the religious character of capitalism is illuminating and liberating, and Christian thinkers have recently been taking it up.[52] It is important for us to hear the anger and passion of Third World Christian voices in their denunciation of capitalism. Costa Rican Methodist theologian Victorio Araya speaks passionately against capital as an economic idol, whose victory is indeed bad news both for the poor and for nature. In the economic logic of capitalism, he says, capital and the law of the market come first, while human beings, their basic needs, and the right to life for all come second. It is apparent that in the following comment Araya has in mind particularly the free-market ideology and functioning of the International Monetary Fund (IMF) and World Bank:

> Capitalism is a system of economic idolatry. Idolatry occurs when humankind deposits its faith and life in something that is not God, but a creation of its own hands....
>
> In the capitalist new market economy, the laws of the market are absolute, untouchable; they can't be changed. They acquire a sacred character that legitimates them as the only possible road to salvation.... "Outside the market there is no salvation...." '"
>
> It is necessary to discern the sacrificial character of capitalism in its demand for human sacrifice.... What is human sacrifice if it is not the slow or rapid death of the millions of the poor in the countries of the South whose life and blood are squeezed out by national or international capital and transferred to the countries

of the North in order that the sacred market remains untouchable and gives life and growth to great capital?[53]

Julio de Santa Ana speaks in a similar vein:

> The laws of the market, which are not independent of the people involved in the market, come to be seen as transcendent. That is, they undergo a process of sociological sacralization. Not only are they given a higher status, they actually become untouchable, like the laws of nature. They become a taboo which must not be shaken.[54]

Hinkelammert expresses his outrage that

> through this policy of total market economy which was promoted by the Reagan government, the eighties of this century became a decade of genocide in the Third World for the recovery of foreign debt, and made a holocaust of nature.[55]

We need to hear the rage of these voices from the Third World, because they shock us into the realization that the capitalist world-economy, while it may have been relatively good for some of us in the First World, has been at the bitter expense of brothers and sisters elsewhere.

And now we have begun to see that the free rein of capital is not good for most of us either. Capital must be de-divinized. As an unquestionable idol, as the great beast, it is nothing but the unfettered profit motive and the control of the economic world by a small number of people in their own interests. In keeping with Marx's analysis of commodity fetishism, it takes on a life of its own and masquerades today under the guise of "Globalization," "New World Order," and "Free Trade."[56] Humanity appears to be in the grip of the great beast. Efforts by democratically elected governments, even social democratic ones (such as the New Democratic Party in Ontario), to organize economic life in the interests of all the people, to redistribute wealth, to provide necessities and opportunities to all, appear to be entirely at the mercy of those who can choose to set interest rates and invest or withdraw capital. Since capital is lodged with and allocated mainly through multinational corporations, themselves larger than many governments, it is beyond the regulative power of any democratically elected government. The logic of capital is such that those who control it do so in their own interests, becoming wealthy and powerful, while most others, especially those not needed by capital, become "throwaway people" and their nations "throwaway nations."[57] Yet capital is simply that accumulated wealth which is required for economic development, to create the possibilities for productivity and employment. Capital is good and necessary, of course, a creature, not evil in itself, but something that must be kept subordinate and instrumental to the well-being of humans and the earth. The democratic control of multinational capital, it must be said, is a gigantic task that no one today appears ready to take on. Ideologically speaking, it is the task for a long-term renewed socialism. Theologically speaking, the false "Lord," capital, must be brought under the Reign of God.

•

The question of a socialist alternative to capitalism is not by any means settled, then, by reference to the failures of Soviet communism. The critique of that historical phenomenon has long been part of socialist thought itself. The collapse of communism, however, cannot be regarded as the "end of history," as though capitalism as it now exists can be regarded as the great answer to our human problems. We need a clearer idea of what constitutes authentic socialism, of the various kinds of socialism that have been tried over the past century and a half, and we need to begin to imagine what possibilities exist for socialism in the future. To begin, let us look to socialist history, especially its originating concepts and practices.

Part III

What Is Socialism?

Chapter 6

A Glance at the Early History

If we wish to think theologically about the historical political reality of socialism and also to move toward a renewed vision of what socialism can be in the future, we need a clear sense of what "socialist" has meant to those who have called themselves by that name. First it is necessary to insist that, historically, socialism is not identifiable with Soviet or eastern bloc communism, and that it is older and much broader than Marxism. Karl Marx has been, certainly, the most influential and perhaps the most powerful intellect in the history of socialism, but Marx entered an existing socialist/communist movement that could already be found in the three countries in which he resided — Germany, France, and Britain. It is not my intention to offer a substantial account of socialist history (this would require at least one whole large volume, and a number of good histories already exist), but only a brief glance, especially at the early history, in order to reach a sense of socialism's original roots and identity. Since every historical account involves interpretation and selectivity, my telling of the story here will of course reflect my concerns and biases. My underlying interest in the telling of the story is the relation of Christian faith to the development of socialist thought and practice, and the question of the appropriateness of socialist options for Christian people. As I have said, if it can be shown that historical socialism, as it has actually existed, has been an unmitigated disaster to the well-being of people; if it can be demonstrated that socialism simply "does not work" — i.e., renders people poorer, more oppressed, and more alienated than they were before (as is often now being said) — then no "theological" reasoning can be used to save it from well-deserved oblivion.

Socialist thought is not, of course, pure ideas fallen from the sky. In accordance with Marx's historical materialist insight into the material basis of social change and the development of ideas, we have to find the historical roots of socialist thought and practice in the rapidly changing socio-economic conditions of eighteenth-century Europe. Socialism, as a constellation of ideas and practice, was in large measure a product of the Industrial Revolution, that technological and economic upheaval that began in England around 1760, and the not unrelated French Revolution, which sent its political tidal wave out over Europe in 1789. The two revolutions were very different, of course, the one being technical and economic, the other political and social, occurring on opposite sides of the English Channel. Both were "revolutionary" in the sense that they were important turning points in the history of humanity. But it is no accident that the French Revolution occurred soon after the "take off" of the Industrial Revolution. In a sense one can regard them as two aspects of one phenomenon — changing material/economic conditions leading to the rising power of the European middle class (the bourgeoisie), the declining power of the feudal aristocracies, and the beginning of the new "liberal" capitalist era. Socialist thought and activity arose, both in France and in England (and to a lesser extent in Germany) as a response to this "dual revolution."[1]

The Industrial Revolution

It is well known that the Industrial Revolution was prepared for over several centuries of improving agricultural technology, rising population, and the development of towns and the middle class, which occurred in western Europe from about the twelfth century and accelerated especially in the sixteenth. The period from the sixteenth to the eighteenth centuries was marked by the rupture of religio-cultural structures, by the appearance of modern philosophy and science, by colonialism and slavery, and by drastic political change. The Industrial Revolution should not be regarded as a sudden bolt from the blue; some authors relativize its significance, noting profound socio-economic changes occurring two or three centuries earlier.[2] The Industrial Revolution itself was apparently triggered in the late eighteenth century by certain new technical innovations. The steam engine, the creation of James Watt in 1784, meant railways and steamships, which expedited the transportation of raw materials from mines to factories and from factories to markets at home and overseas. The cotton gin of Eli Whitney, 1793, meant the rapid processing of cotton and massive increase in textile output. A ready class of capitalist entrepreneurs took advantage of the new opportunities that were inherent, not only in these technical inventions, but also in the increased population, which meant readily available low-cost labor and a hungry market for industrial products. Huge markets in India and North America as well meant that industrialists had no difficulty selling their wares; colonies of the British Empire functioned as a well-protected and limitless source of buyers. Cheap labor, especially in the colonies, and the institution of slavery, helped to supply cheap raw materials and contributed enormously to the low cost of cotton. In 1785 textile output in Britain amounted to only 40 million yards; in 1850 it was 2,205 million yards.[3] The rapid growth of the industrial system and its dependence on steam and the railways after 1830 is indicated by the increase of iron and coal production: in 1830, Britain produced 15 million tons of coal; by 1850 coal output had more than trebled to 49 nine million tons. Iron output of 680,000 tons in 1830 had multiplied by 1850 to 2,250,000 tons.[4] The figures illustrate the incredible acceleration of British industry and economy from the late eighteenth to the mid-nineteenth centuries. These developments spread quickly to Belgium, France, Holland, Germany, and the United States. But in 1850 Britain was still far ahead and able to compound its growth through the exploitation of its huge empire.

Tragically these wonderful material advances of the Industrial Revolution did not benefit, but rather impoverished and degraded the working class of Britain. The economic historian Karl Polanyi declares, at the opening of his book *The Great Transformation,* "At the heart of the Industrial Revolution of the eighteenth century there was an almost miraculous improvement in the tools of production, which was accomplished by a catastrophic dislocation of the lives of the common people."[5] There developed a wealthy capitalist class, which was in a position to maximize its profits unhindered by the feudal obligations of the past. While the serfs of the old feudal system had at least enjoyed a relationship marked by some measure of mutual service and loyalty, the working class (the proletariat) of the new system was strictly a commodity (as Marx would point out), a dehumanized pawn in the economic game of profit maximization, cut off, as Polanyi sees it, from the land and the fabric of meaningful work in community. To understand the appearance of socialism one needs to glimpse the condition of the working class in the early nineteenth century. An individual member of the large labor force had no choice but to work for factory and mine owners, since no other source of employment and income existed. He or she could be made to work ten, twelve, or sixteen hours a day in dreadful conditions for a subsistence wage.

If workers asked for more than the allotted pittance, shorter hours, or better working conditions, they could be easily replaced by members of the huge army of the unemployed who were clambering for a livelihood. To facilitate discipline and smooth operations, as well as low labor costs, women and children were used in large numbers. In the textile industry only about one-fourth of the labor force was made up of men; half were women and girls, one-fourth boys under eighteen.[6] Small boys, as young as seven years, were used particularly in the dark, claustrophobic conditions of the mines, chained to carts of coal as beasts of burden. Great urban slums sprang up, providing minimal, crowded, and soon very ugly housing for the urbanized working force in such rapidly growing centers as Manchester, Birmingham, and Glasgow.

The new economic reality of the early Industrial Revolution produced its first major theorist in Adam Smith, author in 1776 of *The Wealth of Nations*. Smith gave us the classic liberal account of how the economy of a nation functions according to the laws of supply and demand.[7] Society automatically regulates itself to supply what is demanded, he taught. Industry and business will supply what people will pay for. Labor too functions in terms of supply and demand; when plenty of labor is available, wages will be low. Skilled labor, being in shorter supply will be more costly. The labor costs of a man of business must be kept to a minimum of course in order to maximize his profits and the efficiency of the economic process. Smith recommended laissez-faire, that is, the economy should be left alone, must be left free, and must not be interfered with. If allowed to function freely according to natural economic laws it will produce maximum benefit for all. This theory of the "invisible hand" stressed the liberty of each person to seek his or her own economic interest. It is not accurate, though, to characterize Smith's motives as the promotion of greed and selfishness. Much of Smith's argument was in fact directed against the great mercantilist chartered companies that monopolized access to resources and trade in certain sectors and regions under royal/government protection. We may surmise that he would be critical of the anticompetitive aspects of the great corporations of our time, which do all they can to protect themselves from the risk of the market. He was explicitly critical of joint stock companies ruled by managers.[8] Smith's ideas, taken selectively, became the ideology of the liberal capitalism of the Industrial Revolution, and his theories are still cited to back up the so-called "supply side" or "trickle down" free-market economics of contemporary right-wing capitalism. J. K. Galbraith tells us that the acolytes of President Reagan used to wear neckties bearing the picture of Adam Smith, their ideological hero and prophet. But others see Smith very much as a pragmatist and open to an active role for the state.[9] For example, while he generally opposed the fixing of wages by justices of the peace or by law, which he saw as functioning in the service of "masters," he thought that state regulation could be appropriate when it favored workers:

> Whenever the legislature attempts to regulate the differences between masters and their workmen, its counsellors are always the masters. When the regulation, therefore, is in favor of the workmen, it is always just and equitable; but it is sometimes otherwise when it is in favor of masters. Thus the law which obliges the masters in several different trades to pay their workmen in money and not in goods, is quite just and equitable.[10]

Law and government interference in the market, then, according to Smith, would usually serve the interests of the ruling class — a key precept in the later thought of Marx. In fact Marx evidently learned most of his economics from Smith and borrowed from him such concepts as the labor theory of value (discussed again below) and the servitude of the state to capital.

In the next generation, David Ricardo wrote his *Principles of Political Economy* (1817), an analysis of how the capitalist economy operated at that time. Ricardo understood the dynamics of supply and demand, of labor cost and markets, and Marx took a great deal from him also. Ricardo, not a moralist of any kind, calmly described the labor market in terms that must have made the young Marx's blood boil:

> Labor, like all other things which are purchased and sold, and which may be increased or diminished in quantity, has its natural and its market price. The natural price of labor is that price which is necessary to enable the laborers, one with another, to subsist and to perpetuate their race, without either increase or diminution.... The market price of labor... is the price which is really paid for it, from the natural operation of the proportion of the supply to the demand.[11]

It is clear that labor is regarded as a thing, a commodity like any other. This, according to Karl Polanyi, was "the great transformation" — i.e., when The Market became the basic organizing principle of the economy. Nature was transformed into the commodity "land," and work time or labor was abstracted out of life and treated as an exchangeable commodity.

> To separate labor from other activities of life and to subject it to the laws of the market was to annihilate all organic forms of existence and to replace them by a different type of organization, an atomistic and individualistic one.[12]

However, Ricardo included in his thinking a labor theory of value (which he had taken and developed from Locke and Smith and was later taken up by Marx) according to which the economic value of an object is determined by the amount of labor that had gone into its production. Capital — the raw materials, tools and machinery, etc., used in production — were "stored-up labor." Ricardo, himself not a socialist, inspired a later school of Ricardian socialists (such writers as Ravenstone, Gray, and Hodgskin) who challenged the right of the owners of capital to appropriate the profits of industry that had really been produced by the laborers, and indeed attacked the ownership of capital (stored-up labor) by families and individuals. These men, like the French socialists (as we shall see below) recommended various schemes for the ownership of the means of production, including land, by the community of workers, so that the real producers benefited in full from their own labor. Marx's own economic thought (which also featured the labor theory of value), having been informed by the analysis of Smith and Ricardo, built upon the preliminary socialist thought of these Ricardian socialists.

Early Practical Socialism in Britain

It should come as no surprise that socialist ideas and experiments began to occur precisely during the most rapidly accelerating period of the Industrial Revolution.

Robert Owen

The terms "socialist" and "socialism" were first used in Britain in 1827 to describe the ideas and practices of Robert Owen (1771–1858) and his efforts to set up workers' cooperatives.[13] Owen was a child of the working class and one of those rare individuals who was able in young manhood to make himself wealthy as a factory manager and owner. But he turned his talents to the advancement of the working class. He wrote with indignation about the conditions of the working people and condemned child labor, the slums, the poor laws, and the absence of public education.[14] In 1815 he published *Essays on the Principles and Formation of the Human Character* and, in the early 1820s, a magazine, *The New Harmony Gazette*, in which he identified the ills of modern society as essentially moral. Owen was not a religious man in an orthodox sense. He abandoned Christianity early in life, believing that the teaching of Jesus called for narrow individualism and was focused on personal salvation and otherworldly piety.[15] Owen was basically a humanitarian who wanted a cooperative nonexploitative system and recommended "villages of unity and co-operation," an agrarian communal arrangement, first to provide work for the unemployed and later, he hoped, to spread to the whole agricultural sector. In 1824 he founded the London Co-operative Society, which sponsored public debate of social problems and published the *Co-operative Magazine,* which promoted the idea of ownership of the means of production by the real creators of wealth, the workers themselves.

It was here that the word "socialist" was first used, and it carried the definite meaning of worker ownership of the means of production. By this Owen did not mean "state ownership," but rather workers' cooperatives. This was essentially a decentralizing vision, distributing economic power broadly among workers — quite the opposite of the so-called "socialist" state capitalism later associated with Lenin and Stalin.

Owen contributed to the building up of the trade union movement in both Britain and America, and his ideas also became known and influential in France. In 1834, under Owen's leadership and inspiration, the Grand National Consolidated Trades Union attempted a nationwide general strike to be followed by a peaceful takeover by the workers of the means of production. The effort collapsed of course. Owen can be forgiven such naivety, considering that he was an early pioneer in the history of the workers' relations with the capitalist class. The whole movement for a nationally organized labor union was destroyed by fear when the British government exiled six laborers, including two Methodist lay preachers, who had tried to organize farm laborers in the south of England.[16] It became obvious that the humanization of the Industrial Revolution would be a long and difficult struggle.

Owen then returned to his early passion for communal villages. He used his own money to establish such projects in England and in America, which enjoyed some success for a few years, but ultimately collapsed in a hostile environment. Although Owen died a disappointed and apparently defeated man, there is no doubt about the immense value of his experimental efforts in socialist thought and action and of his contribution to the fledgling labor movements in Britain and America.[17] What followed Owen, it may be said, were the labor movement, guild socialism, and the cooperative movement; what followed Marx, by contrast, were Leninist state capitalism and oppressive, centralized communism.[18]

Wesley and the Methodists

It is of particular interest to us here that many committed Christian people were part of the growing socialist labor consciousness of nineteenth-century Britain. Methodism particularly was closely associated with the developing labor movement. John Wesley (1703–91), all his life an Anglican priest and the founding leader of Methodism, had been a devoted monarchist, and in many ways a social and political conservative — not a supporter of the American Revolution and certainly not a "democrat." Nevertheless, he had created in the minds of many of the British working class a great sense of their own value as children of God. His encouragement of decentralized lay authority and participation, stressing the worth of each lay man and woman, called to use his or her natural talents to the full in the service of God, laid the groundwork for an active, democratically minded class of workers. This included women, for Wesley's movement consisted of about twice as many women as men. In the latter period of his life work he lifted up and honored women and their abilities by assigning women to highly responsible tasks as leaders of class meetings, and toward the end of his life's work he was strongly encouraging women as lay preachers.[19]

Wesley lived out much of his life prior to the take-off of the Industrial Revolution, and he is certainly presocialist, yet we find in his thought already a nascent critique of the new capitalist order. He insisted that, because "the earth is the Lord's and the fullness thereof," human beings do not truly own what they possess. Everything is entrusted to us from the Creator. Private property is therefore relativized, and indeed private luxury is theft. For example, in his sermon "On Dress" he declares, "Every shilling which you save from your own apparel, you may extend in clothing the naked.... Therefore, every shilling which you needlessly spend on your apparel is, in effect, stolen from God and the poor."[20] Wesley expressed similar disapproval of large expensive houses and costly food and entertainment; he enjoined, and himself practiced, radical simplicity of life. He denied, against the spirit of that semi-Puritan age, that wealth was a sign of God's favor and instead constantly warned his hearers that wealth and the worship of mammon were the greatest of all dangers to the soul and lead to certain damnation. Wesley believed that Christians should live communally, sharing all things in common, as in Acts 2 and 4:

> All who believed were together and had all things in common; they would sell their possessions and goods and distribute the proceeds to all, as any had need. (2:44)

> Now the whole group of those who believed were of one heart and soul, and no one claimed private ownership of any possessions, but everything they owned was held in common. (4:32)

In fact Wesley was unable to persuade the "people called Methodists" to follow such a policy. Yet such teaching, together with his concepts of stewardship and simplicity of life, constituted in fact a frontal attack on the fundamental presuppositions of the nascent capitalism of his day, and certainly on the consumer capitalism of our day.[21]

After Wesley's death the Methodist movement became much more conservative in many ways, for example, on the question of women's ministries; more and more it reflected the ethos of the dominant rising middle class. But something of Wesley's radicalism survived. By the 1840s Methodists were often in the forefront of the first halting efforts at labor organization. Some historians have argued credibly that many labor leaders received their training as Methodist class leaders and lay preachers and adapted the methods of the class meetings and collection of funds to the organization of labor unions.[22] George Loveless (1808–74) is perhaps the best known of the Methodist "Tolpuddle Martyrs," a fervent lay preacher who applied his Christian convictions by the foundation in 1834 of the "Friendly Society of Agricultural Labourers," for which he and his colleagues were exiled.

The position of Methodism after Wesley's death as a "dissenting" movement, as distinct from the established Church of England, no doubt partly accounted for the inclination of many Methodists (certainly not all) to see themselves as dissenters against the established order generally, so that at times Methodism, in the eyes of some, became more or less synonymous with sedition. Methodist ministers and lay preachers were frequent organizers of unions and strikes, as for example, a serious strike in the north of England in 1844:

> There was a curious element of religion in the strike, on the side of the men. Many of the local preachers were its most active supporters. Prayers for its success were offered up in the chapels; and it was not an uncommon thing for a wayside crowd to join in supplicating the assistance of heaven.[23]

Anglican Christian Socialists

Socialist thought was not by any means absent, though, from the established Church of England. John Ludlow, an Anglican lawyer, Frederick Denison Maurice, clergyman and professor of Divinity at King's College, London, and Charles Kingsley, an Anglican priest, were among the more prominent leaders of the Christian Socialist movement in England after 1848. They warned against the use of religion as "opium," a means of keeping the working class quiet and in order. Their early writings and campaigns against laissez-faire economics and their association of Christianity with socialism did much to pave the way for the later Fabian Society and Labour Party. Maurice mightily opposed the ideas of Herbert Spencer and the "social Darwinists" that competition is the law of the universe. Ludlow declared that socialism, the latest of the forces now at work in modern society, and Christianity, the eldest-born of those forces, are in their nature not hostile but akin to each other; or rather the one is but the development, the outgrowth, the manifestation of the other.[24] They pressed the idea that socialism without Christianity loses its moral basis, and that Christianity without socialism is helpless and stripped of social influence. For Ludlow, Christian socialism was meant to "vindicate for Christianity its true authority over the realms of industry and trade, for Socialism is its true character as the great Christian revolution of the nineteenth century."[25] It was above all a spiritual movement, a church movement... in the largest, deepest sense... which essentially seeks to realize itself in the sphere of industry.[26]

This Christian socialism was committed to peaceful and democratic change, "generation by generation" (i.e., it was not expected to happen overnight). Its watchwords were "Association" and "Exchange" rather than "Competition" and "Profit." They hoped to build up ultimately a "socialist state," but did not envisage massive state ownership. They spoke rather of "collective mastership" — a cooperative system supported and encouraged by the state, built on the "principles of fellowship" and aiming at "organic fullness of life."[27] If these ideas seem just a little vague we should give them credit for having been instrumental in the establishment of the first Workingmen's Association, an early stage of the British labor movement, especially concerned with working-class education. Their specific movement came to an end partly as a result of disagreements among themselves and failure of the mainstream church to support them. But the socialist cause had been advanced a little and further ground laid for the important labor and socialist movements of the next century.

France and Germany

The French Revolution of 1789 was the other great world-shaking event without which it is impossible to understand the development of European socialism. While England had had a political revolution in the mid-seventeenth century, first displacing the monarchy, then restoring it with limited powers, France decisively threw off its monarchical/ aristocratic system just at the beginning of the period of the Industrial Revolution. The concepts of liberty, equality, fraternity, founded in the "Enlightenment" *philosophes* of the eighteenth century, expressed the growing discontent with monarchical and aristocratic rule in a society where property ownership and the possession of money (i.e., economic power) were no longer entirely in the hands of an inherited noble class.[28] The ability of the individual within new technological and economic conditions to achieve wealth regardless of birth created the bourgeoisie, or middle class, and it was primarily this class that was instrumental in throwing off a despotic monarchy that did not serve their interests. The political turmoil, however, very quickly threw up opposition to the newly triumphant bourgeois class. When Marx fled from Prussia to Paris in 1844, he found there an already thriving community of socialists and communists who believed the revolution had not gone far enough.

Noel Babeuf (1760–97) and his followers were revolutionaries of the extreme left who had become dissatisfied with the bourgeois character of postrevolutionary France. Babeuf saw that the beneficiaries of the revolution had not been the rural and urban poor, but the well-to-do middle class. His *Manifeste des Egaux* (*Manifesto of the Equals*) of 1796 is sometimes called the first "communist" document.[29] It called for radical social and economic equality based on the confiscation of the property of the rich, to be brought about by the violent overthrow of the existing bourgeois state and a temporary dictatorship of "the people" through their revolutionary leaders. Since Babeuf did not quite call for the abolition of private property as such, but rather for the egalitarian redistribution of property, it is debatable whether his ideas and movement can be called "communist," but he is widely regarded as the spiritual father of those who later called themselves by that name. His Conspiracy of the Equals was quickly crushed; Babeuf and most of his associates were guillotined in 1797. One survivor of that catastrophe, Philippe Buonarroti (1761–1837), propagated Babeuvist ideas in various parts of Europe for the next forty years.[30]

A leading communist thinker and organizer of the next generation was Etienne Cabet (1788–1856), who published pamphlets in 1841 declaring himself a communist. In his utopian book, *Voyage en Icarie*, he outlined an imaginary communist society in which every kind of social inequality would be overcome, private property would be abolished, and the instruments of production would belong to the whole community. Cabet eventually went to Texas and put his utopian vision into action by establishing "Icaria," one of the earliest cooperative/socialist experiments in the United States, a venture that later moved to Illinois and lasted until 1895, long after his death.[31] Cabet was a devout Christian. He recognized that for Europeans the values of equality and justice were rooted behind the Enlightenment in the biblical tradition. Marx and Engels later dubbed him a "utopian," by which they meant that his ideas lacked sufficient "scientific" historical and economic basis.[32]

Louis Auguste Blanqui (1805–81) was a friendly acquaintance of Marx during his days in Paris and a pre-Marxian thinker and activist whose ideas came closest to what is now known as Marxism-

Leninism. Blanqui, following in the tradition of Babeuf, was a conspir-
ator and organizer of secret societies of discontented segments of the
working class. He had been involved in unsuccessful workers' upris-
ings in 1834 and 1839. He was militantly atheistic, a humanist and a
materialist, as well as a believer in insurrection by terrorist methods,
the dispossession of the rich, and the establishment of an equalitar-
ian society. His elementary critique of capitalism prefigures that of
Marx, in that he held the capitalist system to be inherently unstable
and prone to periodic crises because of the constantly recurring gap
between production and consumption. His expectations, not so much
of the proletariat as of the vanguard of the revolutionary intelligentsia,
prefigured especially the later thought and program of Lenin. He also
spoke of communism as "the final form of association," i.e., the goal
of the revolutionary process, a preview of Marx's idea of communism
as the final stage, following the preparatory stage of socialism.[33]

The organization that Marx actually joined in Paris was the League
of the Just, mainly a group of exiled German communists, which had
its extension in the later Communist League of Brussels. The important leader associated with this organization was Wilhelm Weitling
(1808–71), author of several books, the most famous of which was
The Gospel of a Poor Sinner, in which he proclaimed Jesus as the first
communist. Weitling, though ardently Christian, shared many of the
ideas and attitudes of Blanqui, and like Blanqui, impatient with much
theorizing, wanted an immediate uprising in Germany. Weitling and
Marx clashed publicly in Brussels in 1846, Weitling was humiliated,
and from that time Marx eclipsed Weitling as the dominant figure of
the Communist League.[34] In this context we should not forget Moses
Hess (1812–75), an early Jewish "young Hegelian" friend of Marx.
Hess, though never a leader or great writer, was one of the semi-
nal thinkers of Marx's milieu, preceding him to atheism, materialism,
and communism, linking communism to atheism in a way that Marx
appreciated. Surprisingly, Hess returned to his Jewish faith late in life.

"Communism," then, as distinct from socialism, meant at first that
constellation of ideas and attitudes that we find more or less developed in Babeuf, Cabet, Blanqui and Weitling — the overthrow of the
state, dispossession of the propertied classes, abolition of private property, common ownership of the means of production. Despite Blanqui,
communism, being known as the theory of Cabet and Weitling, was
not particularly associated with atheism until the decisive influence of
Marx and Engels after 1848. "Socialism" is more generally the criti-

cism of capitalism (and may be said to include communism as one of its types) and has taken many forms, originally as a response to the painful impact of the Industrial Revolution on the working class.

One early French Christian utopian socialist was Charles Fourier (1772–1837), who reacted against the unnatural character of industrialism and called for a return to the land under a system of communal ownership and cooperative agriculture, in accordance with "the will of God and Nature." Fourier's ideas and the practical experiments of the *Fourieristes* in France closely paralleled those of Owen in Britain.[35] Followers of Fourier also immigrated to the United States and, like Cabet and followers of Owen, established cooperative communities there.[36]

It appears that the word *socialisme* was first used in French in November 1831 by Alexandre Vinet, a writer in the Protestant newspaper *Le Semeur*.[37] Vinet used the term to mean the opposite of "individualism," a system wherein people work together cooperatively for a common goal, rather than competitively for private gain. Within three months, by February 1833, the term (which had already been used in England six years earlier to refer to Owen's movement) was taken up by the Saint-Simonians.

The Saint-Simonians were a French socialist group that took a more positive attitude to the new technology than that of Fourier. They took their name from an eccentric aristocrat turned revolutionary, Henri de Saint-Simon (1760–1825). He was an enthusiast of technology and a lover of the new bourgeois class of entrepreneurs and scientists. His championing of the cause of producers was read by his followers after his death as a kind of socialism. In 1830, five years after his death, several of them published an influential book purporting to be an exposition of the doctrine of Saint-Simon. It argued that the archaic capitalist ownership of property and the system of family inheritance stood in the way of the massive creation of wealth that was possible with the new technology. It called for an end to the exploitation of one part of society by another, to be accomplished by the public ownership of the instruments of production and the central planning of the national economy by the state, which would be "an association of workers." Such Saint-Simonians as Pierre Leroux and S.-A. Bazard had an immense impact on western socialist thought and formed part of the socialist background that Marx inherited. However, these men saw their socialism as a "New Christianity," the purpose of which was to realize Christ's hopes for society. Besides pressing for a socialist society, they labored for the rights of women and defended the cause of criminals, paupers, and the mentally ill.

Similar in outlook was Louis Blanc (1811–82), who favored a state-regulated economy, but not state ownership of industry. Blanc was particularly suspicious of communist plans to overthrow the state and the dangers of authoritarianism in a communist state. Rather like Owen and Fourier, he therefore wanted worker control of industry through cooperative workshops and farm collectives. After the overthrow of 1848 Blanc was actually in charge of setting up National Workshops for the unemployed, though the system soon collapsed. Blanc based his socialist principles on Christian ethical precepts.[38]

A long-time rival of Marx was Pierre-Joseph Proudhon (1809–65), a father of anarchism, deeply suspicious of the potential authoritarianism of communism. "The community of goods is nothing but the exaltation of the State, the glorification of the police," he warned.[39] Proudhon also rejected private property (by which he meant bourgeois property from which income is earned, not all personal property) and declared (even more drastically than Wesley) *"La proprieté c'est la vol"* (Property is theft). As an anarchist he called for and predicted the disappearance of the state (another preview of Marx) but offered no intelligible explanation of how his social order as "free contract" would actually be organized.

In French communism and socialism, then, we find the origin of many of Karl Marx's ideas, most of which he must have absorbed in the year and a half that he lived in Paris (though their rational and coherent systematization would await Marx's own mature work). We also find already an implicit critique of some of the ideas later known under the name of "Marxism."

In Germany in the 1830s we find Wilhelm Weitling, the Christian socialist whom we have already referred to as a rival of Marx in the League of the Just, after both had fled from Prussian authorities. Franz von Baader (1765–1841) was another German Christian socialist, a medical doctor, then a mining engineer, who became a political and philosophical publicist. He was a democrat (a dangerous radical in monarchical Prussia) who emphasized the right of the people to choose their government. He also called for the stewardship of all things under God, who alone is the true owner of property, and for a Christian cooperative socialist society based on the ethic of the love of God and neighbor. Some historians regard him as the initiator of Christian socialism in Germany, though he did not use the term "socialism," but rather spoke of "Christian social principles":

> Religion in its supreme commandment says: Love God above all, and thy neighbor as thyself. This is the principle of every truly free community of life and every commonwealth, of all true liberty and equality. This is the Christian social principle.[40]

We should also mention the Roman Catholic archbishop of Mainz, Wilhelm Ketteler (1811–77), a saintly and visionary prelate who declared:

> I hear cries for help from among our poor, suffering brethren... Christ is the Way, the Truth and the Life. With him...we can turn the earth into a paradise....Yes, it is my deepest conviction that we could even bring about common ownership of the goods of this world as well as eternal peace along with maximum freedom in our social and political institutions.[41]

Karl Marx

Karl Marx (1818–83) entered critically into this visionary world of German and French socialism and communism, sharing their basic goals, but contemptuous of what he considered its intellectual fuzziness. His overbearing, charismatic personality and superior intellect soon made him a dominant figure in European socialism, and since he was himself not a religious man, he shifted it away from its Christian connections and what he considered its ineffectual "utopianism." Marx despised dreamers who attempted to lead the masses of people on the basis of vague, idealistic notions. Commenting, in 1848, on Saint-Simon, Fourier, and Owen, Marx charged that they

> consider themselves superior to all class antagonisms. They want to improve the condition of every member of society, even that of the most favored....Hence they reject all political and especially all revolutionary action; they wish to attain their ends by peaceful means, and endeavor, by small experiments, necessarily doomed to failure, and by the force of example, to pave the way for the new social Gospel.[42]

Subsequent history leads us to reflect that some of the attitudes that Marx so despised would have served the historical Marxist movement

well. Yet it is beyond doubt that Marx was himself an ethically motivated and truly dedicated man who made enormous personal sacrifices
for his convictions — living most of his life in poverty (in London
after 1848, having fled first Prussia, then France), he and his family often lacking the basic necessities of food and medicine.[43] Marx
was deeply angry about the degradation of working people — not
only that they were poor and overworked, but that their labor had
been turned into a mere commodity to be sold. The worker had become a means to an end, that of making a profit for the capitalist. In
his *Economic and Philosophical Manuscripts* of 1841, written when
he was still a very young man, Marx spoke eloquently of the alienation of the worker under capitalism — alienation from the product
of his labor, from fellow workers, from employers, from the realm
of nature that provides the raw product for his labor, and even from
himself, for the worker has had to sell him/herself as a commodity
on the labor market. Some of the most significant and permanently
valuable socialist thought came from the pen of the young Marx, still
in his early twenties: The worker becomes poorer the more wealth
he produces and the more his production increases in power and
extent.

> The worker becomes an ever cheaper commodity the more goods
> he creates....Labor does not only create goods; it also produces
> itself and the worker as a commodity, and indeed in the same
> proportion as it produces goods....
>
> ...The more the worker expends himself in work the more
> powerful becomes the world of objects which he creates in face
> of himself, the poorer he becomes in his inner life, and the less he
> belongs to himself....
>
> What constitutes the alienation of labor? First, that the work is
> external to the worker, that it is not part of his nature; and that,
> consequently, he does not fulfil himself in his work but denies
> himself, has a feeling of misery rather than well being, does not
> develop freely his mental and physical energies but is physically
> exhausted and mentally debased.[44]

Marx thought that the proletariat were inevitably and permanently
condemned to poverty in capitalism; later, modified and highly developed technological capitalism has shown that this is not necessarily
so. He would surely have been amazed at the level of prosperity of the
North American and western European working classes in the post–

World War II era. Yet this consumer capitalism of the mid- and late twentieth century would not have proved him wrong about the alienation of labor, nor commodity fetishism. Dorothee Soelle, a political theologian of the late twentieth century in the midst of prosperous middle-class Germany, writes poignantly of the same phenomenon, updating Marx's insight for our time:

> The alienation that the Bible calls death is built into life at the most important point — at our work. Being dead is something that is learned; we are educated to be dead. It is in the area of work that life has been fragmented into bits and pieces that we think we can control and manage. But the fragments become meaningless and the whole process is an accommodation to death. . . .
>
> If profit is the one thing to which all else in this life is subordinated, then everything else is of no significance. . . . If life is just a matter of buying and selling, then relationships too become just so many purchasable commodities. Today many perceive the world as just such a supermarket. Absent-mindedly, yet at the same time absorbed in what we are doing, we push our shopping carts up one aisle and down the other while death and alienation have the run of the place. . . . The world is nothing but a supermarket and a factory concerned for bread alone, living for bread alone. Death is the order of the day, and each day we die that dreadful death by bread alone.[45]

Marx was concerned in the same way for the "meaning" or "spiritual" dimension of life that Soelle is appealing for (though he certainly did not use these terms) and thought that meaningful work was essential to a truly human existence. Marx envisaged a situation in which people worked together joyfully for a common end with which they all identified, from which they would all benefit, and in which all would feel pride and the material conditions of life would be rich and varied. For him, the abolition of the private ownership of the means of production and its replacement by social ownership and a "free association of workers" was the key to the end of alienated labor and the idolatry of capital.

We have already referred to Marx's basic theory of historical materialism. Some form of this theory, often considerably modified, has become fundamental to most socialist thinkers since Marx's time. "Materialism" here has nothing to do with the overvaluation of consumer goods (as the term is commonly used in religious rhetoric). Nor was Marx really interested in propagating a "materialist" philosophy or metaphysic, according to which all reality is material. Rather, when Marx spoke of historical materialism, he meant that human history is driven primarily by the struggle to meet material needs. The "mode of production" (the way in which human beings meet their material requirements) and the "relations of production" (the power relations according to which they are organized to meet these material needs) determine the process of history and the structure of societies. Marx had simply observed the great socio-economic events of his time — the Industrial Revolution and the great social changes that had occurred as a result of changes in the mode of production. He wrote:

> Social relations are intimately connected with the forces of production. In acquiring new forces of production, men change their mode of production, their way of earning their living; they change all their social relations. The hand mill will give you a society with the feudal lord, the steam mill a society with the industrial capitalist.[46]

The mode of production, or the state of technology, i.e., the economic base, throws up what Marx called an ideological superstructure which essentially serves the interest of those with economic power:

> The ideas of the ruling class are in every epoch the ruling ideas: i.e. the class which is the dominant material force in society is at the same time its dominant intellectual force. The class which has the means of material production at its disposal, has control at the same time over the means of mental production.[47]

> Morality, religion, metaphysics, and other ideologies, and their corresponding forms of consciousness, no longer retain therefore their appearance of autonomous existence; it is men, who, in developing their material production and their material intercourse, change, along with this their real existence, their thinking and the products of their thinking. Life is not determined by consciousness, but consciousness by life.[48]

Essential to Marx's historical materialism is the recognition of class struggle. "The history of all hitherto existing society is the history of class struggles," he declared in his Communist Manifesto of 1848.[49]

The dominant class, he said, will not give up power willingly. The ruling class will determine the dominant ideology of society and will utilize the spheres of philosophy, law, art, religion, and philosophy to maintain its position. Religion especially, he held, was part of the ideological superstructure that helped people cope with the dreadful conditions of life, rather than inspiring or enabling them to change those conditions. It was the very young Marx who wrote these famous words about religion:

> Religious suffering is at the same time an expression of real suffering and a protest against real suffering. Religion is the sigh of the oppressed creature, the sentiment of a heartless world, and the soul of soulless conditions. It is the opium of the people.
>
> The abolition of religion, as the illusory happiness of men, is a demand for their real happiness. The call to abandon their illusions about their condition is a call to abandon a condition which requires illusions.[50]

Marx's concept of ideology, within his understanding of historical materialism, helps to explain why under capitalism even most of the poor workers believe in the system. This is why he believed a struggle at the level of ideas could never succeed. Utopian socialism, as he saw it, would never come to power through what he called "this fantastic standing apart from the contest"[51] — without a rigorous and disciplined cadre of revolutionaries determined to overthrow the existing order. The organs of the state would have to be seized and a vanguard dictatorship of the proletariat set up if the powers of capital were ever to be controlled by the people. Late in his life Marx wrote of "a political transition period in which the state can be nothing but the revolutionary dictatorship of the proletariat."[52]

Though much of Marx's socialist thought was borrowed from the communist and socialist milieu of the mid-nineteenth century, and much of his analysis of capitalism from the British liberal economists, the manner in which he critiqued, utilized, and systematized the diverse thoughts of others was original and eloquent, and no historian, political theorist, or social scientist has been untouched by the insight of his theory of historical materialism. Even if we modify his theory, e.g., even if we argue for a relatively greater autonomy for the various aspects of what Marx called the superstructure, the theory remains illuminating, indeed indispensable, for understanding processes of social change. Yet, with our present hindsight, it appears tragic that it was his

aggressive brand of communist socialism, cut off from Christian spiritual and ethical foundations, that eventually came to power in Russia
under Lenin. Particularly dangerous (as we see it now with the con-
venient wisdom of hindsight) was the idea of the dictatorship of the
proletariat, which, emphasized and developed by Lenin and utilized
by Stalin, became nothing more than a justification for the oppressive
rule of a party elite. It is debatable to what extent Marx would have
recognized or approved of the outcome of his thought in the Soviet
communism of Lenin, Stalin, or Brezhnev.

An important critique of Marx is found in the "critical theory"
of what came to be known in the 1930s as the Frankfurt school,
especially Max Horkheimer and Theodore Adorno (of the Frankfurt Institute for Social Research), Herbert Marcuse, and later Jürgen
Habermas and others. These are essentially Marxist thinkers who
have attempted to correct serious defects of Marxism that became
visible in Marxist regimes, especially the dominance of technical and
bureaucratic rationality, which they believed had its roots in Marx's
thought itself. Marx, they believed, tended to reduce human *praxis*
to *technē*, or instrumental action.[53] They also criticized the deterministic element in Marx's thought — i.e., the inevitability that the
laws of history would certainly bring about social revolution. Marx
thought that the progress of science and technology, bringing about
the increasing mastery of nature, would create material conditions
for social emancipation. But the Frankfurt thinkers believed that
Marx was wrong to assume that material conditions are sufficient
conditions; he had neglected the subjective conditions required for
self-emancipation. Thus, as Charles Davis comments, Marx "over-
looked the stultifying impact of scientific and technological progress
upon the consciousness of the potential subjects of revolution. He
did not anticipate the technocratic consciousness of one-dimensional
man."[54] The "instrumental reason" that the Frankfurt school criticizes in much Marxist thought is found to be impoverishing of the
full breadth and scope of humanity's rational capacities and can be
seen in the destructive, antienvironmental, and dehumanizing aspects
of countries where Marxism came to power. The domination of nature and the domination of persons were seen to go hand in hand, so
that in practice the originating social and ethical passion of Marx came
to be swallowed up by the technical and deterministic elements of his
thought.[55]

The Social Gospel

"Social gospel," as we have seen above, was a term that Marx used on occasion to describe the Christian version of what he called "utopian socialism." For him it was a term of contempt, but for many Christian socialists in the late nineteenth and early twentieth centuries, the "Social Gospel" became a rallying cry for a revisioning of their whole understanding of the Christian faith. Our purpose here is not so much to discuss the Social Gospel as a theology, but to note the way in which this theological movement critiqued capitalism and linked Christianity to socialism.

The Social Gospel can be defined very broadly to include any theological understanding or practice that emphasizes the responsibility of Christians to seek social justice. It may also be defined more narrowly as the view that "social salvation precedes individual salvation both temporally and in importance."[56] This definition may be too narrow, including only a few of the most radical "social gospellers."[57] Perhaps we may more usefully think of "Social Gospel" as that early twentieth-century movement that emphasized the political and social task of Christianity to improve the quality of human relations on this earth, calling men and women to engage in realizing the Kingdom of God in the fabric of society. "The demand to 'save this man now' became 'save this society now.' "[58] In fact most of the best-known "social gospellers" also saw themselves as socialists.

This theology, like most modern thought, had roots in the Enlightenment and in the nineteenth-century theology of Albrecht Ritschl (1822–89). Ritschl (like his predecessor Schleiermacher) emphasized religious experience and interpreted Jesus' divinity in terms of his consciousness of God. Ritschl also emphasized the teaching of Jesus about the Kingdom of God. Social Gospel theology, picking up Ritschl's emphasis on the Kingdom as well as the New Testament scholarship of the time concerning the historical Jesus and the Kingdom of God, often tended to be "liberal" in its understanding of Christ and salvation. Jesus Christ as Savior and Incarnate God and Christ as risen tended to be downplayed or reinterpreted in a reductive manner. Some who identified themselves with this movement, however, were also quite evangelical and relatively orthodox.[59] The Social Gospel had other non-Enlightenment, nonliberal roots and precursors, including the Methodist tradition of Wesley, as well as some of the other Christian socialists whom we have mentioned above. For our purposes here it seems most useful to look at the socialist Social Gospel thought of the American theologian Walter Rauschenbusch and of the Canadian Methodist Salem Bland.

Walter Rauschenbusch

Rauschenbusch (1861–1918), an American Baptist pastor and professor of church history, represented himself as a theologian who articulated a widespread movement of faith and theology. He saw his task as that of expressing coherently what many Christian social activists were already saying. They were dissatisfied with the older forms of Protestant theology that emphasized forgiveness of sins and eternal life in heaven. They had little patience with what they considered to be obscure doctrines of the two natures of Christ and the Trinity. They wished to get back to the simple message of Jesus about the Kingdom of God. One of Rauschenbusch's later books, *A Theology of the Social Gospel* (1917), clearly laid out the broad outlines for a Social Gospel systematic theology. As for christology, "Jesus had experienced God in a new way." Jesus was "a perfect religious personality."[60] Theology and the church, he thought, had lost touch with the Jesus of the synoptic gospels, the one who preached the Kingdom of love. We must get back behind the doctrines of the incarnation and atonement, he argued, to the things that Jesus was passionately concerned about — the Kingdom of God, which is the "reign of organized righteousness."[61] Not only did the theological understanding of Jesus have to be changed, but also the doctrines of sin and salvation. Here he explicitly follows Ritschl:

> Ritschl, the most vigorous and influential theological intellect since Schleiermacher,... abandoned the doctrine of original sin but substituted the solidaristic conception of the Kingdom of Evil. He held that salvation is embodied in a community which has experienced salvation.[62]

Sin, for Rauschenbusch, is essentially selfishness, but it is necessary to get beyond the merely individualistic idea of sin. "The sinful mind is the unsocial and anti-social mind." The truth of the doctrine of original sin was that "sin is lodged in social customs and institutions."[63]

Social Gospel theology, of which Rauschenbusch is a major representative, accompanied, fueled, and informed the North American socialist movements. Rauschenbusch saw the Social Gospel as the moral power of socialism, which is clearly expressed in a chapter on "The Salvation of the Super-Personal Forces":

> Two principles are contending with each other for future control in the field of industrial and commercial organization, the capitalistic and the co-operative. The effectiveness of the capitalistic method in the production of wealth is not questioned; modern civilization is evidence of it. But we are also familiar with capitalistic methods in the production of human wreckage. Its one-sided control of economic power tempts to exploitation and oppression; it directs the productive process of society primarily toward the creation of private profit rather than the service of human needs; it demands autocratic management and strengthens the autocratic principle in all social affairs; it has impressed a materialistic spirit on our whole civilization.
>
> On the other hand organizations formed on the co-operative principle are not primarily for profit but for the satisfaction of human wants, and the aim is to distribute ownership, control, and economic benefits to a large number of co-operators.[64]

Rauschenbusch dared to expect and hope for the establishment of the Kingdom of God on earth as "the realm of love, and the commonwealth of cooperative labor."[65]

Salem Bland

Bland (1859–1950) can be seen as one among many articulate figures of the Canadian Social Gospel movement. He was a Methodist, later a United Church minister, and a professor at Wesley College, Winnipeg, until his dismissal at the time of his involvement in the Winnipeg General Strike in 1919. I choose to discuss him here not because he was the most significant or influential Social Gospel leader in Canada — that distinction would probably go to J. S. Woodsworth — but because Bland states so clearly a Christian socialist stance that was a widespread (though minority) commitment among Canadian Protestants in the early twentieth century. Bland shared many of the basic intellectual positions of his American contemporary Rauschenbusch. Bland's book *The New Christianity* (1920) is a late expression of views long held by him and many other Social Gospel people. There he accused St. Paul, Hebrews, and the gospel of John of obscuring the teaching of

Jesus with Greek metaphysics and deplored the "perverse exaltation of dogma and orthodoxy.... The Christianity of Jesus means nothing if it does not mean brotherhood. Brotherhood does not mean anything if it does not mean a passion of equality."[66]

Bland divides the past twelve hundred years of Christian history into phases (in a way reminiscent of Marx's division of human history into epochs): (1) the Aristocratic or Feudalistic phase (700–1500); (2) the Bourgeois or Plutocratic or Capitalistic phase (1500–1914); (3) the Labour Phase (1914–). Here he emphasizes that Jesus was a working man and that the growing labor movement of his time, struggling for "brotherhood" and economic justice, was a divine current too strong to be resisted: "Labor and Christianity, then, are bound up together. Together they stand or fall. They come into their Kingdom together or not at all."[67] Bland also categorizes types of historical Christianity geographically and culturally: Jewish, Greek, Latin, Teutonic, and American (including Canada!) — this last form being the most admirable and the wave of the future:

> American Christianity believes in the progressive and aggressive amelioration of things. It believes in this life and its glorious possibilities. It is bent on attaining them as no other sort of Christianity ever was before. It is steeped in optimism. It believes that the leaven of Christianity possesses the power to leaven all the relations and institutions of civilization. It believes that the fulfilment of our Lord's prayer, that God's Kingdom may come and His will be done on earth as it is in heaven, rests with the Church.[68]

Bland had no doubt that socialism and Christianity were essentially tied together. A social system based on competition and profit-making was obviously contrary to "brotherhood." By socialism he clearly meant public ownership. For him an attack on public ownership was an attack on Christianity, "the sin against the Holy Ghost of our age."[69] Sin was essentially capitalism:

> Capitalistic control must pass away. It has, no doubt, played a necessary and useful part in the social evolution. It has shown courage and enterprise. But it has been, on the whole, rapacious and heartless, and its sense of moral responsibility has been often rudimentary. When the managers on whom it depends desert to the side of the workers, it will be patent how little capacity or

service is in capitalism, and how little it deserves the immense
gain it wrung from exploited labor and skill.[70]

Does Christianity mean Socialism? It means infinitely more
than Socialism. It means Socialism plus a deeper, diviner brotherhood than even Socialism seeks.[71]

For those of us who think about these things in the last years of the
same century, Bland's cheerful optimism carries a certain pathos. His
brave hope and life-long struggle within the church and in Canadian
politics for a more just and compassionate society was truly "utopian"
in the best sense. He and his colleagues dared to dream and hope for a
different and better society. We had best listen and admire him and the
movement he represents, both their thoughts and their social achievements, before moving too quickly to accuse them of naivety. There are
important elements of hope and of social criticism in the Social Gospel
that we must carry forward for another new century. We do so in the
painful awareness that the "desertion of managers to the side of the
workers" is not to be expected, and that capitalism and the reign of
profit-making will not soon disappear. The "divine current" combining labor and Christianity has so far been rather successfully resisted.
We sadly recognize that the era of "Labor Christianity" did not begin,
as he hoped it would, in 1914.

We must note that by 1920, the year in which Salem Bland wrote
The New Christianity, an intellectual crisis was already confronting
thoughtful Christians on both sides of the Atlantic. The optimism of
the nineteenth century had been crushed by the colossal and shocking
evil of the Great War. The "Great Depression" of 1929–39 did not
bring about the collapse of capitalism as many hoped; rather, capitalism adapted itself and finally found its way through the mire, in part
by means of war. The mass destruction of World War II, the horrendous disclosures of "Auschwitz," the Hiroshima bomb, all corroded
the Social Gospel confidence in the future. The first volumes of neo-
orthodox theology coincided with Bland's *New Christianity*: Barth's
Epistle to the Romans, 1919, and the scores of articles and books
by Reinhold Niebuhr that began to appear about 1925. But it was
Bland's book that soon appeared dated and unserviceable. These new,
more "biblical" theologies of the day took seriously the depths and
darkness and persistence of human sin and the total dependence of
humanity on God's forgiving and renewing grace. They threw scorn
on hopes for the "establishment of the Kingdom of God on earth"

and returned to more classical (neo-Reformation) doctrines of Christ, salvation, and the end time. These became the contextual and contemporary theologies for a world of pessimism and despair, corresponding to the atheistic existentialist philosophers, novelists, and playwrights of the absurd, who flourished after the First World War (Sartre, Camus, Kafka). For Social Gospel socialists the final injury added to insult was the Stalinist corruption and tyranny of the great socialist breakthrough in the Soviet Union.

Though Social Gospel theology may sound naively optimistic today, many of its insights have reappeared in post-neo-orthodox theology. Moltmann's theology of hope, other European political theologies (Soelle, Metz), the liberation theologies of the Third World, and feminist theologies as well share the Social Gospel's perception of systemic evil and social/structural sin. The call to political discipleship for the transformation of society for greater justice, equality, and compassion (which many Social Gospel people lived out effectively), though not absent from "neo-orthodox" theology, has returned to the forefront since the 1960s. The theology of the Kingdom of God, so stressed by the Social Gospel, has come forward again, so that Rauschenbusch's proclamation of the Kingdom of God as "a vital and organizing energy now at work in humanity"[72] once again has a contemporary ring. And — of particular interest to us here — capitalism has again come under serious theological critique from Christian people as a system of idolatry and inhumanity. Perhaps we need to read the Social Gospel theologians again. They knew that denunciation was not enough and that alternative visions must be advanced. If the socialism that they proposed, or socialism of some description, is not the way to battle with the rule of capital, we must ask whether any alternatives exist.

We shall hear more of the Social Gospel when we come to consider its role in the development of democratic socialism, especially in Canada.

We have not by any means told the whole story of early socialism, nor shall we take space to tell much of the middle history. We shall see a little more of the recent history of different kinds of socialism in the next two chapters. Our glance at the early history has disclosed a story of high political ideals and courage, one of considerable achievement, but also of much failure and defeat. Socialism has not been simply a Christian movement, yet it sprang up out of Christian soil, and Christian people and Christian faith and thought have been an important inspiration and motivating presence in the worldwide socialist movement from its inception. Gregory Baum suggests that in our present religiously pluralist society not only Christianity, but other religious traditions as well can provide inspiration and motivation for socialist politics:

> It seems to me that the great world religions are the major social sources for an ethic of solidarity and self-limitation. Some high-minded individuals may turn to Kant's categorical imperative, but the excessive rationalism of the Kantian ethic prevents it from being widely embraced.... If socialism is to become a mass movement it will have to draw upon the promise of solidarity contained in the ancient religious traditions.[73]

From a Christian perspective, it is crucial that socialism not become absolutized as faith. For Christian socialists, political ideology must remain founded upon faith in God through Jesus Christ and must therefore always be open to adaptation and critique on the basis of faith and practical experience. It is arguable that attention to its biblical roots can assist socialism to avoid the distortions and tyrannies that have been so tragically a part of socialist history.

Chapter 7

Democratic Socialism /
Social Democracy

Socialist movements that developed into political parties have sometimes held the power of government through democratic election in
western European nations, e.g., the Labour Party in Great Britain, the
Social Democratic parties of West Germany, Sweden, and France, etc.
Because this is the form of socialism that we in the western/northern
world know best, it seems important to glimpse some of their history and achievements, to consider the question of their authenticity
as forms of socialism, and to explore their connection to Christians
and the churches. Their histories, as we have noted, go back well into
the mid-nineteenth century and predate Marx and Marxism, having
behind them Christian socialist as well as secular socialist thought.
Similar parties, "democratic socialist" or "social democratic," have
sometimes formed governments — for example, in New Zealand and
in some provinces of Canada. The two terms are not always clearly
distinguished, though some authors insist on a sharp distinction between them.[1] The term "democratic socialist" tends to be used to name
those who call for public/state ownership of the means of production
within a democratic state; "social democratic" tends to refer to those
who play down the importance of public ownership and seek to reach
socialist goals democratically within capitalist structures.[2]

It is possible to make some general statements about these parties. Generally speaking, they began as "democratic socialist" parties
and moved in the direction of "social democracy" (as referred to
above). Before they held power they pushed the political mainstream
or center to the left and influenced the policies of other parties and
governments. Either through pressure while in opposition or by enactment when holding power, they have brought about such socialist
measures as publicly funded medical care, child support and old age
pension schemes, unemployment and welfare income security plans,

133

and maternity leave. In this way they have fostered more compassionate and "friendly" societies and in a large measure eliminated the grosser forms of poverty that were once so visible within the western democracies. They have also pressed for or established various degrees of mixed economy and planned economy in which public ownership and government intervention are used to regulate economic life in the interests of the majority. In these ways they have in fact limited, though certainly not eliminated, the power of private capital. Their influence upon political discourse and upon the actual course of events even lead some commentators to speak of the twentieth as the "social democratic century."[3] Yet these go on within an essentially capitalist economic order, i.e., private ownership and control of the major resources and means of production. The immense social and economic power of private capital and especially multinational capital remains, together with much of the exploitation, injustice and alienation which socialist thought has always deplored. The great ongoing debate about this form of socialism is whether it is authentically socialist, or merely a form of the survival of capitalism.

Fabian Socialism in Britain

An influential, relatively early historical expression of democratic socialism/social democracy is Fabian Socialism in Britain. The Fabians were part of the extremely complex story of British socialism in the late nineteenth and early twentieth centuries as it arose out of the work of Owen, the Methodists, the growing trade union movement, and the Anglican Christian Socialists, as well as Marxism. (Marx died in England in 1883 and his close colleague Engels in 1895.) Many socialist and semisocialist organizations existed in Britain — the Independent Labour Party, the Social Democratic Federation, and other small socialist or labor parties and movements ranging from revolutionary Marxism to reformist gradualism. The Fabians are of particular interest because they represent an approach to socialism that became influential in the twentieth century, i.e., that set of strategies that I have placed under the general heading of democratic socialism/social democracy. Fabian thought became important in the British Labour Party, which has been the main opposition party for most of the twentieth century, and sometimes formed the government. Fabian thought was important also in the development of socialist politics in Canada.

The Fabians began in 1884 as a small group of middle-class intellectuals, distressed by the social misery and economic inequality they saw around them, wanting to think and act together about their social concerns. It is interesting to note that the original impetus came from Thomas Davidson, a Christian socialist guru, who founded the Fellowship of the New Life, devoted to exploring communal living. When he left for America, part of that group broke away to form the Fabian Society, which departed from the idea of communalism and wanted to think its way to some other social strategy. They took their name from an ancient Roman general who, in war against Hannibal, won the day by patiently biding his time until the right moment, as in the line of a poem by John Gay: "Let none object my lingering way/ I gain, like Fabius, with delay."[4] Fabianism originally had to do, then, with taking time to work out the right strategy. The idea of "delay," however, later came to be associated with the concept of evolutionary "gradualism." Fabianism became that gentler and optimistic sort of socialism which eschewed violent revolution, but expressed confidence that socialism was "but the next step in the development of society, rendered inevitable by the changes which followed from the industrial revolution of the eighteenth century."[5] Fabians resembled Marx (and differed from Lenin) in their belief that socialism was an inevitable development arising out of the conditions of capitalism. But they parted from Marxists in rejecting class war, looking for and seeking to assist the gradual, progressive modification of the system by democratic means. The publication of *Fabian Essays* in 1889 helped spawn a large number of local Fabian societies in many parts of Britain and abroad. These essays were highly critical of capitalism, which produced for profit rather than for use, enriching a few and impoverishing the many. Living as they did in a time of great technical and material progress and also in a time of increasing democratization, they believed that the poverty of the masses and gross economic inequality must be, and surely would be, overcome. They identified socialism with social planning under a democratic parliamentary system, together with centralized planning of production and distribution by a government responsible to the people. Fabians, however, did not generally favor nationalization of the means of production, in the sense of national state ownership. Rather, they envisaged land and other means of production passing under the control of local or regional public agencies.[6] One of the main Fabian leaders, Sidney Webb (1859–1947), had great confidence in county councils as vehicles for socialist transformation and was particularly interested in the potential administrative efficiency of a planned economy. His wife, Beatrice (Potter) Webb (1858–1943), thought more in terms of cooperative ownership under the overall authority of elected local councils. They were wary of national governmental authority and saw the need for local control.[7] Another major Fabian socialist leader and associate of the Webbs was the famous playwright George Bernard Shaw, who had a passion for economic egalitarianism, as well as for social efficiency, deploring the unplanned character of capitalism as wasteful. Another was the novelist H. G. Wells, who leaned more toward nationalization and an aggressive political strategy. Although some of their ideas now seem naive in light of historical occurrences since their time, they were creative thinkers who still give us a sense of the great number of possibilities for socio/political/economic organization. Having lived through a time of major material and political change, they had a keen sense that there was nothing necessary or permanent about the existing system. There was a good deal of conflict and disagreement between them, and among them and other socialists of their time. They were part of a ferment of creative thought that, as we have noted, did bear fruit in the actual humanization of the politics of British society in later decades. While the major Fabian leaders were still young, they saw the Labour Party replace the Liberal Party as the main opposition and some of their socialist ideals implemented by Labour governments after 1945.

The Socialist International at Frankfurt

Even larger and more successful democratic socialist movements existed in Germany, France, and other west European nations. As the years passed and the defects of Marxist-Leninist communism became evident, democratic socialism generally moved toward various degrees of "revisionism." Especially after World War II democratic socialism came to mean the welfare state, mixed economy, Keynesian economics, and social equality, i.e., a reformed, managed capitalism.[8] A gathering of democratic socialists from all over the world occurred at Frankfurt, West Germany (not to be confused with the Frankfurt school of critical theory), in 1951. The old Second International (founded in 1889) had died at the beginning of World War I when working-class solidarity gave way to war time nationalist passions.[9] This new Socialist

International indicated that the international socialist movement had learned from historical experience, especially the Soviet experience. This conference declared a sharp distinction between socialism and communism and renounced the centralized state-controlled economy of the eastern bloc:

> Communism falsely claims a share in the Socialist tradition. In fact, it has distorted that tradition beyond recognition. It has built up a rigid theology which is incompatible with the critical spirit of Marxism.[10]

It is interesting that the socialist authors of Frankfurt chose to use the word "theology" — an implicit accusation that communism had become a kind of pseudo-religion. It had ceased to be social theory, subject to adaptation in the light of experience and criticism (what Segundo calls "ideology") and had become a distorted form of "faith." When an ideology is sacralized and placed beyond question or correction, it becomes an absolutist dogmatism and an instrument of tyranny. Theology, of course, is also moribund and corrupted when it becomes dogmatistic, placing itself beyond critique and transformation. The Frankfurt International gathering, however, was positively asserting something essential to socialism when it talked about the decentralization of economic power:

> Socialist planning does not mean that all economic decisions are placed in the hands of the government or central authorities. Economic power should be decentralized wherever this is compatible with the aims of planning.... The workers must be associated democratically with the direction of their industry.[11]

They also stated unequivocally that "without freedom there can be no Socialism. Socialism can be achieved only through democracy." They asserted that socialist planning can be achieved in various ways, depending on the context. Public ownership, which they still espoused, may take the form of nationalization, but may also be municipal or regional in character. They affirmed the socialist value of consumers' or producers' cooperatives. They also affirmed private ownership:

> Socialist planning does not presuppose public ownership of all the means of production. It is compatible with the existence of private ownership in important fields, for instance in agriculture, handicraft, retail trade and small and middle-sized industries.[12]

It is possible to interpret such developments within democratic socialism as a kind of retreat in the face of the already apparent failure of
Soviet communism to nourish freedom and human dignity. Certainly it
can be seen as an attempt to assure western electorates that socialism
does not have to mean totalitarianism. But to see these developments
as retreat is to misunderstand the history of socialism and to make
the common error of simplistically identifying the historical socialist
movement either with Marxism or with Soviet communism. Our historical sketch has shown that socialism has never been a monolithic
movement — that from the very beginning, worker ownership and cooperative enterprise have been important parts of socialist thought,
that historically socialism cannot be identified with state ownership. If
there is a clear, continuous thread to be found in historical socialism, it
is precisely the determination to distribute and democratize economic
power, to limit the political power and social-economic control exercised by private capital, which was seen to be concentrated in a few
hands, and to use democratic power for the economic well-being of
the people. For a long time now most socialists have learned the les-
son of the Soviet experience — that not only private capital, but state
power too is dangerous to human liberty and well-being.

United States

Socialist movements have always had a particularly difficult struggle
to survive and grow in an ideological atmosphere that has been, to
say the least, inhospitable to socialist thought. The American population, having rejected various European tyrannies, fiercely independent
and suspicious of government and governance, did not respond well
to appeals for social cooperation and economic democracy. However,
a substantial and admirable socialist movement struggled for many
years in the United States. It was at first very much a movement of
immigrants, often refugees from socialist defeats in Europe, such as
Etienne Cabet and the French or British followers of Fourier or Owen.
However, these little groups established a tradition that, together with
the labor movement, developed into a substantial political presence.

Marx and Engels had the headquarters of the First International
moved to New York City in 1872. When it died four years later,
American socialists soon formed the Socialist Labor Party in 1877, led
by the Marxist revolutionary Daniel de Leon.[13] A split-off and rival

socialist organization, the Socialist Party of America, was formed in 1901 — a more "revisionist" social democratic style of party. Competition between these parties and divisions between them and the labor unions weakened the socialist movement. Nevertheless, the Socialist Party managed to muster 900,000 votes, 6 percent of the total vote, when its leader, Eugene Debs, ran for the presidency in 1912. The party had, that year, 120,000 dues-paying members, 1,200 elected officials, and over 300 socialist periodicals.[14] As in Canada, socialism in the United States had a major Christian and Social Gospel dimension, including a weekly, *The Christian Socialist*, Social Gospel theologians like Rauschenbusch, and famous preachers like Washington Gladden. A Congregational minister, George Herron, was leader of the Socialist Party for many years.

Norman Thomas, the socialist candidate for president six times between 1928 and 1948, was also, at first, a Social Gospel minister, much under the influence of Rauschenbusch. Thomas was a remarkably courageous and energetic public speaker and author, a campaigner and fighter for the working class, for racial equality, and for social justice of every kind.[15] He was a democratic socialist, calling for socialization of banks, railroads, coal mines, and power and oil industries under public corporations that, under the supervision of government, would plan the national economy, working together with consumer cooperatives and small business.[16] He is sometimes credited with having had significant influence on President Roosevelt in the formation of his New Deal after 1933. Tragically, the American people never responded to his socialist message in large numbers, and Thomas saw the near demise of the movement by the end of his lifetime.

The great neo-orthodox theologian Reinhold Niebuhr was part of this American socialism, having joined the Socialist Party in the 1920s and became a strong supporter and ally of Norman Thomas. Niebuhr, like many others, left his socialism behind by 1940, supported President Roosevelt, and moved toward his famous "Christian realism." The overwhelming anticommunist ideology and propaganda of the postwar period, and in fact the actual corruption and tyranny of the U.S.S.R., made socialism appear to be allied with the dangerous enemy of democracy and freedom. A combination of government suppression and Leninist subversion of the democratic socialist movement effectively undermined socialism as a mass movement, and little more remained beyond a handful of dissenting utopian democratic socialists, including thinkers like Irving Howe and Michael Harrington,[17] organizations like Christians for Socialism, and tiny outposts of Communist and Trotskyite parties.[18] It became impossible to distinguish between communism and socialism in the public mind, and to be "soft on communism" was political suicide for anyone in public life. No doubt it also became impracticable for a theologian like Niebuhr to be taken seriously by mainstream America while espousing "socialist" ideology.

Socialism became a small and marginal movement in the United States; absent from Congress, it has never come close to power, and so social democracy has never had the influence that it has had in western Europe, in Canada, and elsewhere.[19] The socialist historian G. D. H. Cole comments that "in America, broadly speaking, the State did not *rule* . . . , it only intervened for a particular cause . . . , as a rule only when it was brought in as the ally of some pressure group."[20] The reasons for the failure of the American socialist movement to make major electoral gains (as compared with western European nations and Canada) are too complex to be discussed thoroughly here. At any rate, the result of this is that the United States is widely regarded as the most backward of the western democratic nations where economic and social equity is concerned. Linda McQuaig has gathered telling statistics about poverty and social security in the U.S. in her book *The Wealthy Banker's Wife*. Approximately thirty-five million Americans have no medical insurance at all; many more have very inadequate insurance and stand in danger either of receiving deficient medical care or of financial ruin in the case of serious illness or medical emergency. Levels of public health are among the worst among so-called "developed" countries. E.g., the rate of infant mortality in the U.S. in 1989 stood at about ten deaths per one thousand live births, as compared to seven in France, Netherlands, and Canada, and six in Sweden.[21] Americans suffer these very poor levels of public health despite the fact that they spend more of their Gross Domestic Product on health care than any other nation in the world![22] Public spending on social security is lower in the United States (and second lowest in Canada) among all developed western nations (11.5 percent and 12.8 percent of Gross Domestic Product respectively). Social security spending is highest in Belgium, Netherlands, France, and Sweden (all over 20 percent of GDP).[23] By precise comparative statistical measurements, the United States has the smallest "middle class" of any of the industrialized nations (those falling between 0.625 and 1.25 times the median income), the largest middle classes existing in Japan and Sweden and the second smallest middle class in Canada. Again, United Nations statistics on income inequality show that the United States has the highest ratio of inequality of any of the industrialized countries (comparing the incomes of the highest 20 percent to the lowest 20 percent) and Canada the second highest. According to these criteria, nations with the lowest ratio of inequality are Belgium and Sweden. Comparing poverty rates in selected western industrialized countries, United States has the highest poverty rates, Canada the second highest, and Sweden and France the lowest.[24] Provision of public day care and of publicly funded or guaranteed maternity leave are almost nonexistent in the United States, but generously provided in prosperous and economically successful places like France, Germany, and Sweden. A large underclass of the very poor in the United States (disproportionately black), protected by only the most minimal social safety net and hopeless about prospects for a better life, leads to dreadful levels of public, class, and racial violence. As James Laxer comments, the levels of violence in places like Los Angeles (as in the riots of 1992, which left fifty-five people dead, thousands injured, and a billion dollars of property damage) would be seen in most countries as a form of civil war. For example, at the end of the 1980s the murder rate in the United States was approximately 9.0 per 100,000 (as compared to 2.5 per 100,000 in Canada).[25] It is evident that the "triumph of capitalism," found in its purest form in the United States of America, is not the triumph of the people, and that high degrees of social health and human well-being are to be found in nations with strong social democratic traditions.

The Canadian Story

In recent years there have been signs that, under the pressures of globalization, high-tech, free trade, and competitiveness, Canada is moving in the direction of a purer, more American form of capitalism. Particularly, free trade appears to have the effect of integrating the American and Canadian economies, weakening the power of the democratic state to set social and economic priorities, making Canada's relatively social democratic character difficult to sustain.[26] If Canadians are to have the political will to struggle to improve or maintain the levels of social justice they now enjoy, they must know and cherish their history. Particularly Canadian Christians need to be aware of the role of the churches and of Christian socialist thought in the development of what is commonly called the welfare state.

Any discussion of socialism in Canada inevitably focuses on the Cooperative Commonwealth Federation (C.C.F.), 1932–61, which developed out of a number of smaller organizations and later into the New Democratic Party. In terms of the worldwide movement, socialism in Canada began relatively late. There are two matters of particular interest to us here — the involvement of Christians and Christianity in the development of Canadian socialism and the shift from what might be called "democratic socialism" to "social democracy."

The 1890s and early 1900s in Canada saw the appearance of various dissenting political groups — organizations of farmers, of laborers, and of socialist intellectuals, namely, the United Farmers of Alberta, the Independent Labour Party, the Farmers' Political Association, the Socialist Party of Canada, the League for Social Reconstruction, the Non-Partisan League, the Trades and Labour Congress, and others. All of these felt that their political and economic concerns were not being addressed by the Conservative or Liberal parties. They were not, by any means, ideologically monolithic, the urban and labor groups generally tending to be more "socialist" than the farmers. All could be described more as movements than as parties. Walter Young, in his history of the C.C.F., throws light on this distinction:

> Whereas the "pure" party seeks electoral victory, the movement seeks some major social change or reform. The program the party presents to the electorate is designed as a means to victory. The program of the movement is an expression of its ultimate ideals and goals. Success for a party necessarily includes success at the polls; for a movement the same is not true in that its goals may be achieved by another agency stimulated by the mere existence of the movement. . . . A movement seeks fundamental change and may or may not use political means to achieve it; a party seeks power for its leaders through electoral success.[27]

The many protest movements in early twentieth-century Canada arose primarily out of historical conditions similar to those that gave rise to socialism in Europe: the social injustice, poverty, and misery of the cities that accompanied the Industrial Revolution. In Canada there was also a strong element of protest among farmers, especially those who were opening up the vast regions of the west who quickly felt disadvantaged vis-à-vis the developing industrial heartland of the east.[28] Canadian socialism then, deriving much of its impetus from the west in a nation of enormous geographical size, was not by any means purely ideological in character, but heavily mixed with regionalism.

Because Canada was part of Christendom, it is not surprising that resources were found in the Christian tradition to support the victims of injustice. The theological emphasis that accomplished this was the Social Gospel theology that we have discussed above. It is of particular interest to us here to note the role of Social Gospel theology in the development of Canadian socialism.

When we think of the history of socialism in Canada we think first of James Shaver Woodsworth, a man of wonderful courage and tenacity who was the first leader of the Cooperative Commonwealth Federation. Woodsworth, like the first leaders of socialism in the United States, was a clergyman, a Methodist, and son of another prominent Methodist Church leader, and must be seen as part of the Wesleyan Methodist tradition of concern for the poor. There is no evidence that he was under the influence of Marx; rather, it was the British Christian socialist and labor movements, which predated Marx, and the Fabian Society that had formed him in a socialist direction during his time of study in England early in the century. Woodsworth spent some of his early career at All People's Mission in Winnipeg, working with the urban poor, especially the large numbers of non-English-speaking immigrants who were arriving at that time. Frustrated with the limited scope of what he could accomplish through a local city church mission, Woodsworth became involved in social research and advocacy, was heavily engaged with the struggling labor movement of the time, and in 1919 spent time in prison because of his involvement with the Winnipeg General Strike. For a time he was unemployed and he and his family experienced serious poverty. He then found work as a stevedore at the Vancouver docks, doing hard physical labor and becoming a union member. Eventually, in 1921, Woodsworth and one other socialist, William Irvine, were elected to the national parliament, where Woodsworth would remain until his death in 1942.[29] Woodsworth's books, *Strangers within Our Gates* (1909) and *My Neighbor* (1911), reveal the extent to which he identified with the liberal Social Gospel theology of the time.

If we listen to Woodsworth's comments in the *Manitoba Free Press* in 1909 on slum conditions in Winnipeg, we get a feel for the ex-

periences and conditions that created socialists in the early twentieth
century:

> Some of these people may be lazy and shiftless. Small wonder
> when they are forced into conditions which foster idleness, im-
> morality and crime. And behind all, the fact remains that there
> is not work for them. Let me tell you of one little foreign girl.
> She lives in a room in a disreputable old tenement — one of
> those human warrens which are multiplying with great rapidity
> in our city. Her father has no work. The men boarders have no
> work. The place is incredibly filthy. The little girl has been ill for
> months — all that time living on the bed in which three or four
> persons must sleep and which also serves the purpose of table and
> chairs. For weeks this little girl has had itch which has spread to
> the children of the surrounding rooms. She has torn the flesh on
> her arms and legs into great sores which have become poisoned.
> The other day I saw the mother dip a horrible dish rag into the
> potato dish and wash the sores! I took a friend to see the child.
> The mother started to show us the child's arm. The dirty dress
> was stuck in the great open sores. As the scabs were pulled away
> from the quivering flesh the little one writhed and screamed in
> agony.... The little one still lives there in her misery.... Yes, and
> many of the well-to-do are drawing large revenues from this same
> misery. A few months ago it was openly stated before the po-
> lice Commission that the owners of some of the vilest dens in the
> city were our "best" (!) people — our society people, our church
> people.[30]

Woodsworth's personal frustration with what he considered inadequate support from the churches for the socialist as well as the pacifist
causes, together with his own theological liberalism, led him to resign
from the ministry of the Methodist Church in 1918. He then became
involved with the Labour Church — a very liberal Social Gospel body
of left-wing Protestants from many churches. Members of the Labour
Church wanted to continue within their Christian heritage and raise
their children within it, while setting aside what they considered out-
moded dogmas, emphasizing instead the ethical and the social/political
dimension of Christianity.

It is certainly true that the socialist cause in Canada has never
had the support of more than a minority of the membership of the
churches. Yet Protestant clergy and other church members were promi-

nent among the leadership of the movement. Prominent Protestant socialists besides Woodsworth and Bland were Methodists A. E. Smith, Ernest Thomas, William Ivens, and A. J. Irwin, and Presbyterians J. G. Shearer and William Irvine.[31] At times even the institutional church could make public pronouncements of a socialist kind, as at the Methodist General Conference held at Hamilton in 1918, which called for public insurance and welfare systems, a mixed economy and tighter governmental control of the private sector, and indeed "nothing less than a complete social reconstruction."[32]

Such Social Gospel calls for a cooperative social order no doubt had a part, perhaps a major part, in preparing public consciousness for social measures that were later enacted, and (if Gramsci is at all correct) this is important. Social change must find its strength in the people's awareness and common will. Still, all of this would have had little effect without the practical work of social activists and politicians. A dramatic "socialist" event occurred in 1926 when the tiny democratic socialist "ginger group" in parliament held the balance of power when no party won a clear majority. Under Woodsworth's leadership, the balance of power was used to keep Mackenzie King's Liberals in power in exchange for the agreement that universal old age pensions would be instituted.[33]

The Cooperative Commonwealth Federation, founded in 1932 at Calgary as a federation of leftist organizations, chose J. S. Woodsworth as its first leader. It produced a program that called for "the establishment of a planned system of social economy for the production, distribution and exchange of all goods and services." It also wanted "socialization of the banking, credit and financial system of the country, together with the social ownership, development, operation and control of utilities and natural resources."[34] The following year at Regina the C.C.F. set forth its agenda more fully in the Regina Manifesto. Showing some awareness of the dangers of communism as seen in the Soviet Union, it assured the public that "the new social order at which we aim is not one in which individuality will be crushed out by a system of regimentation." It was firmly committed to democratic electoral politics. It stated clearly,

> we do not believe in change by violence. We consider that both the old parties in Canada are the instruments of capitalist interests and cannot serve as agents of social reconstruction, and that whatever the superficial differences between them, they are

bound to carry on government in accordance with the dictates of the big business interests who finance them. The C.C.F. aims at political power in order to put an end to this capitalist domination of our political life. It is a democratic movement, a federation of farmer, labor and socialist organizations, financed by its own members and seeking to achieve its ends solely by constitutional methods.[35]

Besides socialization of the "financial machinery" it called for "socialization (Dominion, provincial or municipal) of transportation, communications, electric power and all other industries and services essential to social planning and their operation under the general direction of the planning commission by competent managements freed from day to day political interference." However it assured the farmers that it supported "security of tenure for the farmer upon his farm on conditions to be laid down by individual provinces." It also pledged "encouragement of producers' and consumers' cooperatives."[36] Among other things, it called for publicly organized health, hospital, and medical services:

> Health services should be made at least as freely available as are educational services today. But under a system which is still mainly one of private enterprise the costs of proper medical care, such as the wealthier members of society can easily afford, are at present prohibitive for great masses of the people. A properly organized system of public health services including medical and dental care, which would stress the prevention rather than the cure of illness, should be extended to all our people.[37]

Over the years that followed the C.C.F. favored a variety of methods for subordinating capital and profits to the needs of people. It was the first to advocate many policies that were eventually instituted by governments (usually of the Liberal Party) and took credit for not only old age pensions (clearly Woodsworth's and Irvine's achievement in the minority parliament of 1926) but also family allowances, unemployment insurance, and hospital insurance programs, as well as the establishment of the Wheat Board and the inclusion of oats and barley under the Board's jurisdiction.[38] These measures achieved to some extent a "welfare state" within capitalism, but also a degree of public regulation or planning in the economy, and in that way limited the operation of the individualistic "free" market and the power of profit-oriented capital.

•

Of special interest to us here is the Fellowship for a Christian Social Order (FCSO), a national organization formed in the depths of the depression in 1934 (just two years after the formation of the C.C.F.). This organization was a "fellowship of fellowships," forming local groups throughout the country for the sake of studying and finding ways to promote a "Christian social order." By this they meant a society in which fellowship and friendship were the hallmarks, i.e., a socialist society founded upon the "religion of Jesus":

> Until we take as our steadfast objective, not missionary-evangelization and social service as we have been wont to project them, but the whole field of human existence to be transformed according to the radical maxims of Jesus, we are not joining the battle at the fundamental point, and, though the setting up of divine righteousness in the world may be done by someone, it will never be done by us.[39]

The existence of such "base" or grassroots communities of Christians was extremely important — who can measure the degree of influence such an organization had on public awareness? The Fellowship regarded itself as a "Kingdom of God movement," clearly socialist in the Social Gospel tradition:

> Believing as we do that there are no distinctions of power and privilege within the Kingdom of God, we pledge ourselves to the service of God and to the task of building a new society in which all exploitation of man by man and all barriers to the abundant life which are created by the private ownership of property shall be done away.[40]

It is remarkable that such ideas were sufficiently widespread and popular that in 1933 the Toronto Conference of the United Church of Canada was willing to pass by majority vote a resolution that in effect called for a socialist society. Professor John Line of Emmanuel College, Toronto, and his colleagues of the Committee on Evangelism and Social Service presented to the conference a proposal calling for "the socialization of banks, natural resources, transportation and other services and industries which, under private ownership, gave too much power over the subsistence of the people to special interests."[41]

Roger Hutchinson tells us that this was not an isolated instance, since a similar report was adopted by the Montreal and Ottawa Conference, and that a study done at the time demonstrated a growing ecumenical consensus about the discrepancy between capitalism and Christian teachings.[42]

Members of the Fellowship published an important book in 1936, *Towards the Christian Revolution,*[43] edited by McGill biblical scholar R. B. Y. Scott and Queens philosopher Gregory Vlastos, in which Christian socialist ideas were spelled out from the point of view of various theological disciplines, by academics (theologian John Line and ethicist King Gordon, in addition to Vlastos and Scott) and pastors (R. Edis Fairbairn and J. W. A. Nicholson), and also from the perspective of politics and economics (especially by economist Eugene Forsey and classicist Eric Havelock). While members of the FCSO sounded very much like the Social Gospel Christians and were no less radical in their socialist aspirations for society, these Christian socialists of the 1930s had moved away from the optimism of the earlier Social Gospel. John Line, for example, preferred to speak of "Religious Radicalism," which shared in the postwar disillusionment, recognizing a tragic strain in human existence:

> The Religious Radicalism represented by this book . . . is very different from the pre-war social gospel. It seeks a more deep-going diagnosis of man's need, and for that reason is more inward and in a true sense more religious. . . . The present radical gospel sees that man's redemption is unattainable without fundamental spiritual reorientations; it sees too that in man's present state and by reason of the unity of life these involve in their very beginnings the regeneration of the individual spirit and the re-creation of social life.[44]

Line reflects the neo-orthodoxy of the time, calling for a critical reappropriation of "Evangelicalism" and a "revival of faith in the deity of Jesus."[45] In his doctrines of sin and judgment and in his political ethics, Line's theology, written within the context of the depression, closely resembles the political theologies and liberation theologies that were to appear more than thirty years later:

> Thus the theology of Religious Radicalism will be eschatological; it will picture God as judging the world and taking sides. And this will dictate the strategy of a revolutionary Christianity,

which will clearly include alignment with the forces God is using to accomplish the next stage in man's deliverance. . . .

For this revolution seeks to end the strife and injustice that are contrary to the will of God, and to convert human society into a divine commonwealth of righteousness and love. Revolutionaries who have this goal are workers together with God.[46]

It was a hopeful, energetic, and intellectually vital movement, and no doubt left a longstanding legacy to both the church and Canadian society. But the depression was followed by the war, and a very different kind of social mood set in. As European socialists had learned at the time of the First World War, national and ethnic loyalties tend to take precedence over class loyalties when the nation seems threatened from the outside. The Fellowship for a Christian Social Order did last, however, until after the war, and ceased operations in 1945. It had been weakened during the war by the controversy over pacifism and by tensions between moderates and radicals.[47] James Woodsworth himself was a life-long pacifist, unshakably opposed to Canada's participation in war. Here his Social Gospel Christianity and the teaching of Jesus about nonviolence were decisive. However, when he could not carry his party with him in his antiwar stance in 1939 at the beginning of World War II, he effectively lost the leadership role, though certainly not the respect and affection of his party. When he died in 1942 he was succeeded by a former schoolteacher (an Anglican layman), M. J. Coldwell.

The election of a C.C.F. government in Saskatchewan in 1944 was, however, an important breakthrough in which the fruits of the Social Gospel could be seen. That government took power as the first socialist jurisdiction in North America under the leadership of T. C. Douglas. He, like Woodsworth, was a Christian minister and, like Rauschenbusch, a Baptist. Douglas also was clearly a man of the Social Gospel and continued to occupy pulpits throughout his province during his long tenure as premier. His government pioneered with hospital insurance, establishing in 1947 the first universal prepaid hospitalization in North America, and eventually full medicare, becoming a model for later developments across the country. The Saskatchewan C.C.F. also implemented some public ownership of industry, establishing small crown corporations in timber, tannery, printing, buses, and relatively larger ones in potash, coal, and silica.[48] The experiment met with a mixture of failure and success. This provincial government constantly had to assure North American capital investors that it was not communist, for fear of major capital strike or pullouts of investment and widespread unemployment. Rapid progress was made through government planning in the construction of highways, in rural electrification, and in the diversification of the economy. Gradually less emphasis was placed on the party's policies for state-owned industry.[49] The C.C.F. government was continually reelected for nearly twenty years (1944–62), culminating with its enactment of universal government-sponsored medicare against the vigorous opposition of the medical profession, the opposition Liberal and Progressive Conservative parties, and most of the media. A few years after the struggle to establish medicare in Saskatchewan it was launched as a national program by the federal Liberal government of Lester Pearson, a minority government with parliamentary support from the New Democratic Party. The N.D.P. (successor to the C.C.F.) has often held office since in the province of Saskatchewan, and governments of other parties that have held office have generally not dared to set aside its "socialist" achievements.

Both the successes and frustrations of the C.C.F. in Saskatchewan had their influence on the national direction of the party. A major policy declaration from Winnipeg in 1956, at a time when C.C.F. popularity was low in most of the country, indicated its development from a movement into a party. The younger party leadership, prominent among them David Lewis, a future leader, stressed the need for shaping policies that stood some chance of success at election time. The Winnipeg Declaration proudly spoke of "many of the improvements...wrung out of unwilling governments by the growing strength of our movement." Yet it noted that, despite great improvements, Canada still suffered from much poverty and inequality. It continued to call for a planned economy and saw this as more urgent than ever in the face of technological development. Forty years later the declaration of 1956 seems prophetic:

> Unprecedented scientific and technological advances have brought us to the threshold of a second industrial revolution. Opportunities for enriching the standard of life in Canada and elsewhere are greater than ever. However, unless careful study is given to the many problems which will arise and unless there is intelligent planning to meet them, the evils of the past will be multiplied in the future. The technological changes will produce

even greater concentrations of wealth and power and will cause widespread distress through unemployment and the displacement of population.[50]

The difficulties that arose with state ownership in Saskatchewan, as well as the strong anticommunist feeling in the country (partly because of the well-known abuses of the Soviet Union and great defense expenditures in Canada and NATO generally, precisely to ward off communism) apparently influenced the C.C.F. to move away from their strong emphasis on state ownership. The Winnipeg Declaration is much less specific on this subject, continuing to affirm public ownership only in general terms, while also explicitly affirming private enterprise:

> The CCF has always recognized public ownership as the most effective means of breaking the stranglehold of private monopolies on the life of the nation and of facilitating the social planning necessary for economic security and advance. The CCF will, therefore, extend public ownership wherever it is necessary for the achievement of these objectives.
>
> At the same time, the CCF also recognizes that in many fields there will be need for private enterprise which can make a useful contribution to the development of our economy. The co-operative commonwealth will, therefore, provide appropriate opportunities for private business as well as publicly owned industry.
>
> The CCF will protect and make more widespread the ownership of family farms by those who till them, of homes by those who live in them, and of all personal possessions necessary for the well-being of the Canadian people.
>
> In many fields the best means of ensuring justice to producers and consumers is the co-operative form of ownership. In such fields, every assistance will be given to form co-operatives and credit unions and to strengthen those already in existence.[51]

It is apparent here that, probably for the reasons suggested above, the C.C.F. was beginning to back away from its earlier clear policies of public ownership and thinking more and more about other ways to empower individuals or smaller groups, as opposed to the great corporations. Dissenters within complained that the C.C.F. had become like other parties, wanting " ... Success, Victory, Power; forgetting that the main business of socialist parties is not to form governments but to change minds."[52] Yet others, like David Lewis, believed that electoral success, actual influence, and the power to change things were more important than ideological purity. It would be true to say that the C.C.F. had become (in Walter Young's terms) less a movement and more a party, seeking victory at the polls. Social Gospel concepts and idealism were heard less often in the postwar boom time, with Social Gospel theology largely superseded not by "Religious Radicalism," but by Barthian or Niebuhrian neo-orthodoxy and "Christian realism" in the churches.[53]

The shift that was visible from Regina in 1933 to Winnipeg in 1956 was further evident in the founding convention of the New Democratic Party in 1961, which elected T. C. Douglas as its first leader. This development followed the decimation of the C.C.F. in the Diefenbaker Conservative sweep of 1958 and consisted of a new and stronger alliance between the C.C.F. and the labor movement. The party's platform spoke only in generalities about public ownership, promising to "expand public and co-operative ownership for such purposes as the operation of utilities, the development of resources, the elimination of monopoly concentrations of power."[54] It called for tax policies to divert funds from private to public investment, a guarantee of jobs for all who were able and willing to work, and the expansion of the health and social security network.

We cannot tell the whole story here. Our interest is to note the transition from "democratic socialism" to "social democracy." The debate and the historical development in Canada was highly reminiscent of earlier debates and histories in western Europe. To what extent should socialists seek economic betterment for working people within the capitalist structures, which were obviously not going to disappear quickly? Should socialists opt for a measure of political power and influence, precisely by advocating less radical programs, so gaining the confidence and support of a cautious electorate? Or should they persistently seek a comprehensive program of public ownership? There was even disagreement as to whether public ownership should be a socialist goal at all. The general move away from policies of public ownership was obviously a practical adjustment to the reality of political life in a North America thoroughly dominated by capitalist ideology. The withdrawal from policies of public ownership resulted, for some, from a loss of confidence in its effectiveness and efficiency, and for others from a realization that it was simply not saleable in the ideological atmosphere of North America. In the Canadian N.D.P., what appeared to some to be betrayal and retreat was vigorously resisted by the so-called "Waffle" group, who preferred to "waffle to the left" rather than "waffle to the right." But for most members of the N.D.P., "a medicare in the hand is worth two utopias in the bush."[55]

It is noteworthy that the New Democratic Party, like the C.C.F. before it, became well known as a nationalist party, suspicious of economic dependency upon the United States and supportive of Liberal governments when they attempted, though not very effectively, to assert a greater degree of economic independence (e.g., the establishment of the publicly owned petroleum company, Petro-Canada, and guidelines placing limits on foreign investment). The New Democrats have persistently rejected free trade with the United States and with Mexico. This is all of a piece with its distrust of multinational corporations and their economic power. If the nation state, or provincial or municipal governments, cannot impact the economic life of the nation, the power of big capital obviously grows more and more beyond the reach of democratic control and priorities.[56]

Neither C.C.F. nor N.D.P. have ever held federal governmental power in Canada, though they have held office provincially in Saskatchewan, Manitoba, British Columbia, and Ontario. Increasingly, in the circumstances of the 1970s to the 1990s, they have found it difficult to expand the socialist agenda of social democracy. Can it be (as some authors, such as Michael Lebowitz, suggest[57]) that the economic circumstances of a new high-tech multinational capitalist world have rendered such an agenda impossible? Will daring strategies have to be found if the achievements of social democracy are to be preserved or extended? In changing circumstances, perhaps this will entail, eventually, a return to the older democratic socialist commitments of the C.C.F. Or will it require, given the power of the capitalist world-system, a new and unprecedented "multinational socialism"?

Sweden

Sweden is one among the several western European nations that have, from time to time, elected a social democratic party to government and is often pointed to as an example of the success of democratic socialism. In Sweden the Social Democratic Party held the power of government from 1932 to 1976 — forty-four years of uninterrupted power. Though it regained power later, it was defeated again in 1991, replaced by a center right party, then returned to power again in September 1994. The Swedish story is important and instructive, exhibiting, as in Canada and elsewhere, the move away from policies of nationalization or state ownership toward a combination of economic planning and welfare measures with private ownership of capital.

The Social Democratic Party of Sweden was formed in 1889, including within itself Marxist elements, Swedish Lutherans, and those who were influenced by British-style Fabianism and German Social Democratic patterns. As late as 1920 the Swedish socialists were calling for public (state) ownership of all natural resources, but allowing for some private ownership in business and industry. Throughout the 1920s the demands of electoral politics forced a gradual change in policy, so that, by the time they came to power during the depression in 1932, plans for large-scale nationalization were largely abandoned.[58] The challenge of the depression years was met by modest socialist measures, such as unemployment insurance and pensions. Rhetoric of class conflict was dropped, and the party spoke of itself as a "party of the whole nation." In the decades that followed a kind of "functional socialism" evolved, wherein the power of government was used to sponsor a cooperative relationship between state power, capital, and labor. This has been one of the most impressive examples of a planned economy. Government pursued a strategy of regulating investment, selective subsidization, and supervision of foreign trade. Extensive regulation of industry, however, did not hamper industry and productivity, but rather encouraged it. Government actually served the interests of Swedish-based privately owned industry, especially in cars and trucks and other technologically specialized areas. Large Swedish multinational corporations (Volvo, Saab-Scania, Atlas, Copco, and Electrolux are among the best known) were enormously successful partly because of government encouragement by tax incentives, research and development funding, and promotion of international sales through the use of the diplomatic corps abroad.[59] In this respect Swedish social democracy actually resembles the government interventionism characteristic of east Asian capitalism. Such practices could be regarded simply as the co-optation of social democracy by capitalist interests. However, we may also see it as an alignment of socialist with nationalist concerns in a relatively small nation. Considering how much was accomplished for the well-being of workers, it is facile, I think, to dismiss Swedish social democracy as a genuine form of socialism. Sweden achieved a very high average standard of living, at times the highest in the world, very low unemployment rates, and the world's lowest statistics in infant mortality. Swedish socialism's nationalistic attitude and caution with regard to foreign investment helped to maintain the decisive influence of democratically elected government as over against foreign multinationals.[60] Further, "Sweden has an unusual wage structure. Its system of so-called 'solidarity wages' is one in which wage differentials among skill levels and across industries are among the lowest in the world."[61] Because of a combination of the planned economy, wage settlements, worker ownership and welfare programs (universal medical care, child care, etc.), the gap between rich and poor was very significantly reduced. The socio-economic character of the country has apparently helped to shape cultural and moral attitudes: "Conspicuous consumption is taboo in Sweden."[62]

Attempts within the labor movement to radicalize "wage earner funds," i.e., to greatly increase worker ownership of the means of production, were resisted in the 1970s, and again in the early 1990s, both by capital and by some workers. By 1976, when the Social Democratic Party was defeated, something of the neo-conservatism that was to come forward elsewhere in the western world was already at work in Sweden, the power of capital and the demands for profits asserting themselves. This was accompanied by disunity within the labor movement as well. Some commentators on Sweden have warned that the defeat of the strategy of wage earners' funds, due to capitalist opposition and worker disunity, was a very serious reversal for socialism in Sweden and has led to a significant turn to the right.[63] Very recently, Sweden, like other nations in the western/northern world, is experiencing major public debt problems, inflation, and growing unemployment, and the conservative government (defeated in 1994) was beginning to trim the social welfare system.[64] Yet the parties that took power after 1976 and after 1991 did not dare to dismantle the highly popular network of social democratic measures in a major way. Levels of social security, medical care (including dental care), day care, and maternity leave all remain very high, indeed remarkably high compared with anything found in either the United States or Canada. Even under governments ruled by parties other than the Social Democratic, Sweden has remained in a sense a "socialist" nation. Sweden has its problems in terms of unemployment and debt, but its problems are minuscule compared to those of the U.S. or Canada.[65] It has reached a high degree of social and economic equality and high levels of productivity, prosperity, health, and education, together with political freedom, high worker satisfaction, and industrial peace. Similar, if less notable social democratic success, can be found in Norway and Denmark, Germany, the Netherlands, Belgium, and (to a much lesser extent) in Britain and Canada.

Should a country like Sweden really be called "socialist"? Or is it quite simply a capitalist country — "capitalism with a human face"? The Social Democratic government did establish a very large public sector, especially in social services, employing up to 31 percent of the work force.[66] The government also set up several publicly owned industries, but while the Social Democrats have been out of power "the bourgeois coalition governments nationalized more private industry during the first three years of their six years in office than the [Social Democratic Party] did throughout its entire forty-four year incumbency."[67] The Swedish state came to own twenty-eight companies, under a state holding company, but "approximately 90 per cent of Swedish industry remained in private hands with only about 6 per cent controlled by the national government."[68] Gregg Olsen, commenting on this, insists that the departure from nationalization or state ownership in favor of economic planning was not an indication of reduced commitment to "socialism":

> Any strategy which was solely based on the socialisation of key Swedish industries would only address those problems which resulted from private property rights, not those occurring from the excessive reliance of those enterprises on market mechanisms.[69]

State ownership, as we have seen, can have other problems, such as bureaucratization and the inefficiencies of "state capitalism" (e.g., the Soviet Union) and does not by any means guarantee the democratization of the work place or the de-alienation of labor. Even state-owned industries or public utilities within political democracies do not guarantee a happy or fulfilled working class; workers may remain as far removed as ever from decision-making powers about working conditions or investment.[70] If "socialism" is about a quality of social cooperation and solidarity and the democratic control and exercise of economic power, then a high degree of socialism does indeed exist in social democratic states like Sweden. While socialism is not fully realized in Sweden or anywhere else (nor will it ever be) this is surely one of the most admirable societies in the world.

Particularly admirable, since the reelection of the Social Democrats in 1994, has been the major role of women in parliament and government.[71] Women members of the party, prior to the election, seriously threatened to establish a women's party, which would have badly damaged the Social Democrats' chances in the election. Sweden votes according to a system of proportional representation; voters cast ballots for parties, not candidates, and the parties submit candidate lists. Under pressure from its women members (in what was called the "Support Stocking Revolt") and with the support of many men, the Social Democrats voted that its candidate lists would consist of half women, half men. Once elected, Prime Minister Ingvar Carlsson appointed women to half of the cabinet posts — easily the most gender-equal government in the world. Some young women, mothers of small children, have been appointed to cabinet; their husbands are able (like all parents), if they choose, to stay home for a full year to care for their children on 90 percent of their regular wages. Such provisions have a powerful impact on the ability and willingness of women to pursue careers. Public deficit and other economic problems are not likely to be solved in Sweden by cutbacks on parental leave or child care programs. Can it be true that socialism and feminism really do need each other? Is this not the triumph of socialism and of the people as well, both women and men?

Despite all these social achievements, it does not follow that the Swedish model is the correct or best one for every part of the world or for all historical circumstances. What has been achievable in Sweden may not be achievable everywhere. No doubt the racial and cultural unity of that nation contributes to its stability and social peace. It remains to be seen, further, whether in the high-tech decades ahead, such mixed, capitalist, and government-planned economies and social democratic systems of wealth reallocation can coexist with the great power of mobile and privately owned multinational corporations. Perhaps the relatively low level of foreign ownership in Sweden will continue to give that nation a greater degree of self-determination than is possible in places like Canada. However, the arguments of Browne and Lebowitz (see chapter 3) and Panitch and Swartz,[72] raise questions about the continuing viability of such "social democratic" strategies for limiting the power of private capital in our changing technological world.

•

Democratic socialist and social democratic parties have clearly had a major humanizing impact on their societies. Nevertheless, they are criticized by some socialists, e.g., some members of the so-called "New Left," who believe that democratic socialism/social democracy is too compromised with the dominant capitalist system. While the term "New Left" can refer to a fairly broad range of radical socialists, the most extreme kinds of "new leftists" have favored a strategy of mass strikes and boycotts and generally the promotion of social chaos, which, they hope, will lead to significant structural change. Gradual amelioration of social conditions within capitalism, as promoted by social democracy, is seen as nothing but an adaptive modification and survival mechanism of the capitalist system itself, and therefore counterproductive. The New Left itself, since its prominent appearance in the upsets of the 1960s, has not succeeded in moving the world toward a socialist order.[73] However, their warning to democratic socialists should not go unheeded. The latter always stand in danger of being co-opted by the reigning system.

Chapter 8

Socialism in Its Many Varieties

The Question of Definition

How can we usefully define socialism in a way that honors its history and its best thought and practice? And what kind of socialism, if any, should we support or aspire to in face of the collapse of communism and the present failure and injustice of global capitalism? It is still very common for writers about socialism to define it in terms of "the abolition of private property in means of production."[1] Another defines socialism more broadly, better reflecting the historical variety of socialisms: "the predominance of state, social and co-operative property and the absence of large-scale private ownership of the means of production."[2] Two Canadian authors propose that socialism means "taking capital away from the capitalists, and democratizing control over the instruments and processes of production, distribution, and communication, to the end of transforming their capitalist and undemocratic content and function."[3] Others object to the confusion of socialism with statism:

> Socialism is social ownership and control of the means of production, not state ownership and control of the means of production. A socialist society is a producer's society.... The producers own and control the means of production and democratically decide what is to be produced.... This includes the clear possibility of letting market forces play a role in production.[4]

The brief glimpse of the history of socialism that we have recounted so far makes it clear that *socialism is not one thing*. From the beginning socialist theorists and practitioners have varied and disagreed about both goals and methods. Yet they have enough in common that they are all recognizable as "socialist." In light of the history, what constitutes the unity of all the socialisms? Socialism, as a worldwide and historical movement has very blurry boundaries, and perhaps it is best

159

that this should be so. Heresy hunting and "doctrinal purity" is to be avoided if at all possible, not only in religious but also in political circles. I would propose first a very broad and general definition: *Socialism is the movement that strives to make of human society a community of friends, promoting and emphasizing economic cooperation for the benefit of all the people and placing the economic interests of all the people ahead of the interests of a few.* Socialism, thus defined very broadly as an idea and a goal, makes friendship the supreme value for human society, and is clearly congruent with the Christian ethical commitment to love of neighbor. Community and human solidarity are valued more highly than competition, maximization of profit, or even productivity. In this very broad sense, people who do not call themselves socialist may nevertheless contribute to the "friendly society" by promoting aspects of mutual cooperation within a capitalist society.

Yet a more specific definition at the level of methods or strategies is also required to distinguish socialists from ethically motivated persons who reject socialism as a concept. Socialism also offers, typically, some political/economic prescription or strategy, but these differ from one socialist group to another, and in various times and places. In this sense, *Socialism is that movement which seeks to use democratic political power to limit and regulate the power of the private ownership and control of capital.* Or, to state both the general and the specific more briefly: *Socialism is the effort to distribute and democratize economic power among all the people, for the sake of creating society as a community of friends.* This inclusive understanding of what constitutes "socialism" implies that it is not helpful to define it in terms of one particular political or economic strategy. It is essential, of course, that some particular strategy be undertaken or advocated; socialists, whether individual citizens, politicians, or parties, cannot be vague about their actual goals and policies. However, strategies must and will change according to particular circumstances. It may be public, i.e., state ownership and control of a national or regional economy, or some degree of this; it may consist of state welfare measures within an essentially capitalist system and a mixed economy; it may encourage cooperatives or worker ownership within a planned economy under the direction of a democratically elected government. From its beginnings in the mid-nineteenth century, socialists have been divided about the role of the state. Some socialisms have great faith in government; other socialisms are highly suspicious of the potential tyranny of state power. Besides political/philosophical or ideological differences of this kind, based in various actual experiences, socialisms vary according to the historical circumstances with which they live. The cliché is all too true: "Politics is the art of the possible." But all socialist strategies have in common not just the striving after justice and human well-being (many liberals and conservatives share this with socialists) but also the drive toward the democratization of capital and the limitation of the power of private capital.

To enlarge on our definition, we may characterize socialism as essentially utopian (using the term positively). It is common for people to speak of "achieving socialism" as a social goal or ideal. (It is rare, by contrast, for people to speak of "achieving capitalism" — an economic state of affairs that seems to occur all too spontaneously.) Every particular socialism is a critical analysis of the human economic condition under the dominance of capital and a hopeful, visionary strategy for changing it. For Christian socialists, socialism is an attempt to move toward "no place" — (that which has never yet been seen in history) and thus to approximate the "Reign of God" within the conditions of history.

Christians especially are aware that, given the reality of human sin and the refusal of human beings to be *for the neighbor,* socialism (society as a community of friends) will never be fully realized in history as we know it. A good society, a community of friends, requires good, friendly people. Yet it is our calling always to "strive first for the Kingdom of God and his righteousness" (Matt. 6:33) and thus never to be satisfied with the "unfriendly," essentially competitive kingdom of capital. For Christian socialists, then, the quest for socialism in the political realm is a quest for signs, pen-ultimate approximations, or parables of the Reign of God.

Our brief glance at the history shows that the term has been used in widely divergent ways from the beginning, and this continues to be so today. I have said that some political phenomena that have called themselves "socialist" should not be so-called. National Socialism (Nazism), being anti-Semitic, fascist, and capitalistic, should certainly not be included among the types of socialism. And I have argued that the communism or monopoly state capitalism that developed in the Soviet Union, though it began with an intentionally socialist revolution, has to be regarded as having ceased to be socialist. Using the definition of socialism suggested above, the same would have to be said of the communist regimes of eastern Europe prior to

1989. It seems useful to identify and briefly describe some of the major kinds of socialist movements, parties, or governments that have developed since the earlier history sketched in the previous chapters. Our purpose here is not to describe, analyze, or assess them with any thoroughness, but simply to indicate the contemporary varieties of socialism and to consider the degree to which they can be regarded as successful in realizing socialist goals.

What Are the Other Socialist Alternatives?

We have already discussed at various places in this book the two major and most historically visible forms of socialism:

- The state-owned communism of the Soviet Union and eastern Europe (which, I have argued, ceased to be truly "socialist" in terms of that word's original and broader meaning; see chapter 3), and

- Democratic socialism/social democracy (which has achieved a great deal, but is always in danger of becoming co-opted by capital; see chapter 7).

I shall now mention or discuss briefly other forms of socialism existing in our contemporary world — Euro-Communism, Third World communisms, and African socialism, but consider at a little more length the broad movement known as worker ownership, cooperativism, and communitarianism.

Euro-Communism

Powerful communist parties (as distinct from socialist parties) exist in such western European nations as France, Italy, and Spain. Though such parties have never held total governmental power, they have sometimes formed part of governing coalitions, and are represented in parliaments, and have sometimes had considerable influence on governments. They are to be located ideologically (from a western point of view) to the "left" of the democratic socialist/social democratic parties, calling more persistently for public (state) ownership. Their histories go back, as we have seen, to early communist/socialist thought in the mid-nineteenth century and the days of the Second International after 1889, and they should not be regarded as offshoots of Soviet communism. They can be distinguished from social democratic parties in Europe by their early support for Lenin and the Russian revolution and by their participation in the Third International (Comintern) set up by Lenin in 1919, which involved a break with "reformism" associated with such leaders as Bernstein and commitment to the defense of the soviet republics.[5] While they sometimes seemed to be the captives of Stalinism, in more recent years they generally insisted upon their independence from Moscow, according to the principle of "polycentrism" as articulated, for example, by the Italian Communist Party leader Palmiro Togliatti,[6] though this, of course, was no longer a problem after the collapse of communism in the Soviet Union. They are often neo-Marxist in some sense, informed to various degrees by the neo-Marxist thought of the Frankfurt school or other kinds of "revisionism." They wish to be elected democratically rather than to seize power by violent revolution.

Chinese Communism

Chinese communism (also discussed in previous chapters) resembles in many ways that of the Soviet Union — oligarchic party rule and a dearth of political freedom or worker control — and so it is debatable whether it should be described as "socialist." It deserves particular attention here because of its relevance to Third World development and the enormous size of the Chinese nation, consisting as it does of about one-fourth of the world's population.

Chinese communism was founded and developed under the leadership of Mao Tse-Tung (1893–1976), who came to power by violent revolution in 1949, and it is now generally accepted that he consolidated his power by a wave of mass killings. Maoism featured state ownership and control of industry and state collective farms. It has always rejected the Stalinist and Brezhnev doctrine of the leadership of the Soviet Communist Party, insisting on its own peculiarly Chinese form of communism. It is also neo-Marxist, or a kind or revisionism, in that it was originally built not upon the proletarian class but almost entirely upon the peasant class in a predominantly agricultural nation. Maoism was an attempt to overcome the injustice and oppression of an ancient feudal society, further corrupted by the presence of western/northern economic colonialism. Mao also emphasized the need for "permanent revolution" and ongoing self-criticism and social change. He sought to build an independent, self-sufficient nation, a goal with some credibility in such a huge nation, possessing vast territory and

nearly every natural resource. Despite the near totalitarian nondemo-
cratic and tyrannical character of Chinese communism (so evident in
recent events), which is indefensible and cannot be condoned, Chinese communism must be credited with incomparable achievements
in rapid industrialization and in the overcoming of poverty, disease,
and illiteracy (see details in chapter 5).[7] It provides a noncapitalist
or postcapitalist model of development. What has to be noted here,
however, is that in the post-Mao era, China has moved significantly
away from "pure" communism, finding it desirable to introduce elements of a market economy. The story of socialism here is, as ever, an
ambiguous one.

Other Third World Communism

Under this heading can be included the Communist or Marxist governments of Cuba, North Korea, Angola, Mozambique, and Ethiopia.
It is beyond the scope of this book (and the competence of the author) to describe or analyze all of these, except to note that all of
them have been, in some measure, supported by the U.S.S.R. or China
as, in some measure, outposts of their empires (just as much of the
capitalist Third World has been part of the American/west European
neo-colonial empire).

Cuba, after Castro's brave revolution of 1959, was isolated in the
western hemisphere by the hostility of the United States, which, after the failure to destroy the revolution militarily, made it impossible
for Cuba to receive international credit or to engage in significant
trade except with the Soviet Union and the eastern bloc. This severely
circumscribed its opportunities for economic development. It soon
became a client state of the Soviet Union and developed a state-
controlled command economy on the model of its powerful sponsor.
It continued to be heavily dependent on a single product, sugar,
and, having relatively little natural endowment, has not succeeded (as
China did) in its attempt to industrialize. It thus suffers from many of
the same problems as the Soviet Union, including the failure to democratize politically. Cuba remains very poor and, like China, has
not accomplished any great breakthrough in agricultural productivity. Still, Cuba has not exhibited the same gross divergences between
rich and poor as are to be found in most of the Caribbean and
Latin America, and, through the relatively humane and enlightened
attitudes of its communist leaders, has, until recently, outdone most

of the Third World in its fight against disease, infant mortality, and illiteracy.[8] The loss of its powerful Soviet sponsor and the continued hostility of the United States points to its probable imminent collapse.

Mozambique, Angola, and Ethiopia have grim and very complex colonial histories and dreadful internal divisions, which are legacies of the colonial past. Efforts to build a form of Marxist/Leninist communism in Mozambique and Angola have been grievously frustrated by debilitating internal divisions, encouraged, until recently, by the destabilization strategies of apartheid South Africa.

African Socialism

Many of the leaders of postcolonial Africa have borrowed the word "socialism" to describe their political programs or aspirations. They have been critical of the western European capitalism, which dominated them for so long during the period of old colonialism, recognizing that their nations' peoples and resources were exploited precisely by profit-oriented capitalist societies. Kwame Nkrumah, first president of independent Ghana in west Africa, developed, under the influence of Lenin's thought, a theory of "neo-colonial" and "neo-imperialist capitalism." He pointed out in his book on neo-colonialism that, though they had gained political independence, postcolonial nations were still dominated economically by their former masters or other western capitalist nations.[9] Nkrumah, in his meticulous presentation of information and analysis of the "Oppenheimer Empire," of the Anglo-American Corporation, and of mining and various other industries in Africa, showed how resource wealth and the value of African labor were exported out of Africa to enhance the wealth of a northern/western elite and an even smaller African elite. Nkrumah was an important early contributor to "dependency theory," which (though later modified) has been an important tool of liberation theologians and other theorists for understanding Third World poverty.

Nkrumah and his successors, however, have not succeeded in combating neo-colonialism, as is so evident in Ghana's (and Africa's) impoverishment under the Structural Adjustment Plans of the I.M.F. and World Bank — examples of neo-colonialism par excellence.

At a conference of independent African nations at Dakar in 1962 a number of African leaders rejected both Marxist socialism and liberal capitalism as foreign to African culture. Leopold Senghor, president of Senegal, called for "African Socialism," rejecting Marxist class struggle (since, he said, in Africa there are no classes) and capitalist individualism, since African traditional societies have been communal in nature.[10] Unfortunately, African communalism has had to live within a world dominated by international capital in the form of multinational corporations, powerful institutions like the International Monetary Fund, and the fierce trade competition of capitalist nations. African economic and political elites have in large measure colluded with these forces, so that the utopian African socialism envisaged in the early 1960s has not materialized.

Perhaps the most impressive African socialist experiment was the *Ujamaa* socialism of Tanzania, under the leadership of Julius Nyerere. Nyerere is a devout Christian, educated, like most modern African leaders, in Christian mission schools and motivated by high ideals for society. *Ujamaa*, or "familyhood," was a truly visionary effort to build a friendly society, organizing this mainly rural nation around communal villages. It opposed both capitalist exploitation and Marxist class conflict and sought to honor elders and to value the work of all equally. The Arusha Declaration of Nyerere's party and government in 1967 declared that "all citizens together possess all the natural resources of the country in trust for their descendants." It explicitly declared itself "democratic socialist." This was understood to mean that "it is the responsibility of the state to intervene actively in the economic life of the nation..., and so to prevent the accumulation of wealth to an extent which is inconsistent with a classless society." They committed themselves to see that "government exercises effective control over the principal means of production and pursues policies which facilitate the way to collective ownership of the resources of this country."[11] Nyerere valued "democracy," attempting to achieve this within one-party consensus, but there are allegations of oppressive "persuasion" and imprisonment of dissenters.

To assess the success or failure of *ujamaa* is not a simple matter. Much was achieved in terms of justice and equality in basic health care, education, and the provision of necessities to all the people. Yet there was much dissatisfaction about the shortage of both consumer goods and foreign exchange. The high ideals and ambitious goals of *ujamaa*, requiring a "change of heart" among the people, no doubt required much more time, and Tanzania lived under the constant competitive pressure of the international capitalist system. Nyerere's successors have, sadly, largely abandoned his socialist ideals, and Tanzania has been subjected, like so much of the Third World, to a Structural Adjustment Plan.

Worker Self-Management: Yugoslavia

A historical example of a political socialism that operated in a decentralized way, maximizing the decision-making power of workers, has been Yugoslavia.[12] In 1948 Yugoslavia broke away from Soviet domination and developed its own kind of socialism. Although since the death of Tito and the later collapse of eastern European communism, the Yugoslavian nation has fallen apart into ethnic chaos, for decades a highly successful and relatively free worker control socialism existed there, which is of interest to our current concerns about the future of socialism.

Yugoslavian socialism was, of course, a political socialism, imposed by the state. It is said to have been relatively the freest and least oppressive of the eastern European communist nations, yet it could not be described as a political democracy, and this is a serious failure. However, though government was authoritarian, workers in Yugoslavia enjoyed a high degree of autonomy and personal dignity in a system of worker self-management of factories. Workers of a given firm (large industries being publicly owned, but co-owned by the workers) exercised democratic control of the operation of their firms and at the same time competed in the market place with other firms, so that the interests of the consumer, worker, and factory incentives and efficiency were built into the system.[13] Small-scale exceptions were allowed: private craftsmen, restaurant owners, and others who employed up to five people were not subject to the worker-control provision.[14] This system eliminated, or at least reduced, some of the worst features of capitalism: the alienation of wage-labor and the powerlessness of workers in their work place. Workers could feel a strong sense of identification with the productive process and were rewarded for the productivity of their firm and for the popularity of their product with the consumer. Evidently there were tensions and conflicts in the system. Self-management, well developed at the grassroots level, had its limitations; being controlled by an undemocratic, authoritarian state obviously left much to be desired. However, worker self-management proved far more successful than the bureaucratic command economy typical of the Soviet Union and most of eastern Europe. Between 1952 and 1960 Yugoslavia recorded the highest growth rate of any country in the world.[15] Yugoslavian industrial output increased five-fold and the per-capita income of Yugoslavian workers increased three and a half times in twenty years[16] — statistics rivalling those of China in its success at rapid industrialization. Industrial output and industrialization are not, of course, the only measure of a good socio-economic system, but the ability to provide improved material standards of living to large populations is not by any means irrelevant to the assessment of systems.

Worker Ownership/Cooperativism

The term "socialism" can also refer to the efforts of workers to own and control the means of production among themselves, i.e., worker ownership of companies, or the cooperative movement. Communitarianism (a term describing a very diverse phenomenon of communal, cooperative economic life) is a closely related concept. Worker ownership can also be part of capitalism, when private companies encourage their employees to own shares — a circumstance that does not usually give workers very much influence or power, though they may have a small share in the company profits.[17]

But cooperative worker ownership is quite different. As defined and described by one of the early socialist experiments, the "Rochdale Pioneers" in 1844, it is distinguished from capitalist companies or corporations in that it specifically aims to empower workers and consumers to produce and distribute for use, rather than for profit. Its membership is open. It often differs from ordinary capitalist organization in that every member of a cooperative is an equal voting member. It is not shares that vote, but people.[18] Co-ops tend to emphasize education of their members in the philosophy of cooperativism. Returns on investment are often limited, since the accumulation of riches is not its goal. Earnings of the cooperative are commonly reinvested or distributed according to the degree of participation.[19]

This is actually close to the most original concept of socialism, as in the efforts of Robert Owen and his associates. Cooperatives often cooperate among themselves and assist each other, but cooperativism has the value of including elements of competition and incentive, in that worker-owned cooperatives still compete with each other and/or with companies and corporations for the consumers' business, while reinvesting or distributing the power of capital widely among those who actually work and produce. It can exist within a mixed system that combines state, worker, and other kinds of private ownership.[20] Widespread cooperative worker ownership together with private ownership, and social planning by a democratically controlled government, could conceivably work well and promote the "community of friends" for the benefit of all the people in an imperfect world. Gregory Baum, speaking of "Pope John Paul II's Socialism," characterizes the social vision of cooperative socialism in this way:

> It defines itself against the centralized, authoritarian collectivism of the Soviet bloc. ... It demands, first, that workers become co-owners and be co-responsible for the policies of their industries, and, second that the central planning supervised by the government take place in a manner that allows for the interplay of many different institutions and local interests.[21]

But what is the history of this kind of socialism, and is there any evidence that it can succeed or survive? We have already seen a measure of success in the early experiments of Robert Owen and his colleagues, though those early experiments did not last very long. Following upon Owen's efforts, a large and important cooperative movement existed in Britain for many years. A particularly famous and influential example of cooperativism was the highly successful Rochdale Society of the "Rochdale pioneers," formed in England in 1844 (during the depression of the "hungry forties").[22] A key leader here was Charles Howarth, who helped formulate what are commonly regarded as the principles of "Cooperation" (a term used synonymously with "Socialism'). Another major leader of "Cooperation" was the Christian socialist E. V. Neale, who held up the vision of "Christian Cooperation" as a model for "Christian civilization." Cooperativism often took the form of consumers' cooperatives, in which citizens banded together cooperatively in wholesaling of goods to consumers to bypass profiteering. The Cooperative League, through which cooperatives cooperated among themselves to maximize their effectiveness, was formed in 1852. Producers' cooperatives also developed in Britain from the mid-nineteenth century, for example, the Working Tailors Association, formed in 1850, promoting self-governing workshops among tradespeople, and the Guild of Cooperators, formed in 1878, facilitating, among others, the Frameworkers and Guilders Association Permanent Building Society.[23] By 1936, Eugene Forsey, writing about the achievements of cooperatives, recorded that in Britain the cooperative societies had a membership of over seven million, with almost three hundred thousand employees, and capital of over 150 million pounds (UK). Together they were the largest single distributive business in the country, the largest dealers in butter, sugar, bacon, and dried fruits in the British Empire, and the world's largest buyers of Canadian wheat. They operated successful shoe factories and flour mills and the world's largest tea business. They were heavily involved in life and accident insurance and credit unions, and they operated as well over two hundred factories and productive industries! Forsey informs us that at that time cooperatives did three-quarters of all the business in Iceland, one-third in Finland, and 40 percent in Sweden. Stockholm, he tells us, had over eighty thousand people in cooperative homes. These are a few selective statistics to indicate that, as Forsey says, "it works and works well and on a large scale."[24]

An early twentieth-century socialist theory and movement closely associated with the cooperative movement was sometimes called "syndicalism" or "guild socialism." Socialists of this persuasion were always suspicious of the power and control of the state and favored instead "worker control." Leading British thinkers along these lines were the Christian socialist A. J. Penty, A. R. Orage, Anglicans N. Figgis and the "Red Vicar" Conrad Noel (who wrote a socialist *Life of Jesus*), historians R. H. Tawney and G. D. H. Cole, and Archbishop William Temple.[25] In Britain the National Guilds movement cherished a plan for state-chartered guilds of workers based on trade unions to take over the management of industry as agents of the whole community. The great concern here was for the freedom and dignity of the worker in the work place and the abolition of "wage-slavery." It was not poverty but abject dependence and insecurity that most motivated this movement. It wanted to diffuse social power and responsibility widely among all the people through their workers' associations, guilds, or unions, making individuals and groups as much as possible the masters of their own lives and the conditions of their work.[26] Of course this scheme never came to power. Much disagreement among guild socialists themselves and lack of power to actually implement their plans meant that capitalism went on as usual (though eventually modified by the influence of the unions and of the Labour Party).

The reality is that cooperativism and worker ownership, especially producers' cooperatives, have always suffered under the fierce opposition and competition of large corporately owned capital. This was already evident when Eugene Forsey wrote in 1936. He pointed out that cooperativism is severely restricted by the bargaining strength and price-cutting capacity of great corporations.

> The first limitation results from the fact that capitalism is no longer competitive but monopolistic.... 1936 is not 1844.... [Any] important industrial enterprises which co-operatives may undertake on this continent will have to fight not the small individual or family business but giant corporations. Only in exceptional cases can they hope for success.[27]

Cooperativism had considerable success in Britain, where it had started very early, and in countries on the fringe of major capitalist development; it was less successful in North America. One of the great limitations on cooperativism — and this was already visible in 1936 in Britain as well as this continent — was that they simply could not compete with the great corporations in the production of producers' goods — coal, steel, machinery, and other heavy industry products. Prices, supply, and demand for these major items were prone to great fluctuation. Cooperatives were able to survive in the area of consumers' goods — food, clothing, even housing, etc. — partly because of the relative stability of demand in these industries. The enormous scale of investment required in heavy industry was beyond the reach of the little people who were able to set up cooperatives in smaller and more stable fields.[28] It is well known that since World War II cooperativism has declined, since large, sometimes multinational capital began to invest massively in the fields in which cooperativism had succeeded, i.e., the field of consumer goods and distribution.

Socialists of the Marxist persuasion have typically criticized cooperativism as an ineffective tool for putting control of economic power into the hands of workers. Since cooperatives cannot compete with large-scale capitalist enterprise in producers' goods and more recently have not been able to compete either in consumers' goods, whether in production or distribution, they cannot bring economic power under democratic control. They cannot control the monetary system, nor the allocation of major investment for heavy industry; they cannot provide overall social/economic planning, nor full employment, nor can they determine environmental or social priorities. Thus Forsey commented:

> Cooperation is still weak and politically neutral. It can make working class income go farther without touching the income of

the capitalist class. What better device could any one invent for heading off socialism....?

Only the capture of political power and the transfer to the state of at least the main industries and services now in capitalist hands can bring in the new economic order.[29]

Since Forsey wrote, the limitations and dangers of state ownership of industry have now also become painfully evident, not least to Forsey himself. Unfortunately, however, his critique of the limitations of co-operativism is still relevant. Proponents of cooperativism today know that they cannot hope to replace multinational corporate capitalism in the foreseeable future. Severyn Bruyn, for example, a contemporary proponent of a communitarian alternative to capitalism and socialism (which he identifies with state ownership), recommends that the opponents of the dominant capitalism should support alternative networks. He names six elements of "communitarianism" that already exist and that deserve support: community land trusts, worker cooperatives, community financial institutions, consumer organizations, community development corporations, and industrial trade associations.[30]

Communitarianism

Concepts of cooperativism, communalism, and communitarianism overlap, and there is no generally accepted precise usage of these terms. Older forms of "communalism" can be seen as precursors of today's "communitarianism." German and Swiss Mennonites and Hutterites have a long history, going back to the sixteenth century, of alternative economy in the form of community, cooperative ownership, and control of land and instruments of production, a tradition that still survives with vitality in many places. These older communalisms sought to free people from ecclesiastical and feudal tyrannies and to enable them to live out their understanding of Christian community in their economic life. The communitarian experiments found in our contemporary cities are quite different of course; they do not usually have an explicitly religious base and do not separate themselves off from the larger culture. But they do resemble those older communalisms as movements of protest and alternative economy. Like the older communes, today's cooperatives and communitarian experiments do not foresee taking over the economy. Their members merely wish to live their own lives with greater freedom and integrity and to meet real needs in a practical, economically viable way in the face of an economic system that often does not serve their interests.

A broad and diverse communitarian phenomenon has been identified in both the United States and Canada (implementing precisely what Bruyn, above, speaks of), i.e., cooperative day care and after-school child care centers, co-op gardening, food and housing cooperatives, community repair organizations, popular loan funds and local credit unions, common kitchens, street patrols to reduce crime, etc. These are all ways in which people seek to gain greater control of their lives and environments, escaping the control of both large corporations and governments. The concept is not new, as we have seen: people without great financial resources or power come together co-operatively to meet their own local needs, to some extent freeing themselves of the control of large privately owned corporations, and governments as well, which often seem remote and beyond the control of electors.

A growing movement in the United States toward community land trusts (CLTs) is particularly exciting, in that it attempts in a creative way to address the urgent problem of housing and homelessness and the spiraling price of land for productive ends. Chuck Matthei, in *Sojourners,* tells the story within the context of theological reflection.[31] These are democratically organized nonprofit corporations that own land for the sake of making it available to individuals, families, or organizations for residential, agricultural, or commercial purposes. The CLT has as one of its goals the protection of property from monopolization, absentee ownership, and speculation, allowing individuals the benefits of ownership, security, and even legacy for their heirs, as long as they actually use or live on it. Some CLTs take the form of limited-equity cooperatives, where residents own a share, but the transfer value is limited to ensure affordability, or mutual housing associations (MHAs, nonprofit housing corporations), which provide low-cost housing subject to deed and resale restrictions.

In Canada some housing coop projects have enjoyed the support of government funding and have often been undertaken with church initiative. Cooperative ownership of housing is shared by families according to their financial capacity: payment from each according to their ability to pay; housing to each according to their need.[32] Surely this is a micro-form of "socialism," made possible only by certain "social democratic" measures of the state, yet operating within capitalist structures. Unfortunately, it remains a tiny phenomenon within a basically capitalist housing market.

In the United States, where there has been less state support for such ventures, it has been especially the churches that have provided facilities, personnel, volunteers, and investment capital. Matthei cites examples of community land co-ops in Cincinnati and Syracuse; of a pastor/organizer sponsored by the Methodist Church and assigned to work with CLTs in Atlanta; of CLTs supported by the Roman Catholic archdiocese of New York; of a house of Dominican sisters who donated land for such a purpose in Ohio. "There are now more than 100 CLTs across the country and many individual co-ops or MHAs. Yet their numbers are still limited and most of this development takes place in low-income communities where the need is most urgent and where these models have obvious advantages over conventional market or public sector options."[33] Those who lead this movement do not wish to see it as solely a "poor people's policy," however, and hope that mainstream society will move in this direction. An instrument for furthering this movement is the "Equity Trust Fund," an organization that invites gifts from the social appreciation in property to be used to meet the needs of those who are disadvantaged by the land and housing market. Equity gifts from individuals or organizations are used to provide loans or grants to community land trusts or mutual housing associations. Churches and religious orders, which are often property rich, are among the prime participants in this movement.

While such phenomena have never been entirely absent from the scene, the circumstance that has led to a new emphasis on efforts of this kind is precisely the specter of major, widespread, and enduring unemployment in the industrial sphere and the growing impotence of so many to provide housing for themselves or their families, or places or opportunities for business. In the first thirty years or so following World War II people became increasingly dependent upon both large corporations and governments to provide employment, as well as goods and services. But, as we have noted elsewhere, the new technological/economic situation is such that increases in economic growth can be produced without employing more people. Indeed in our post-Keynesian world, in which high profits, inflation, and unemployment apparently go hand in hand, economic growth can be accompanied by net job reduction.[34] New investment in high-tech may increase Gross National Product but decrease employment (what in the recent recession has been called a "jobless recovery") leading to increased homelessness and general impoverishment. It would be highly optimistic, at least at this time, to suggest that community land trusts, grassroots cooperatives, and neighborhood mutual help organizations will solve these problems by taking over and controlling the mega-dimensions of complex industrial processes — mass production of cars, household appliances, aircraft, energy production, etc. At least no one knows how this could happen in the foreseeable future. Yet emphasis on small-scale informal or alternative economy is one way that imaginative people defend themselves against the large impersonal structures that are market-dominated and profit-driven and therefore do not serve the needs of people for useful and meaningful employment.

In a detailed study of "informal economic activity" David Ross and Peter Usher analyze the various informal structures that are in fact a major, but largely forgotten and neglected aspect of the total socio-economic scene. The household, they point out, "produces by far the greatest part of the entire national output of childcare and household care. As well ... some households are partly or largely self-sufficient in such things as food, clothing and energy production."[35] Illegal or quasi-legal economic activity is more and more common, as when the services of skilled tradespeople are exchanged without goods and services tax or income tax (the so-called "underground" economy). Informal economy, strictly speaking, as these authors define it, is typically "unquantified, unrecorded, uncounted," designed to provide sustenance rather than profits. Local neighborhood cooperatives in either goods or services involve group decision-making and flexible work routines and are characterized by "the absence of capital accumulation for its own sake, by the reduced emphasis placed on money, by direct concern for the community, the environment and the welfare of future generations and by more cooperation."[36] Again, it is often Christians (but not exclusively Christians) who are at the forefront of developments of this kind.[37]

Are such organizations and movements and the people involved with them to be called "socialists"? We must be wary of applying the term to people who would explicitly reject it. Some local organizations of mutual aid and cooperation would be highly suspicious of "socialism," seeing it as a form of state control of people's lives. Often neighborhood associations are formed precisely to resist the incursions of government, whether national, state/provincial, or municipal into local communities.[38] As we have seen, it is a very old tradition of socialist thought to be suspicious of government, which is often seen to be in the pocket of the ruling class. In fact there is much of the socialist spirit about this phenomenon. In that it emphasizes cooperation and constitutes resistance to the reigning capitalist/corporate structure and is to some extent an alternative strategy for survival and humanization, it appears to be an authentic manifestation of the socialist vision. Indeed it is very close to the original "socialist" vision of Robert Owen and others like him in Europe. In that it empowers people and in some degree democratizes economy and creates some degree of independence from the power of big capital, it can be called "socialist" in the broad sense in which the concept has been defined here.

Analysts and proponents of this development have been wary of describing it as "socialist" for good reason. Harry Boyte, in his book *Backyard Revolution* (analyzing this phenomenon as it exists in the United States), complains that social democrats (or in the U.S. "liberal Democrats" of the left) tend to create social service structures that ruthlessly turn citizens into dependent clients.[39] He argues that socialist or left-wing movements have historically been inattentive to complex cultural and religious traditions. In terms reminiscent of the great socialist theoretician Gramsci, Boyte charges that socialists have tried to cut off people from "their past, their folkways, and their group identities.... From the pinnacles of 'advanced thinking,' voluntary associations like the family, the church, and ethnic traditions tend to appear as backwaters of culture."[40] His comments about the church are particularly relevant to us here. The church is one of the most important aspects of what Boyte calls the "populist tradition," which is "more organic, more culturally rooted than that of classic socialism or liberalism." He sees a revival of the tradition beginning in the 1970s arising out of primary institutions such as family, church, union locals, neighborhood associations.[41] What he calls "the citizen revolt" seeks to transfer power to human communities in all their cultural diversity, envisaging an "alternative future not dominated by mega-institutions, whether corporate or state."[42]

What these analysts describe as informal or alternative economy, or communitarianism, citizen revolt, or democratization, are, as I have said, truly socialist in spirit and may harbor clues to a viable way forward, both for the historical socialist movement and for society. That it constitutes a form of resistance to the rule of capital and promotes human society as a "community of friends" is clear. By itself, plainly enough, it is not *the solution*. But it may be an important part of a solution, if recognized and encouraged by democratic governments and combined with increased worker ownership and control of major industry. We may see such strategies as transitional, as preparing and strengthening structures and networks that will be ready for the time of crisis that lies ahead — an ecological and economic crisis that will convince large numbers of people in many nations of the unviability of the present capital-dominated world-system.[43] Barnet and Cavanagh speak eloquently about such strategies:

> Globalization from below . . . is proceeding much faster than most of us realize. Local citizens' movements and alternative institutions are springing up all over the world to meet basic economic needs, to preserve local traditions, religious life, cultural life, biological species. . . . The great question of our age is whether people, acting with the spirit, energy and urgency our collective crisis requires, can develop a democratic global consciousness rooted in authentic local communities.[44]

Such strategies, I suggest, deserve the widespread support of Christian people and the churches in that, in their modest way, they serve the interests of the marginalized and the vulnerable, "lift up the humble and meek," and "fill the hungry with good things."

•

For more than 150 years, then, socialists of many stripes have applied energy, imagination, and courage to the problem of the political and economic organization of society as a "community of friends." Differing circumstances — socio/economic, political, and ideological — have thrown up very different concepts and strategies, and "socialism" cannot be limited or defined by any one of them.

The story is neither all gloomy nor all shining and bright. And the history of socialism is young.

Concluding Theological
Reflections

Chapter 9

Christian Socialism: A Tradition Not to Be Abandoned

We began by asking questions about the theological appropriateness of "ideological" commitment for Christians, particularly about the suitability of socialism as a political commitment, and about the future viability of historical socialism in face of the present "triumph of capitalism." Is socialism indeed the best political commitment for those who confess Jesus as Lord, who strive to live out the love of neighbors and to realize the highest possible degree of justice and freedom, as these are understood out of Christian faith?

Speaking Theologically

We have noted the overwhelming dominance of "capital" in contemporary human affairs. Some have likened the dominance of capital in the global economy to the "principalities and powers" that Paul speaks of in Ephesians:

> For our struggle is not against enemies of blood and flesh, but against the rulers, against the authorities, against the cosmic powers of this present darkness, against the spiritual forces of evil in the heavenly places. (Eph. 6:12)

Others have likened "capital" to the great beast of Revelation 13:

> They worshipped the beast, saying "Who is like the beast and who can fight against it?" (Rev. 13:4)

Emphatically, this is not to say that individual capitalists or every capitalist institution or practice can be identified as demonic. On the contrary, it does mean that a system, or an abstraction like "the market," can dominate human beings as a kind of false god. We know

181

that systems and ideologies are often more powerful than the individuals who create them or who are caught up in them. The risen Christ is the ground of our hope that no such "beast" can rule utterly or forever, and it is he who in the meantime empowers and inspires us to find ways to resist.

Theologically, we began with some elementary points: No political ideology or system, not even socialism, can be absolutized or divinized by Christians. Every ideology and every political program, including every socialist one, is open to critique and revision in light of the lordship of Jesus Christ and in light of its practical contribution to the universal "community of friends." Nor can Christian faith be defined exclusively in terms of any particular political commitment. Yet Christians are called, as those who follow after the crucified and risen Jesus, to be hopeful and faithful stewards for the growth of God's Reign in the world, striving for the realization, in a measure, of love, justice, and peace in the human community, with a special bias for those who are marginalized, oppressed, or poor. This means, in our global context, that capital is not "lord." At the same time we have to remain soberly realistic about the limitations of human achievement in history. Further, such commitment means that Christians will have to operate out of particular social analyses and strategies, i.e., they will have to live and act in accordance with some explicit, particular political/ideological stance.

Definitions/Distinctions

We have defined the term "socialism" in a pluralist way; we have acknowledged that socialism has taken many forms. But essentially what socialists share is a commitment to society as a community of friends, where economic and political power are taken out of the hands of the few and widely distributed among all the people. Socialism has to do with the democratization of economic power, so that social priorities are decided upon by the whole community, and not by those who happen to enjoy massive property rights.

When these objectives are seriously promoted, the result is not reformist but "revolutionary" in the best sense, i.e., a change of direction (a social *metanoia* — repentance or conversion), and "radical" in the best sense (getting to the roots of problems). "Revolution" is not necessarily sudden; "radicalism" must be distinguished from extremism. Socialist visionaries and leaders, from Robert Owen to James Woodsworth, from Rosa Luxemburg to Julius Nyerere, have long since learned that such profound change is exceedingly difficult to achieve and maintain and involves lengthy and sustained resistance to those whose interests lie either in their own aggrandizement or in the continued dominance of private capital.

Lenin saw correctly that there is nothing inevitable about social transformation and that only determined struggle would bring it about. "Gradualism" in the sense of "economism" or "inevitabilism" is not to be trusted, and history has shown Lenin to be right about this. Yet Rosa Luxemburg pointed out the great danger of elitist, bureaucratic rule as merely another form of tyranny, despite the "socialist" slogans. Gramsci saw correctly that so-called "revolution" may be superficial and short lived if the masses of the people are not convinced, not ready, and not on board. True revolution and true radicalism require time and need massive "on-the-ground" social/cultural/religious preparation. Local and national networks of people who share a socialist, cooperative, or communitarian inspiration, Christian people and others, need to prepare the ground for truly radical social transformations that may lie ahead, but that may appear gradually.

Successes/Failures

As I have said, the story of socialism is highly ambiguous. At worst we could easily decide, in light of it, that socialism is simply a failed concept, something noble and idealistic, naive about the depths of human selfishness, and so impractical and finally destructive in the real world. The failures and distortions that have gone under the name of "socialism" have been sufficiently ruinous to the lives of millions that we should not be surprised at the hatred this term provokes. If this were the whole story, Christian theologians and ethicists should certainly cease their denunciations of capitalism and cease to call themselves "socialist." These are the kinds of conclusions to which many have come in the past few years. Certainly no amount of abstract theological or ethical reasoning could fortify a Christian socialism if historical socialism could be shown to be simply impracticable or essentially destructive.

However, I believe I have shown in this brief study that there is enough solid achievement and success in what has been, in fact, a relatively brief socialist history to encourage socialists to go on refining their theories and practices. After all, what are the alternatives? State communism has failed, and capitalism is failing too. The failure of capitalism in Africa and Latin America is indisputable and dramatic. The sweatshops and export processing zones, the child labor, infant mortality, and deepening poverty in so much of the world is surely proof enough that humanity must seek new social and economic structures. I have argued here that the failure of capitalism in North America is becoming more and more visible. The recurring fits of high unemployment, now the apparent permanence of widespread structural unemployment, the reappearance of child labor, the gross injustice, alienation, violence, and spiritual emptiness, as well as the ecological irresponsibility of capitalism as we know it, means that capitalism is not a viable or ethically defensible choice for humanity's long-term future.

Naming the Alternative

It is common, it is politically correct, and indeed it is almost universal among theologians to deplore capitalism; but unfortunately such denunciation is rarely accompanied by the annunciation of a socialist alternative. A recent example of this is found in a paper by Cedric Mayson, of the South African Council of Churches, on the eve of the 1994 elections:

> Christianity and the economic system known as Capitalism are intrinsically opposed. The Gospel means good news to the poor: Capitalism is bad news. The Gospel is about unity: capitalism is divisive. The Gospel is global: the benefits of capitalism cannot be globalised because the profits of the affluent are derived from the marginalisation of the poor. The Gospel is opposed to apartheid: apartheid was racist capitalism.... The Gospel demands an economy viewed from the side of the poor: capitalism springs from the views of the affluent. The Gospel demands for a social and economic system which benefits the poor require a fundamental reassessment of how wealth is produced and how it is shared, including the role of work, wages, responsibility, and leisure.... The Gospel believes that the Earth belongs to God

and all the children of God, and denies the absolute right of private ownership of land and wealth which empowers one person to enjoy luxuries whilst millions lack food, water, land, homes, clothes, or social amenities. Capitalism lauds and promotes the accumulation of private wealth: Jesus stated repeatedly that the worship of Mammon and the pursuit of riches was a hellish occupation. The Gospel criticizes the affluent: capitalism blames the poor. . . . but if capitalism is fatally flawed, what is the alternative? It is not the task of the Church to spell out political and economic details, it is certainly our task to contribute broad *direction.*[1]

Mayson goes on to speak creatively of grassroots democracy and of local ecumenical clusters in a manner reminiscent of what in North America is sometimes called communitarianism. However, the dangerous word "socialist" is studiously avoided, and the task of spelling out political and economic details is disavowed. Yet the socialist tradition, including Christian socialism, is a rich and valuable tradition that needs to be named; we need to be aware of the historical socialist struggle, of its failures and successes, as a tradition upon which we can build in order to find a direction away from capitalism and toward real concrete alternatives.

We know that the search for alternative social structures is not a simple matter and the demonization of everything "capitalist" is not helpful. In the absence of what Gramsci called "cultural socialism," or a massive change of heart among human beings, we still need in the decades to come a system that includes such ostensibly capitalist elements as competition and financial incentive, both to work and to invest. Christians, in view of their understanding of the reality of sin, cannot seriously expect the realization of a perfect socialistic community of friends within human history as we know it. This would entail the appearance within history of the conditions of the consummated Kingdom of Heaven on earth. As Christians, though, we know that the Spirit's work of personal sanctification and transformation can indeed change hearts and that revolutionary social change toward social wholeness can be brought about by the leavening power of even a small minority of dedicated individuals. The Christian mission, Christian education and nurture, social action and spirituality must attend to the mutual reinforcement of personal and social transformations. Nor is the work of God's Spirit in the world limited to Christians or the church. Others too, often more effectively than Christians, advance the cause of human solidarity and the wholeness of creation, and so serve the Reign of God.

Ambiguities/Utopia

The historical ambiguity of socialism does not constitute, I think, good reason to abandon socialist thought and practice. Rather it is good reason for recognizing that socialism is, in a positive sense, utopian and visionary in nature. Society as a community of friends — where the rule is "From each according to his ability, to each according to his need" — is truly a "no place" in history and will continue to be so. Yet it is possible to resist the injustices and cruelties of the world, to struggle toward the community of friends, and to approximate it in various ways. Socialism (as distinct from liberal, reformist capitalism) is truly and positively utopian in that the community of friends is always a goal earnestly strived for, but never perfectly achieved.

Nor is it possible or desirable to prescribe one form of socialism or one method of attaining it for the whole world or for all times. As I have argued above, forms of resistance or approximations to a socialist utopia will surely take different forms in different places and will be accomplished by many methods — by small or large socialist measures within a capitalist system, together with mixed economies, when this can be accomplished politically; by worker/cooperative ownership and/or state ownership and so on. Every kind of socialist strategy has its weaknesses and limitations as well as strengths:

Cooperative and communitarian efforts are extremely valuable and important means of resisting and limiting the power of big capital, but by themselves they remain on the margins of the economic order and are simply too weak to grasp the reins of macro-economic power for all the people without the support and encouragement of government.

State socialism in the sense of massive state-ownership, on the other hand, appears prone to become bureaucratic, monopolistic, oppressive, and inefficient.

Democratic socialist or social democratic parties and governments, though they have achieved much, often seem powerless to pursue a radical, cooperative agenda, lacking the economic clout of big capital, vulnerable to the attacks of the dominant ideology and the caprice of public opinion, and even more vulnerable to the mobility and independence of multinational firms. But the new high-tech and internationalization of capital render them relatively impotent, even when they hold governmental power.

A Multinational Socialism?

The impotence and marginalization of the various socialisms, and indeed of government in our time, raises the question whether a multinational socialism has become necessary. Of course the socialist movements have always had an "internationalist" character, and this has been so because capitalism has always been a multinational phenomenon. And this is more true today than ever. As we have seen, the "world-system" is more than ever an integrated "imperial" economy, ravaging the ability of elected governments to pursue social goals for the well-being of people. Barnet and Cavanagh comment:

> According to . . . the *Economist,* the world's top 300 industrial corporations now control more than 25 percent of the world's $20 trillion stock of productive assets. But these footloose business enterprises in a world of weakened governments hold the power to veto a range of crucial political decisions across the planet. In the world economy, as in a large public corporation, powerful minority stockholders can end up in control.[2]

No one has taught us better than the social and economic historian Immanuel Wallerstein that "the capitalist world-economy is precisely a system in which the basic economic processes are located in a zone far larger than any political authority."[3] This is why he feels constrained to speak in visionary terms of a "socialist world government." This seems dream-like and utopian indeed. But may there not appear circumstances so dire and so universal — whether in the form of widespread poverty or ecological destruction — that democratic electorates around the world will demand international democratic cooperation to bring the power of capital under control? Wallerstein argues that the capitalist world-system came into existence, and it is not necessary or eternal; it had a beginning and it will have an ending. He likens capitalism to a "hydra-headed monster . . . lumbering along to its doom" and declares that the world today is faced not with inevitable progress, but a real historical choice:

> This is neither impossible nor inevitable. The alternative possibility is the creation in the next 100 years of a socialist world order,

one based on a system of production for use . . . , one which will result in a reasonably egalitarian distribution of resources, time, space, and social roles. Such a system will not be utopia, nor beyond history. And it is quite impossible to predict its institutional forms. But this alternative would indeed be progress.[4]

It is also possible that dire circumstances will lead instead to a ghastly international fascism, generated by privileged elites successfully controlling "democratic" processes. But Wallerstein's vision is worth contemplation:

> A socialist government when it comes will not look anything like the USSR, or China, or Chile, or Tanzania of today. Production for use and not for profit, and rational decision on the cost benefits (in the widest sense of the term) or alternative uses is a different mode of production, one that can only be established within the single division of labor that is the world-economy and one that will require a single government.[5]

It is clear that such a solution is very remote indeed. If such a century-long (or centuries-long?) project were ever to come to fruition, the groundwork for it would have to be laid in many local communities of individuals "spinning their own transnational webs to embrace and connect people cross the world."[6] If we have learned anything from Gramsci, we know that such a futuristic vision can be realized only if it begins to take shape in many small places, at community, municipal, state/provincial, and national levels, taking account of and respecting the cultural and religious sensitivities of peoples. It will mean networks of cooperation among all kinds of people struggling for change. All the small struggles at local and national levels are necessary if large numbers of people are to be ready for a multinational socialist transformation in the future. This will require a tolerant openness among all people struggling for change.

Meanwhile: Socialist Pluralism/Penultimate Goals

Rosemary Radford Ruether, often seen as an uncompromising feminist/socialist, is one who pleads for a tolerant socialist pluralism. In the United States, she argues, suspicions among democratic socialists, Christians for Socialism, Marxist/Leninists, and other radical social critics, merely plays into the hands of the power of private capital:

> Most of all, a new socialism must seek alliance with all the existing bases of American radicalism; with neighborhood community organizing; with the environmental movement; with radical minority movements; with the women's movement, especially as that relates to poor and working-class women; to labor unions, especially the new union efforts among disenfranchised workers; with antiwar and anti-imperialist movements. It should develop indigenous leadership to provide alternative strategies when corporations shut down plants and threaten the livelihood of entire towns. It needs a good network among church and synagogue leaders who are often effective links to local communities.[7]

The larger socialist project — i.e., a worldwide community of friends — has always been an uphill resistance to great odds and will continue to be so, but socialist history shows that penultimate goals can be realized.

In North America and western Europe the efforts of minority democratic socialist parties to limit the power of capital and to redistribute wealth and power within capitalism (i.e., the welfare state) are very important and very vulnerable and generally should, I believe, be supported. Herb Gamberg, in his recent article "What Is Socialism?" would disagree. He argues, "The growth of the modern welfare state...has nothing to do with socialism. The greater engagement of the state with the economy at all levels has arisen as an attempt to save capitalism, rather than altering it."[8] It is an old debate. I would contend that small victories — extremely valuable in themselves for human well-being — help to create a situation and a social awareness that is ripe for more fundamental breakthroughs. The achievement of medicare and of universal pension plans in Canada, for example, has created a situation in which people assume and expect that medical care and old age security are rights for all citizens. An essential service has been raised beyond the vicissitudes of the market and at least a minimally decent standard of living made available to all the aged. These are indeed socialist achievements. Surely from the perspective of the 1840s, or the 1920s, these are truly "utopian" achievements! In light of them, mere pessimism is not in order. Perhaps we may hope that, precisely because of the experience of living in a "welfare state," increasing deterioration of the economic conditions of working and unemployed people will move the public to demand significant structural change, perhaps even more state/public ownership and greater worker control of industries and work places, perhaps even international agreements among democratic nations to put limits on the power of capital.

Spiritual Character of the Socialist Movement

As for the democratic socialist parties that we are familiar with in Canada and western Europe, it will be important for them to know who they are, to remember their history, and to be clear about their goals. They will have to become more intensely aware of the essentially spiritual (not necessarily religious) character of their historical roots. Socialism, like any other human phenomenon, is subject to systemic sin in the form of distortion and corruption — whether to co-option by the power of capital or to tyranny and domination. Gamberg makes a very important point about the need for a high quality of leadership:

> a type of powerholder unprecedented in history, people who are modest in their material existence, honest in their dealing with the public and other party members, possessing a high degree of consciousness and identification with oppression of all kinds (class, gender, national, racial etc.) and demonstrating a respect for democracy within the party and for its extension to ordinary citizens.[9]

Such an ideal of humble leadership is not far from the footwashing Christ whom Christians follow: "If I, your Lord and Teacher, have washed your feet, you also ought to wash one another's feet" (John 13:14). The spiritual vision offered above also closely resembles the Christian feminist vision of nonhierarchical authority and leadership.[10] Yet it is not only leaders who must exhibit such qualities. A socialist society, as a cooperative community of friends, requires genuinely "friendly" people — not merely individualists, but people of integrity who will not abuse the system, who will not misuse medicare and welfare provisions, who will serve the public gladly and devotedly through their work, who will not demand excessive levels of personal compensation. Gamberg's description of the qualities of desired leaders closely resembles what Christians, especially Methodists, commonly call "sanctification" — a work of the Holy Spirit.

The formation of "good people" is assisted by a "good society," but the good society cannot function without good people. A revolutionized or "converted" society can neither arrive nor survive without "converted" people — people of integrity, generosity, and compassion. Social transformation, then, exists in dialectical tension with personal transformation, and this calls for a process of human spiritualization. For Christians, at the personal level, this means living more and more from and within God's gracious love disclosed in Jesus, living in gratitude for the forgiveness of sins, living in the hope and joy of the resurrection, and thus reaching out joyfully to others in a community of sharing and solidarity.

Is it "excessively utopian" to envisage a worker-managed, cooperatively owned system, planned, supervised, and encouraged under freely elected democratic governments? How would we ever get from here to there, especially in an increasingly "international" world, wherein governments and electorates have less and less power to determine priorities? How and when will democratic electorates around the world cooperate to bring capital truly into the service of people? I do not pretend to know the answer to these colossal questions. Yet the cultivation of cooperative and communitarian networks of people who together resist existing capitalist structures and growing awareness among all the people of the urgent need to change are surely essential to any future social transformation. For Christians, the spiritual, educational, and outreach work of the church can be a powerful instrument, moving and motivating people toward the establishment of the friendly community. The accumulated wisdom of historical socialist experience affords much to be built upon for future generations. We know a good deal more about socialism now than we did a hundred years ago, or fifty, or even five years ago.

I believe there is more than enough that is positive in socialist history to move Christians to conclude: This tradition must not be abandoned. As people of Exodus and Resurrection, we are called to dream about the future of God's world.

Notes

Chapter 1: Political Theology and Ideology

1. Stanley Hauerwas and William H. Willimon, in their book *Resident Aliens* (Nashville: Abingdon, 1990), argue "that the political task of Christians is to be the church rather than to transform the world.... Political theologies, whether of the left or of the right, want to maintain Christendom, wherein the church justifies itself as a helpful, if sometimes complaining, prop for the state" (38). This apparent attempt to be neutral about the great social issues of the day, equating "left" and "right," while somehow staying above all the political controversies, is surely naive and illusory.

2. See discussion by Joyce Nelson, "Dr. Rockefeller Will See You Now," in *Canadian Forum*, January–February 1995, 7–12.

3. Pamela Constable, "Leftist Rebels Learn the System," in *Toronto Star*, May 5, 1993, A17.

4. Peter Cook, "Yes, but How Can South Africa Grow?" in *Globe and Mail*, Toronto, February 9, 1995, B2.

5. See W. Merkel, "After the Golden Age: Is Social Democracy Doomed to Decline?" in C. Lemke and G. Marks, eds., *The Crisis of Socialism in Europe* (Durham, N.C.: Duke University Press, 1992).

6. Rosemary Radford Ruether, "Sexism and the Liberation of Women," in E. C. Bianchi, ed., *From Machismo to Mutuality: Essays on Sexism and Woman-Man Liberation* (New York: Paulist, 1976). See also Ruether's *Disputed Questions: On Being a Christian* (Nashville: Abingdon Press, 1982), 88–89.

7. Marsha Hewitt, "The Socialist Implications of Feminist Liberation Theology," in *Studies in Religion* 22, no. 3 (1993): 328. See in this article a discussion of Ruether's socialism and the historical relationship between socialist thought and the women's movement.

8. Roger Hutchinson, writing about method for ethical thought, speaks of "comparative ethics" as a discourse that calls for an attitude of listening and respect toward those who adopt other ethical or religious stances: "the protocols and categories developed for cross-cultural studies and interfaith and ecumenical dialogue [may be] applied to debates within a particular religious group.... That is, the general orientation, norms and substantive judgments of one group are not presumed to be normative for all factions within a particular denomination" (*Prophets, Pastors and Public Choices: Canadian Churches and the Mackenzie Valley Pipeline Debate* [Waterloo, Ont.: Wilfrid Laurier University Press, 1992], 2). We may also speak of "comparative ideology" in the same spirit of tolerance, while insisting that tolerance does not imply detachment or lack of commitment.

9. See the thorough discussion by Clodovis Boff of "theology of the political" as "second theology," which I shall discuss later (*Theology and Praxis: Epistemological Foundations*, trans. R. R. Barr [Maryknoll, N.Y.: Orbis, 1987]).

10. Jürgen Moltmann, "A Political Hermeneutic of the Gospel," in *On Human Dignity* (Philadelphia: Fortress Press, 1984).

11. Significant volumes of Christian-Marxist dialogue include John C. Bennett, *Christianity and Communism* (New York: Association Press, 1948); Roger Garaudy, *From Anathema to Dialogue*, trans. L. O'Neill (New York: Herder and Herder, 1966); Donald Evans, *Communist Faith and Christian Faith* (Toronto: Ryerson Press, 1964); Giulio Girardi, *Marxism and Christianity* (New York: Macmillan, 1968); José Míguez Bonino, *Christians and Marxists* (Grand Rapids: W. B. Eerdmans, 1976); Milan Machovec, *A Marxist Looks at Jesus* (London: Darton, Longman and Todd, 1976).

12. Gustavo Gutiérrez, *A Theology of Liberation: History, Politics and Salvation*, trans. C. Inda and J. Eagleson (Maryknoll, N.Y.: Orbis, 1973), 232–39.

13. Ed Broadbent, "Introduction: Some Thoughts on Socialism," in Simon Rosenblum and Peter Findlay, eds., *Debating Canada's Future: Views from the Left* (Toronto: James Lorimer & Co., 1991), 4.

14. Marvin Stauch argues this point against deconstructionism in his article, "Postmodern Socialism: Self, Community, and Power," in *Socialist Studies Bulletin* 33 (July–August–September 1993): 23. Also William D. Lindsey offers a critical study in "Richard Rorty: The Homelessness of Liberalism," in *Ecumenist* 1, no. 1 (November–December 1993): 17–20.

15. George Grant, "An Ethic of Community," in Michael Oliver, ed., *Social Purpose for Canada* (Toronto: University of Toronto Press, 1961), 21.

16. Karl Polanyi, "The Essence of Fascism," in John Lewis, Karl Polanyi and Donald Kitchin, eds., *Christianity and the Social Revolution* (London: Victor Gollancz, 1935), 361.

17. Boff, *Theology and Praxis,* xxviii, and Part One.

18. Robert T. Osborn, like many liberation theologians, argues that "the poor are hermeneutically and soteriologically privileged" (see *The Barmen Declaration as a Paradigm for a Theology of the American Church* [Lewiston, N.Y.: Edwin Mellen Press, 1993], 115).

19. A similar point is made by Jürgen Moltmann, when he speaks of "political hermeneutic" as an interaction of reflection and action: "Political hermeneutic therefore rejects pure theory in theology just as it does blind activism in ethics. Its model is a differentiated theory-praxis relationship in which theory and praxis, thinking and doing, mutually drive each other forward.... They constantly overlap so that theory must incorporate practice and practice must incorporate theory" ("Political Hermeneutic of the Gospel," in *On Human Dignity*, 107–8).

20. See a helpful discussion of "God and the Market Logic," in M. Douglas Meeks, *God the Economist: The Doctrine of God and Political Economy* (Minneapolis: Fortress Press, 1989), chap. 3.

21. The Barmen Confession in H. G. Locke, ed., *The Church Confronts the Nazis: Barmen Then and Now* (Lewiston, N.Y.: Edwin Mellen Press, 1984), 22–23.

22. Ibid.

23. Eberhard Busch, *Karl Barth: His Life from Letters and Autobiographical Texts*, trans. J. Bowden (Philadelphia: Fortress, 1976), 235. See also Robert P. Erickson, "The Barmen Synod and Its Declaration: A Historical Synopsis," in H. G. Locke, ed., *The Church Confronts the Nazis.*

24. Rosemary Radford Ruether, *To Change the World: Christology and Cultural Criticism* (London: SCM, 1981), 1, 3.

25. See discussion by A. James Reimer, "The Theology of Barmen: Its Partisan-Political Dimension," in *Toronto Journal of Theology* 1, no. 2 (Fall 1985): 155–74. Also, Jürgen Moltmann "Barth's Doctrine of the Lordship of Jesus Christ," in *On Human Dignity*, 83.

26. Osborn, *The Barmen Declaration as a Paradigm for a Theology of the American Church*, 65.

27. See my article, "Social Analysis and Theological Method: Third World Challenge to Canadian Theology," in H. Wells and R. Hutchinson, eds., *A Long and Faithful March* (Toronto: United Church Publishing House, 1989).

28. For a thorough analysis of "contextuality" in theology, see Douglas John Hall, *Thinking the Faith: Christian Theology in a North American Context* (Minneapolis: Fortress Press, 1989).

29. Karl Marx and Friedrich Engels, *The German Ideology*, ed. R. Pascal (New York: International Publishers, 1947), 39. However, sometimes Marx used the word neutrally to mean the consciousness of a culture, i.e., "the whole immense superstructure..., the legal, political, religious, artistic or philosophic — in short, ideological forms" that are operative in a society (see Karl Marx, *A Contribution to the Critique of Political Economy* [New York: International Publishers, 1970], 20–21).

30. E.g., Gustavo Gutiérrez, *A Theology of Liberation*, revised ed., trans. C. Inda and J. Eagleson (Maryknoll, N.Y.: Orbis, 1988), 137.

31. See Paul Ricoeur, who insists on the unavoidability of ideology, in "Science and Ideology," in J. B. Thompson, ed., *Hermeneutics and the Human Sciences* (London: Cambridge University Press, 1981). See also my article, "Ideology and Contextuality in Liberation Theology," in J. Antezana, ed., *Liberation Theology and Sociopolitical Transformation* (Burnaby, B.C.: Simon Fraser University Press, 1992).

32. Juan Luis Segundo, *Faith and Ideologies*, trans. J. Drury (Maryknoll, N.Y.: Orbis, 1984), 25. See a substantial study of Segundo on ideology by Marsha Aileen Hewitt, *From Theology to Social Theory: Juan Luis Segundo and the Theology of Liberation* (New York: Peter Lang, 1990).

33. Juan Luis Segundo, *The Liberation of Theology*, trans. J. Drury (Dublin: Gill and Macmillan, 1977), 102.

34. Osborn, *The Barmen Declaration as a Paradigm for a Theology of the American Church*, 101.

35. Segundo, *The Liberation of Theology*, 107, 181.

36. Elizabeth Johnson, *She Who Is* (New York: Crossroad, 1993).

37. Jürgen Moltmann, with Elisabeth Moltmann-Wendel, *Humanity in God* (New York: Pilgrim Press, 1983), 106. These connections were made classically by Augustine in *De Trinitate* and also developed recently by Leonardo Boff, *Trinity and Society* (Maryknoll, N.Y.: Orbis, 1987). See my articles, "The Trinity and

the Good News," I and II, in *Touchstone* 8, no. 2 (May 1990), and 8, no. 3 (September 1990).

38. For example, the Christian socialist organization the Fellowship for a Christian Social Order in the 1930s and 1940s in Canada. See Roger Hutchinson, "The Fellowship for a Christian Social Order," in H. Wells and R. Hutchinson, eds., *A Long and Faithful March* (Toronto: United Church Publishing House, 1989).

39. Jürgen Moltmann, "Barth's Doctrine of the Lordship of Jesus Christ," in *On Human Dignity*, 95.

40. Osborn, *The Barmen Declaration as a Paradigm for a Theology of the American Church*, 93.

41. Elizabeth A. Johnson, "Redeeming the Name of Christ," in C. M. LaCugna, ed., *Freeing Theology: The Essentials of Theology in Feminist Perspective* (San Francisco: HarperSanFrancisco, 1993), 126–27.

42. See Medellín Documents, in J. Gremillion, ed., *The Gospel of Peace and Justice: Catholic Social Teaching since Pope John* (Maryknoll, N.Y.: Orbis, 1976), 445–76; and Puebla Final Document, no. 1134, in J. Eagleson and P. Scharper, eds., *Puebla and Beyond* (Maryknoll, N.Y.: Orbis, 1979), 279.

43. Gutiérrez, *A Theology of Liberation*, 272–79; see also a discussion of class struggle by Gregory Baum, in *Theology and Society* (New York: Paulist Press, 1987).

44. Gutiérrez, *A Theology of Liberation*, 273–74.

45. Gutiérrez quoted by Arthur F. McGovern, *Liberation Theology and Its Critics* (Maryknoll, N.Y.: Orbis, 1989), 148. For shifts in Gutiérrez's social analysis, see the preface to the revised edition of *A Theology of Liberation*, 1988. For a discussion of changes in Gutiérrez's thought on socialism, see Marsha Hewitt, "Liberation Theology and the Emancipation of Religion," in *Scottish Journal of Religious Studies* 13, no. 1 (Spring 1992): 21–35.

46. See the discussion by Lee Cormie, "Liberation Theology and Dependency Theory: Revisiting the Debate," in *Ecumenist* 2, no. 1 (January–March 1995): 1–8.

47. Leonardo Boff, interviewed by José María Vigil, "Liberation Theology: Option for the Poor and Socialism Today," in *Letter to the Churches*, nos. 311, 312 (August 1994).

48. Karl Barth, *Church Dogmatics*, vol. 2, pt. 1, ed. G. W. Bromiley and T. F. Torrance (Edinburgh: T. & T. Clark, 1957), 386.

49. The point is made by Gregory Baum in his article, "Class Struggle and the Magisterium: A New Note," in *Theology and Society* (New York: Paulist Press, 1987).

Chapter 2: Utopia and the Gospel of the Reign of God

1. See Michael Lerner, *The Socialism of Fools: Anti-Semitism on the Left* (Jerusalem and Oakland, Calif.: Tikkun Books, 1992), 4.

2. Arend T. Van Leeuwen, *Christianity in World History: The Meeting of the Faiths of East and West* (London: Edinburgh House, 1964).

3. Lesslie Newbigin, *The Gospel in a Pluralist Society* (Grand Rapids: Wm. B. Eerdmans Co., 1989), 90.

4. Ibid., 91.

5. Karl Marx, *The Communist Manifesto*, in R. C. Tucker, ed., *The Marx-Engels Reader* (New York: W. W. Norton & Co., 1978), 495.

6. Paul Tillich, *The Socialist Decision*, trans. F. Sherman (New York: Harper and Row, 1977), 122.

7. Reinhold Niebuhr, *Moral Man and Immoral Society* (New York: Charles Scribner's Sons, 1932; 1960 ed.), xx.

8. Ibid., 197.

9. Reinhold Niebuhr, *Christian Realism and Political Problems* (New York: Charles Scribner's Sons, 1953), 36–37.

10. Jürgen Moltmann, *Experiences of God*, trans. M. Kohl (Philadelphia: Fortress, 1980), 11–12. This basic insight is worked out thoroughly in his *Theology of Hope: On the Ground and the Implications of a Christian Eschatology*, trans. J. W. Leitch (London: SCM, 1965).

11. Gustavo Gutiérrez, *A Theology of Liberation: History, Politics and Salvation*, trans. C. Inda and J. Eagleson (Maryknoll, N.Y.: Orbis, 1973), 136.

12. Ibid., 136.

13. Ibid., 139–40.

14. Thomas More, *Utopia*, ed. G. M. Logan and R. M. Adams (Cambridge: Cambridge University Press, 1975).

15. Leonardo Boff, *Jesus Christ Liberator* (Maryknoll, N.Y.: Orbis, 1979), chap. 7.

16. Jürgen Moltmann, *The Way of Jesus Christ: Christology in Messianic Dimensions*, trans. M. Kohl (London: SCM, 1990), 219.

17. Ibid., 258.

18. Jürgen Moltmann, *The Spirit of Life: A Universal Affirmation*, trans. M. Kohl (Minneapolis: Fortress Press, 1992), 96.

19. Franz Hinkelammert, *The Ideological Weapons of Death: A Theological Critique of Capitalism* (Maryknoll, N.Y.: Orbis, 1986), 128.

20. Moltmann, *The Way of Jesus Christ*, 274.

21. Elizabeth Johnson, "Redeeming the Name of Christ," in Catherine Mowry LaCugna, ed., *Freeing Theology* (San Francisco: HarperSanFrancisco, 1993), 132.

22. See substantial developments of the theology of stewardship by Douglas John Hall, *Christian Mission: The Stewardship of Life in the Kingdom of Death* (New York: Friendship Press, 1985).

23. Gutiérrez, *A Theology of Liberation*, 151–52.

24. Ibid., 177.

25. See Reinhold Niebuhr on sin in *The Nature and Destiny of Man*, vol. 1 (New York: Charles Scribner's Sons, 1943), chaps. 7–9.

26. Jon Sobrino, *Christology at the Crossroads: A Latin American Approach*, trans. J. Drury (Maryknoll, N.Y.: Orbis, 1978), 53.

27. Rosemary Radford Ruether, *Disputed Questions: On Being a Christian* (Nashville: Abingdon, 1982), 100–101.

28. Juan Luis Segundo, *Grace and the Human Condition*, trans. J. Drury (Dublin: Gill and Macmillan, 1980), 125.

29. Ibid.

30. See Introduction to More's *Utopia*, xxvii.

31. George Grant, "An Ethic of Community," in Michael Oliver, ed., *Social Purpose for Canada* (Toronto: University of Toronto Press, 1961), 4.

32. Rosemary Radford Ruether, *To Change the World* (London: SCM, 1981), 22–23.

33. See Bonhoeffer's discussion of the relation of the ultimate to the penultimate, and of "radicalism" and "compromise": *Ethics*, trans. and ed. E. Bethge (London: SCM, 1955), 85–89.

34. John Wilson, *The Meaning of Socialism: A Community of Friends* (Toronto: Woodsworth Memorial Fund, 1971).

Chapter 3: Soviet Communism: The Tragedy of Utopia

1. One distinction is in the usage of Marx, who thought of socialism as an earlier stage and communism as the final stage of the revolutionary process. The distinction between communism and socialism as existing phenomena became clearer after 1919 when Lenin set up the "Third International" (also called the Comintern), made up of parties around the world that supported the Russian revolution. See James R. Ozinga, *Communism: The Story of the Idea and Its Implementation* (Englewood Cliffs, N.J.: Prentice-Hall, 1987), 110.

2. Ibid., 101.

3. Immanuel Wallerstein, *Geopolitics and Geoculture: Essays on the Changing World-System* (New York: Cambridge University Press, 1991), 88.

4. The "First International" refers to the First International Workingmen's Association with which Marx was associated, founded in 1864; it moved to the U.S. in 1872, did not flourish, and died in 1876. The Second International was founded in 1889 and lasted until World War I.

5. Eugene Forsey, "A New Economic Order," in Gregory Vlastos and R. B. Y. Scott, eds., *Towards the Christian Revolution*, 1936 (Kingston, Ont.: Ronald P. Frey and Co., 1989), 139.

6. Karl Marx, *Critique of the Gotha Program*, in R. C. Tucker, *The Marx-Engels Reader* (New York: W. W. Norton & Co., 1978), 531.

7. V. I. Lenin, *What Is to Be Done?* trans. S. V. and P. Utechin (Oxford: Clarendon Press, 1963), 58, 59.

8. Ibid., 63.

9. Eduard Bernstein (1850–1932), having been influenced by the Fabians during a time in Britain, is associated with "Revisionism," a more moderate and gradualist form of socialism than that of Lenin. In 1899 he wrote a book titled *Evolutionary Socialism* (see Ozinga, *Communism: The Story of the Idea and Its Implementation*, 79).

10. Lenin, *What Is to Be Done?* 66.

11. See V. I. Lenin, *State and Revolution* (New York: International Publishers, 1932), 20.

12. V. I. Lenin, "Writings on the Commune," in Karl Marx and V. I. Lenin, *The Civil War in France: The Paris Commune* (New York: International Publishers, 1940), 121–22.

13. Lenin, *What Is to Be Done?* 132.

14. Stephen Gill and David Law, *The Global Political Economy: Perspectives, Problems and Policies* (Baltimore: Johns Hopkins University Press, 1988), 304.

15. G. D. H. Cole, *A History of Socialist Thought* (London: Macmillan, 1960), vol. 3, pt. 1, 460.

16. Lenin, quoted by Gerry van Houten, "Socialism Today: Renewal or Retreat," in Jos. Roberts and Jesse Vorst, eds., *Socialism in Crisis? Canadian Perspectives* (Winnipeg: Society for Socialist Studies/Fernwood Publishing, 1992), 127–28.

17. Ibid., 128.

18. Ozinga, *Communism*, 81.

19. Rosa Luxemburg, "Leninism or Marxism?" in B. D. Wolfe, *The Russian Revolution and Leninism or Marxism?* (Westport, Conn.: Greenwood Publishers, 1961), 88.

20. Ibid., 71–72.

21. Gill and Law, *The Global Political Economy*, 305.

22. Alvin Y. So, *Social Change and Development: Modernization, Dependency and World-System Theories* (Newbury Park, Calif.: Sage Publications, 1990), 188.

23. Gill and Law, *The Global Political Economy*, 302–5.

24. Statistic quoted by Peter Burns, "The Problem of Socialism in Liberation Theology," in *Theological Studies* 53, no. 3 (September 1992): 509.

25. Statistics cited by Michael Novak, *Will It Liberate?* (New York: Paulist, 1986), 104–5.

26. See the comment by Stephen Handelman, "Russian Fascism Reaches Out from a Long, Sinister Past," in *Toronto Star*, December 19, 1993, E5.

27. Peter Berger, "Capitalism and Socialism: Empirical Facts," in Michael Novak, *Capitalism and Socialism: A Theological Inquiry* (Washington, D.C.: American Enterprise Institute for Public Policy Research, 1979), 87.

28. See the discussion of Reagan and the neo-conservative "roll back" of communism by D. Broad and Lori Foster, "Uncle Sam's 'New World Order': Triumph of Capitalism?" in R. Bourgeault et al., eds., *1492–1992: Five Centuries of Imperialism and Resistance* (Winnipeg and Halifax: Society for Socialist Studies/Fernwood Publishing, 1992), 253–72.

29. Immanuel Wallerstein, *The Capitalist World-Economy* (New York: Cambridge University Press, 1979), 90.

30. Paul Browne, "Reification and the Crisis of Socialism," in *Socialism in Crisis?* 27–28.

31. See Gregory Baum, "Religion and Socialism," in *The Social Imperative* (New York: Paulist Press, 1979), 168.

32. See discussion of Gramsci by Stephen Gill and David Law, *The Global Political Economy*, 63–64, 76–78.

33. Anne S. Sassoon, ed., *Approaches to Gramsci* (London: Writers and Readers Publishing Cooperative Society, 1982), 15–16.

34. See, e.g., his discussion of the ideological effects of music, in a letter to his mother (Antonio Gramsci, *Letters from Prison*, ed. and trans. L. Lawner [London: Jonathan Cape, 1973]).

35. Franco de Felice, "Revolution and Production," in Sassoon, *Approaches to Gramsci*, 198.

36. Gramsci, *Letters from Prison*, 42.

37. E. J. Hobsbawm, "Gramsci and Marxist Political Theory," in Sassoon, *Approaches to Gramsci*, 24.

Chapter 4: North American Capitalism: Just What Is Wrong?

1. See the insightful studies of capitalism by Immanuel Wallerstein, *The Modern World System: Capitalist Agriculture and the Origins of the European World Economy in the Sixteenth Century* (New York: Academic Press, 1977), and *The Capitalist World Economy* (New York: Cambridge University Press, 1979).

2. Paul W. McCracken, "The Corporation and the Liberal Order," in M. Novak and J. W. Cooper, eds., *The Corporation: A Theological Inquiry* (Washington, D.C.: American Enterprise Institute for Public Policy Research, 1981), 43. Also, Chong-Sik Lee tells how the "economic miracle" of capitalist South Korea has outstripped the communism of North Korea. See "South Korea: The Challenge of Democracy," in Steven M. Goldstein, ed., *Minidragons: Fragile Economic Miracles in the Pacific* (New York: Ambrose Video Publishing, 1989), 144–82.

3. McCracken, "The Corporation and the Liberal Order," 45.

4. See a defense of capitalism by Robert Benne, *The Ethic of Democratic Capitalism: A Moral Reassessment* (Philadelphia: Fortress Press, 1981), 10.

5. John Kenneth Galbraith, *The Culture of Contentment* (Boston: Houghton Mifflin Company, 1992), 7–9.

6. John Maynard Keynes, whose book of 1936, *The General Theory of Employment, Interest and Money* (New York: Harcourt, Brace and World) became decisive for dealing with the great depression and efforts to prevent another after World War II, called for active government participation and regulation of the economy, and thus a relativization of laissez-faire. "Post-Keynesian" economics, emphasizing the manipulative power and control of corporations, is not original to Galbraith, but is credited especially to Joan Robinson and her colleagues at Cambridge. See Alfred Eichner, ed., *A Guide to Post-Keynesian Economics* (White Plains, N.Y.: M. E. Sharpe, 1979).

7. Galbraith, *The Culture of Contentment*, 20.

8. John Kenneth Galbraith, *The New Industrial State* (New York: New American Library, 1967), 18. See a discussion of Galbraith and economists who disagree with his view in R. Benne, *The Ethic of Democratic Capitalism*, 101–19.

9. John Kenneth Galbraith, *Economics and the Public Purpose* (New York: New American Library, 1973), 270–74.

10. Galbraith, *The Culture of Contentment*, 138. Similar analyses of "democratic" government under capitalism are basic also to Marxists of the Frankfurt school, e.g. Jürgen Habermas, *Legitimation Crisis*, trans. T. McCarthy (London: Heinemann, 1977).

11. Galbraith, *The Culture of Contentment*, 23.

12. Ibid., 27.

13. Ibid., 26.

14. Ibid., 55–56.

15. Ibid., 61.

16. Galbraith, *Economics and the Public Purpose,* 263–74. Note that R. Benne, commenting on Galbraith, regards him as a democratic socialist (*The Ethics of Democratic Capitalism* [Philadelphia: Fortress Press, 1981], 115).

17. Galbraith, *The Culture of Contentment,* 7–10.

18. Richard J. Barnet and John Cavanagh, *Global Dreams: Imperial Corporations and the New World Order* (New York: Simon and Schuster, 1994), 348.

19. See a defense of democratic capitalism by Peter Berger, "Capitalism and Socialism: Empirical Facts," and "Capitalism and Socialism: Ethical Assessment," in Michael Novak, ed., *Capitalism and Socialism: A Theological Inquiry* (Washington, D.C.: American Enterprise Institute for Public Policy Research, 1979). See also Michael Novak, *The Spirit of Democratic Capitalism* (New York: Simon & Schuster, 1982).

20. Eric Kierans and Walter Stewart, *The Wrong End of the Rainbow: The Collapse of Free Enterprise in Canada* (London: Collins Publishers, 1988), 13, 130.

21. Ibid., 133. See also Ben Smillie, *Is Everyone Right?* (Saskatoon: St. Andrew's College, 1992), 64.

22. Michael Czerny and Jamie Swift, *Getting Started on Social Analysis in Canada* (Toronto: Between the Lines, 1988), 66.

23. Ibid., 69. See also Kierans and Stewart, *The Wrong End of the Rainbow,* 133.

24. Czerny and Swift, *Getting Started on Social Analysis in Canada,* 37.

25. Ibid., 38–39.

26. Ibid., chap. 7.

27. "Dr. Rockefeller Will See You Now: The Hidden Players Privatizing Canada's Health Care System," in *Canadian Forum* 73, no. 836 (January–February 1995): 7–12.

28. Barnet and Cavanagh, *Global Dreams,* 356.

29. Ben Smillie, *Beyond the Social Gospel: Church Protest on the Prairies* (Toronto: United Church Publishing House, 1991), 18. Smillie is citing information from the *Star Phoenix* (Saskatoon), June 3, 1989, from the National Farmers' Union, and the Farm Debt Review Board (Smillie, *Beyond the Social Gospel,* nn. 15 and 16, 152).

30. Marilyn J. Legge, *The Grace of Difference: A Canadian Feminist Theological Ethic* (Atlanta: Scholars Press, 1992), 81.

31. Ibid., 102, 105, 106.

32. Greenbook of the United States House of Representatives, United States, quoted by Galbraith, *The Culture of Contentment,* 13–14.

33. Barnet and Cavanagh, *Global Dreams.*

34. Ibid., 331.

35. Peter Burns, "The Problem of Socialism in Liberation Theology," in *Theological Studies* 53, no. 3 (September 1992): 510.

36. Czerny and Swift, *Getting Started on Social Analysis in Canada,* 96.

37. See James Laxer, "Republican Victory Marks the Failure of Democracy," in *Toronto Star,* November 20, 1994, E3.

38. See Alvin Y. So, *Social Change and Development,* 238.

39. Ibid., 241.

40. Ibid., 239–40.

41. Ibid., 246.

42. Barnet and Cavanagh, *Global Dreams,* 344.

43. Ibid., 321.

44. Ibid.

45. Ibid., 333.

46. Cy Gonick, "Socialism: Past and Future," in Jos. Roberts and Jesse Vorst, eds., *Socialism in Crisis? Canadian Perspectives* (Winnipeg: Society for Socialist Studies/Fernwood Publishing, 1992), 213.

47. This is well said by Axel Dorscht, "Politics of Transformation and the Process of Social Change," in *Socialism in Crisis?* 151.

48. Benne, *The Ethic of Democratic Capitalism,* 136.

49. See comparative OECD statistics on economic growth in several western industrialized nations, showing superior productivity gains between 1979 and 1989 in France, Belgium, Sweden, etc. compared to Canada, the U.S. and Norway, cited by Linda McQuaig, *The Wealthy Banker's Wife: The Assault on Equality in Canada* (Toronto: Penguin Books Canada, 1993), 17.

50. Michael Novak, *The Spirit of Democratic Capitalism* (New York: Simon and Schuster, 1982), 15.

51. Ibid., 197.

52. Michael Lebowitz, "The Limits and Possibilities of Social Democracy: A Marxist View." Lebowitz's paper was presented to the Society for Socialist Studies, May 1991, and is available from the national office, 471 University College, University of Manitoba, Winnipeg, Manitoba, Canada, R3T 2M8.

53. Quoted by Richard Gwyn, " 'Economic Constitution' Tilts Power to Corporations," in *Toronto Star,* November 10, 1993, A27.

54. Lebowitz, "The Limits and Possibilities of Social Democracy," 4.

55. Ibid., 5.

56. Ibid., 7.

Chapter 5: Capitalism and the Third World

1. See Victorio Araya, "Good News to the Poor in the Wesleyan Tradition: An Ethical and Pastoral Reflection from the Third World on the 500th Anniversary of the European Invasion of Abya-Yala," paper read at the Oxford Institute of Methodist Theological Studies (Oxford, August 1992), 1.

2. Franz Hinkelammert, "The Crisis of Socialism in the Third World," in *Focus* 104 (September–October 1991): 1.

3. See Jürgen Habermas, "The Hermeneutic Claim to Universality," and Paul Ricoeur, "Critique of Ideology," in G. L. Ormiston and A. D. Schrift, eds., *The Hermeneutic Tradition* (Albany: State University of New York Press, 1990).

4. Here we touch upon the great debates about hermeneutics and the human sciences found in the work of Gadamer, Ricoeur, and Habermas. See Gregory Baum, "Social Science as Critical Humanism," in *The Social Imperative* (New York: Paulist Press, 1979), 148–67; see also my discussion of this issue in "Social Analysis and Theological Method: Third World Challenge to Canadian Theology,"

in H. Wells and R. Hutchinson, eds., *A Long and Faithful March* (Toronto: United Church Publishing House, 1989), 210–12.

5. See a discussion of liberal or "equilibrium" economics by Robert Gilpin, *The Political Economy of International Relations* (Princeton, N.J.: Princeton University Press, 1987), 26–31.

6. E.g., the viewpoint of Talcott Parsons, as discussed by Alvin Y. So, *Social Change and Development* (Newbury Park, Calif.: Sage Publications, 1990), 20–23. See discussion of functionalist versus dialectical approaches to social science interpretation by Clodovis Boff, *Theology and Praxis* (Maryknoll, N.Y.: Orbis, 1987), 57–60. Robert Gilpin also makes this distinction (*The Political Economy of International Relations*, chap. 2), though he adds a discussion of economic nationalism. Alvin So also contrasts functionalist theories, which he associates with "modernization" theory, with dialectical theories, which he associates with "dependency" theory, while adding "world-systems analysis" as a distinct type.

7. See Introduction to So, *Social Change and Development*.

8. Ibid., part 1.

9. See the discussion of center/periphery by Fernando Henrique Cardoso and Enzo Faletto, *Dependency and Development in Latin America*, trans. M. M. Urquidi (Berkeley: University of California Press), 1979 (Spanish original, 1971).

10. So, *Social Change and Development*, part 2.

11. Among Immanuel Wallerstein's books are *The Capitalist World-Economy* (Cambridge University Press, 1979); *The Politics of the World-Economy* (Cambridge University Press, 1984); *Geopolitics and Geoculture* (Cambridge University Press, 1991).

12. So, discussing the thought of Immanuel Wallerstein, in *Social Change and Development*, 195.

13. See a thorough study of the World Bank Structural Adjustment Programs by John Mihevc, "The Changing Debate on Structural Adjustment Policies in Sub-Saharan Africa: Churches, Social Movements and the World Bank," Ph.D. diss., Toronto School of Theology, 1992.

14. See, for example, World Bank, *Accelerated Development in Sub-Saharan Africa: An Agenda for Action* (Washington, D.C.: World Bank, 1981), 5.

15. Susan George, *The Debt Boomerang: How Third World Debt Harms Us All* (London: Pluto Press, 1992), xv–xvi.

16. UNICEF, *The State of the World's Children*, cited by John Mihevc, "The Changing Debate on Structural Adjustment Policies in Sub-Saharan Africa," 5.

17. Barnet and Cavanagh, *Global Dreams*, 252.

18. Ibid., 253.

19. Ibid., 333.

20. See the discussion by Alvin So, *Social Change and Development*, 246–51.

21. Maurice Meisner, *Mao's China and After: A History of the People's Republic* (London: Collier Macmillan, 1986), 436–37.

22. Ibid., 400.

23. Ibid., 474, 481, 484.

24. So, *Social Change and Development*, 252–56.

25. See basic growth statistics in Janet E. Hunter, *The Emergence of Modern Japan: An Introductory History since 1853* (London: Longman Group UK, 1989), 307.

26. Wallerstein, *Geopolitics and Geoculture*, 19–25.

27. Barnet and Cavanagh, *Global Dreams*, 405.

28. Ibid., 404.

29. Ibid., 406.

30. See Karel von Wolferen, *The Enigma of Japanese Power* (London: Macmillan, 1989).

31. Phillip Oppenheim, *Japan without Blinkers: Coming to Terms with Japan's Economic Success* (Tokyo: Kodansha International, 1992), 137.

32. Ibid., 200.

33. Hunter, *The Emergence of Modern Japan*, 66, 184–86.

34. Ibid., chap. 9.

35. Ibid., 133.

36. Oppenheim, *Japan without Blinkers*, 205.

37. Quoted by ibid., 200.

38. Ibid., 61.

39. Wallerstein, *The Capitalist World-Economy*, 76.

40. Steven Goldstein, *Minidragons: Fragile Economic Miracles in the Pacific* (New York: Westview Press, 1991), 11.

41. Chong-Sik Lee, "South Korea: The Challenge of Democracy," in ibid., 155.

42. Barnet and Cavanagh, *Global Dreams*, 285.

43. Chong-Sik Lee, "South Korea: The Challenge of Democracy," 147.

44. Oppenheim, *Japan without Blinkers*, 319–21.

45. See Paul Tillich, *The Encounter of Religions and Quasi-Religions*, ed. T. Thomas, Toronto Studies in Theology 37 (Lewiston, N.Y.: Edwin Mellen Press, 1990), 31–36.

46. Karl Marx, *Capital*, trans. B. Fowkes (New York: Vintage, 1977), 1:163.

47. Franz J. Hinkelammert, *The Ideological Weapons of Death*, trans. P. Berryman (Maryknoll, N.Y.: Orbis, 1986), 6–7.

48. Marx, *Capital*, 1:229.

49. Quoted by Hinkelammert, *The Ideological Weapons of Death*, 23.

50. Marx, *Capital*, 1:482. For further development of the idea of capital as the great beast of the apocalypse, see Stephen Willey, "Voices of the Hinterland: 'Who Is like the Beast and Who Can Fight against It?'" paper delivered to the Society for Socialist Studies, Charlottetown, P.E.I., May 1992.

51. Marx, quoted by Hinkelammert, *The Ideological Weapons of Death*, 23.

52. See John Mihevc, "The Changing Debate on Structural Adjustment Policies in Sub-Saharan Africa: Churches, Social Movements and the World Bank," Ph.D. diss., Toronto School of Theology, 1992. Mihevc analyzes the capitalist ideology of the World Bank as a kind of religious fundamentalism, complete with concepts of sin, salvation, heresy, etc.

53. Araya, "Good News to the Poor in the Wesleyan Tradition," 3–4.

54. Julio de Santa Ana, "Sacralization and Sacrifice in Human Practice," in World Council of Churches Commission on the Churches' Participation in Development, *Sacrifice and Humane Economic Life* (Geneva: W.C.C., 1992), 20.

55. Franz Hinkelammert, "The Sacrificial Cycle as a Justification for Western Domination: The Western Iphigenia in Latin America," in W.C.C., *Sacrifice and Humane Economic Life,* 72.

56. See the analysis of globalization and free trade by political scientist James Laxer, *False God: How the Globalization Myth Has Impoverished Canada* (Toronto: Lester Publishing, 1993).

57. Araya, "Good News to the Poor in the Wesleyan Tradition."

Chapter 6: A Glance at the Early History

1. E. J. Hobsbawm, *The Age of Revolution: Europe 1789–1848* (London: Weidenfeld and Nicolson, 1962), 11.

2. E.g., Immanuel Wallerstein, *Unthinking Social Science: Limits of Nineteenth-Century Paradigms* (Cambridge: Polity Press, 1991), 41–50.

3. Hobsbawm, *The Age of Revolution,* 54.

4. Ibid., 61.

5. Karl Polanyi, *The Great Transformation* (1944; Reprinted: Boston: Beacon Press, 1957).

6. Hobsbawm, *The Age of Revolution,* 66.

7. George Lichtheim, *The Origins of Socialism* (London: Weidenfeld and Nicolson, 1969), 104, 129; also Hobsbawm, *The Age of Revolution,* 289.

8. See the comment by John Kenneth Galbraith, *The Anatomy of Power* (Boston: Houghton Mifflin Co., 1983), 111–13; also *The Culture of Contentment* (Boston: Houghton Mifflin Co., 1992), 99.

9. See Spencer J. Pack, *Capitalism as Moral System: Adam Smith's Critique of the Free Market Economy* (Brookfield, Vt.: Edward Elgar, 1991), 1; also Galbraith, *The Culture of Contentment,* 98–99.

10. Adam Smith, *An Inquiry into the Nature and Causes of the Wealth of Nations,* ed. E. Cannan (New York: Modern Library, 1937), 142.

11. David Ricardo, quoted by Lichtheim, *The Origins of Socialism,* 127.

12. Polanyi, *The Great Transformation,* 163.

13. J. F. C. Harrison, *Robert Owen and the Owenites in Britain and America* (London: Routledge and Kegan Paul, 1969).

14. See Norman Penner, *From Protest to Power: Social Democracy in Canada, 1900–Present* (Toronto: James Lorimer & Co., 1992), 4.

15. See Gregory Baum, "Karl Polanyi on Ethics and Economics," unpublished lecture, 1993, 32.

16. Joyce Marlow, *The Tolpuddle Martyrs* (London: Andre Deutsch, 1971).

17. See G. D. H. Cole, *A History of Socialist Thought* (London: Macmillan, 1953), vol. 1, 86ff., 120ff.

18. See Gregory Baum, "Karl Polanyi on Ethics and Economics," 24.

19. See Paul Chilcote, *She Offered Them Christ* (Nashville: Abingdon, 1992).

20. *The Works of the Rev. John Wesley,* ed. Thomas Jackson, 3d ed., 14 vols. (London: Wesleyan Methodist Book Room, 1872), 7:20.

21. See a number of articles linking Wesley's theology to liberation theology, in Theodore Runyon, ed., *Sanctification and Liberation* (Nashville: Abingdon,

1977). See also Theodore Jennings, *Good News for the Poor: Wesley's Evangelical Economics* (Nashville: Abingdon, 1991).

22. A major debate has occurred among historians around the Halévy thesis (of French historian E. Halévy) that Methodism was a stabilizing influence in Britain and warded off a bloody revolution of the kind that occurred in France, providing an outlet for the energies and passion of the bourgeois and working classes and an alternative, orderly, and gradualist method of social reform (a thesis that some historians reject). According to one's ideological predisposition, such a stabilizing influence can be regarded as salutary or as a harmful form of "opium." See Runyon, *Sanctification and Liberation*, 15–16.

23. Henry Pelling, *A History of British Trade Unionism* (London: Macmillan & Co., 1963), 37, 74.

24. John Ludlow, quoted by H. W. Laidler, *History of Socialism* (London: Routledge and Kegan Paul, 1968), 726.

25. Torben Christensen, *Origin and History of Christian Socialism, 1848–54* (Copenhagen: Universitetsforlaget I Aarhus, 1962), 154.

26. Ibid., 155.

27. Quotations taken from Christensen, *Origin and History of Christian Socialism*, 154–56.

28. Note Wallerstein's analysis of the French Revolution as a World-Historical event, not so much enthroning the bourgeoisie, who were already largely in place in the economic sphere, but establishing "liberal" ideology, which became so important for the capitalist world-economy (*Unthinking Social Science*, 7–22).

29. Lichtheim, *The Origins of Socialism*, 21.

30. Cole, *A History of Socialist Thought*, vol. 1, 11ff.

31. Ibid., 362.

32. Ibid., 27–30; see Friedrich Engels, *Socialism: Utopian and Scientific*, in R. C. Tucker, ed., *The Marx-Engels Reader* (New York: W. W. Norton & Co., 1978). Engels wrote of so-called "utopian socialism" in an ironical and patronizing way: "The Utopians' mode of thought...is the expression of absolute truth, reason and justice, and has only to be discovered to conquer all the world by the virtue of its own power" (693).

33. Lichtheim, *The Origins of Socialism*, 62–68.

34. Ibid..

35. Ibid., 31–38.

36. Cole, *A History of Socialist Thought*, vol. 2, pt. 1, 362.

37. John Cort, *Christian Socialism: An Informal History* (Maryknoll, N.Y.: Orbis, 1988), 101, 110.

38. Lichtheim, *The Origins of Socialism*, 78–82.

39. Pierre-Joseph Proudhon, *Système des contradictions economiques*, 2:328, quoted in ibid., 92.

40. Quotation from Cort, *Christian Socialism*, 186.

41. Ibid., 188.

42. *Communist Manifesto*, in Tucker, *The Marx-Engels Reader*, 498.

43. See David McLellan, *Karl Marx: His Life and Thought* (London: Macmillan, 1973).

44. Karl Marx, *Economic and Philosophical Manuscripts*, in Erich Fromm, ed. *Marx's Concept of Man* (New York: Continuum, 1961), 95, 96, 98.

45. Dorothee Soelle, *Death by Bread Alone: Texts and Reflections on Religious Experience*, trans. D. Scheidt (Philadelphia: Fortress, 1978), 8–9.

46. Karl Marx, *The Poverty of Philosophy*, in T. Bottomore, trans., *Karl Marx: Selected Writings in Sociology and Philosophy* (New York: McGraw Hill, 1956), 95.

47. Marx, *German Ideology*, in Tucker, *The Marx-Engels Reader*, 172.

48. Ibid., 150.

49. Ibid., 473.

50. *Contribution to the Critique of Hegel's Philosophy of Right: Introduction*, in Tucker, *The Marx-Engels Reader*, 54.

51. K. Marx and F. Engels, *Manifesto of the Communist Party*, in ibid., 498.

52. *Critique of the Gotha Program*, in Tucker, *The Marx-Engels Reader*, 538.

53. Max Horkheimer, *Critique of Instrumental Reason* (New York: Seabury, 1974).

54. Charles Davis, *Theology and Political Society* (Cambridge: Cambridge University Press, 1980), 118.

55. See the sympathetic critique of critical theory itself from a feminist standpoint, by Marsha Hewitt, "Woman, Nature and Power: Emancipatory Themes in Critical Theory and Feminist Theology," in *Studies in Religion* 20, no. 3 (Summer 1991): 267–79.

56. This is the definition of William R. Hutchison, *The Modernist Impulse in American Protestantism*, 2d ed. (New York: Oxford University Press, 1982), 165.

57. See the discussion by Phyllis Airhart, *Serving the Present Age: Revivalism, Progressivism and the Methodist Tradition in Canada* (Montreal: McGill–Queen's University Press, 1992), 104–5.

58. Richard Allen, *The Social Passion: Religion and Social Reform in Canada, 1914–28* (Toronto: University of Toronto Press, 1971), 6.

59. See Phyllis Airhart, "Christian Socialism and the Legacy of Revivalism in the 1930's," in H. Wells and R. Hutchinson, eds., *A Long and Faithful March* (Toronto: United Church Publishing House, 1989), 30–40.

60. Walter Rauschenbusch, *A Theology for the Social Gospel* (Macmillan Co., 1917; Nashville, Abingdon Press edition), 154.

61. Ibid., 52.

62. Ibid., 125.

63. Ibid., 50, 60.

64. Ibid., 111.

65. Ibid., 55.

66. Salem Bland, *The New Christianity* (1920), introduction by Richard Allen (Toronto: University of Toronto Press, 1973), 23.

67. Ibid., 55.

68. Ibid., 66.

69. Ibid., 28.

70. Ibid., 17.

71. Ibid. 22.

72. Rauschenbusch, *A Theology for the Social Gospel*, 165.

73. Gregory Baum, "The Catholic Left in Quebec," in Colin Leys and Marguerite Mendell, eds., *Culture and Social Change* (Montreal: Black Rose, 1991), 153.

Chapter 7: Democratic Socialism / Social Democracy

1. The distinction is drawn, for example, by Michael A. Lebowitz, "The Limits and Possibilities of Social Democracy," paper for the Society for Socialist Studies, May 1991. See our discussion in chapter 4 above. See also W. Paterson and A. Thomas, *Social Democratic Parties in Western Europe* (London: Croom Helm, 1977).

2. A sharp distinction is drawn by scholars holding opposing views: Henry Milner and Arthur Milner, "Social Democracy versus Democratic Socialism: The Question of Public Ownership," and Leo Panitch and Donald Swartz, "The Case for Socialist Democracy," in Simon Rosenblum and Peter Findlay, eds., *Debating Canada's Future: Views from the Left* (Toronto: James Lorimer & Co., 1991).

3. W. Merkel, citing R. Dahrendorf, "After the Golden Age," in C. Lemke and G. Marks, eds., *The Crisis of Socialism in Europe* (Durham, N.C.: Duke University Press, 1992), 136.

4. G. D. H. Cole, *A History of Socialist Thought* (London: Macmillan, 1960), vol. 3, pt. 1, 106.

5. Edward Reynolds Pease, *History of the Fabian Society*, quoted by Cole, ibid., 112.

6. Cole, *A History of Socialist Thought*, vol. 3, pt. 1, 114–15.

7. The idea of locally based socialism persists in Britain. See Robin Murray, "New Directions in Municipal Socialism," in Ben Pimlott, ed., *Fabian Essays in Socialist Thought* (London: Heinemann, 1984).

8. See W. E. Paterson and A. H. Thomas, *The Future of Social Democracy* (Oxford: Clarendon Press, 1986), 3–5.

9. James R. Ozinga, *Communism: The Story of the Idea and Its Implementation* (Englewood Cliffs, N.J.: Prentice-Hall, 1987), 84.

10. *New International Review* (Winter 1977): 6.

11. Ibid., 8–9.

12. Ibid., 7–9.

13. Cole, *A History of Socialist Thought*, vol. 2, pt. 1, 365.

14. John Cort, *Christian Socialism*, 222.

15. Gary J. Dorrien, *The Democratic Socialist Vision* (Totowa, N.J.: Rowman & Littlefield, 1986), chap. 3.

16. Norman Thomas, *The Choice before Us: Mankind at the Crossroads* (New York: Macmillan Co., 1932), 219–21.

17. Irving Howe is one such surviving democratic socialist, who asserts the continuing importance of socialist utopianism. See "The Spirit of the Times," in *Dissent* (Spring 1993): 131–33. See also the works of the American socialist intellectual Michael Harrington, e.g., *The Next Left: The History of a Future* (New York: H. Holt, 1987); *Socialism: Past and Future* (New York: Arcade, 1989).

18. Rosemary Radford Ruether, *Disputed Questions* (Nashville: Abingdon, 1982), 85.

19. See John Cort, *Christian Socialism*, 222–81.

20. Cole, *A History of Socialist Thought*, vol. 3, pt. 2, 783.

21. Statistics quoted by Linda McQuaig, *The Wealthy Banker's Wife: The Assault on Equality in Canada* (Toronto: Penguin Books Canada, 1993), 83.

22. James Laxer, *False God: How the Globalization Myth Has Impoverished Canada* (Toronto: Lester Publishing, 1993), 53.

23. Ibid., 16.

24. Ibid., 165, 100, 34.

25. Laxer, *False God*, 55.

26. The Ecumenical Coalition for Economic Justice, *Reweaving Canada's Social Programs: From Shredded Safety Net to Social Solidarity* (Toronto: Ecumenical Coalition for Economic Justice, 1993), 52, 129–30.

27. Walter D. Young, *The Anatomy of a Party: The National CCF, 1932–1961* (Toronto: University of Toronto Press, 1969), 3–4.

28. See Ben Smillie, *Beyond the Social Gospel: Church Protest on the Prairies* (Toronto: United Church Publishing House, 1991), chap. 6.

29. Kenneth McNaught, *A Prophet in Politics: A Biography of J. S. Woodsworth* (Toronto: University of Toronto Press, 1959).

30. Quoted by McNaught, *A Prophet in Politics*, 56–57.

31. See Richard Allen, *The Social Passion: Religion and Social Reform in Canada, 1914–1928* (Toronto: University of Toronto Press, 1971), 76, 85–86, 99–100.

32. Ibid., 71.

33. Young, *The Anatomy of a Party*, 8.

34. Calgary Programme, 1932, in ibid., 303.

35. Regina Manifesto (1933) in ibid., 303–5.

36. Ibid., 306–7.

37. Ibid., 39.

38. Young, *The Anatomy of a Party*, 245.

39. John Line, quoted by Roger Hutchinson, "The Fellowship for a Christian Social Order: 1934–1945," in *A Long and Faithful March*, 20.

40. FCSO Basis of Agreement, 1936, quoted by Hutchinson, ibid., 24.

41. Ibid., 20.

42. Ibid.

43. R. B. Y. Scott and Gregory Vlastos, eds., *Towards the Christian Revolution* (Willett Clark & Company, 1936; Kingston, Ont.: Ronald P. Frey & Co., 1989).

44. Line, "The Theological Principles," in ibid., 40.

45. Ibid., 49.

46. Ibid., 48, 50.

47. Hutchinson, "The Fellowship for a Christian Social Order: 1934–1945," 27.

48. Norman Penner, *From Protest to Power: Social Democracy in Canada, 1900–Present* (Toronto: James Lorimer & Co., 1992), 118.

49. See Ivan Avakumovic, *Socialism in Canada: A Study of the CCF–NDP in Federal and Provincial Politics* (Toronto: McClelland and Stewart, 1978).

50. Winnipeg Declaration of Principles of the Co-operative Commonwealth Federation, in Young, *The Anatomy of a Party,* 315.

51. Ibid., 315.

52. Carlyle King, president of the Saskatchewan C.C.F., quoted in ibid., 127.

53. Barth himself, however, continued to espouse democratic socialism. Niebuhr, while he abandoned socialism as such, continued to be heavily involved in the politics of social justice in the United States.

54. Quoted by Avakumovic, *Socialism in Canada,* 93.

55. Walter Young, "Regina Thirty Years Later," in *Canadian Forum* 43 (September 1963): 126.

56. See the discussion of "nationalization within the global economy" and the need for national policies to "encourage the challenging of industrial giants on the part of small-sale businesses and entrepreneurs" by Herman E. Daly and John B. Cobb, Jr., *For the Common Good: Redirecting the Economy Toward Community, the Environment, and a Sustainable Future* (Boston: Beacon Press, 1989), 174, 291.

57. Lebowitz, "The Limits of Social Democracy within Capitalism: A Marxian View"; see chap. 4.

58. Gregg M. Olsen, "Swedish Social Democracy and Beyond: Internal Obstacles to Economic Democracy," in *Regulating Labour: The State, Neo-Conservatism and Industrial Relations,* ed. L. Haiven, S. McBride and J. Shields (Winnipeg: Society for Socialist Studies; Toronto: Garamond Press, 1990).

59. Michael E. Porter, *The Competitive Advantage of Nations* (New York: Free Press, 1990), 352.

60. See Eric Kierans and Walter Stewart, *Wrong End of the Rainbow: The Collapse of Free Enterprise in Canada* (Toronto: Collins Publishers, 1988), 207–8.

61. Porter, *The Competitive Advantage of Nations,* 343.

62. Ibid.

63. See the comment by Leo Panitch and Peter Findlay, "The Case for Socialist Democracy," in Simon Rosenblum and Peter Findlay, eds., *Debating Canada's Future,* 43.

64. David Crane, "Sweden, Once a Model for Us, Faces Its own Economic Crisis," in *Toronto Star,* May 16, 1993, A1, A12.

65. See the remarkable statistical comparisons cited in Linda McQuaig, *The Wealthy Banker's Wife* (Toronto: Penguin Books Canada, 1993), chaps. 3 and 4.

66. Porter, *The Competitive Advantage of Nations,* 347.

67. Olsen, "Swedish Social Democracy and Beyond," 183.

68. Ibid.

69. Ibid., 184.

70. The point is made by Ed Broadbent, "Introduction: Some Thoughts on Socialism," in Rosenblum and Findlay, *Debating Canada's Future,* 2.

71. Bill Schiller, "The Support Stocking Revolt," in *Toronto Star,* November 19, 1994, A1, A22.

72. Leo Panitch and Donald Swartz speak of the "collapse of social democratic reformism" (*Debating Canada's Future,* 47).

73. See the discussion of the New Left by Richard Lowenthal, "The Future of Socialism in the Advanced Democracies," in L. Kolakowski and S. Hampshire, eds., *The Socialist Idea* (London: Weidenfeld and Nicolson, 1974), 228–30.

Chapter 8: Socialism in Its Many Varieties

1. Andrew Levine, *Arguing for Socialism* (New York: Routledge and Kegan Paul, 1984), 7. Also Herman E. Daly and John B. Cobb, Jr., in their excellent book on alternative systems: "Socialism is defined by government ownership of the means of production with allocation and distribution by central planning, but with some reliance on the market when central planning gets overwhelmed." Yet they recognize that some socialists "support, as we do, decentralization of political and economic power, worker ownership of factories or participation in their management, and the subordination of the economy to social goals, democratically defined" (*For the Common Good: Redirecting the Economy: Toward Community, the Environment, and a Sustainable Future* [Boston: Beacon Press, 1989], 13, 15).

2. Alec Nove, *The Economics of a Feasible Socialism, Revisited* (London: Unwin Hyman, 1991), 245–46.

3. Leo Panitch and Donald Swartz, "The Case for Socialist Democracy," in Simon Rosenblum and Peter Findlay, eds., *Debating Canada's Future: Views from the Left* (Toronto: James Lorimer & Co., 1991), 33.

4. Dean E. Frease and Erling Christensen, "Socialism vs. Capitalism," paper for the Society for Socialist Studies, Victoria, B.C., May 1990, 3.

5. Immanuel Wallerstein, *The Politics of the World-Economy: The States, the Movements and the Civilizations* (New York: Cambridge University Press, 1984), 117.

6. James R. Ozinga, *Communism: The Story of the Idea and Its Implementation* (Englewood Cliffs, N.J.: Prentice-Hall, 1987), 222.

7. See Maurice Meisner, *Mao's China and After* (London: Collier Macmillan, 1986).

8. See L. H. Theriot, "Cuba Faces the Economic Realities of the 1980's," in J. L. Horowitz, ed., *Cuban Communism* (New Brunswick, N.J.: Transaction Publishers, 1991).

9. Kwame Nkrumah, *Neo-Colonialism: The Last Stage of Imperialism* (New York: International Publishers, 1965).

10. Oswald Hirmer, *The Gospel and the Social Systems* (Kampala, Uganda: St. Paul Publications-Africa/Daughters of St. Paul, 1981), 105.

11. See Julius K. Nyerere, *Ujamaa — Essays on Socialism* (London: Oxford University Press, 1968), 14–15.

12. David Schweickart, *Capitalism or Worker Control? An Ethical and Economic Appraisal* (New York: Praeger Publishers, 1980) 48–49, 137–38.

13. See Gregory Baum, *The Priority of Labor* (New York: Paulist Press, 1982), 55–56.

14. Rudolf Bicanic, *Economic Policy in Socialist Yugoslavia* (Cambridge: University Press, 1973), 34.

15. Branko Horvat, *The Yugoslav Economic System: The First Labor-Managed Economy in the Making* (White Plains, N.Y.: International Arts and Sciences Press, 1976), 3.

16. Elizabeth Mann Borgese, Introduction to I. Adizes and E. M. Borgese, eds., *Self-Management: New Dimensions to Democracy* (Santa Barbara, Calif.: ABC-Clio, 1975), xx.

17. See the discussion of worker ownership by Daly and Cobb, *For the Common Good*, 298–304.

18. Harry C. Boyte, *The Backyard Revolution: Understanding the New Citizen Movement* (Philadelphia: Temple University Press, 1980), 134.

19. Michael Schaaf, *Cooperatives at the Crossroads: The Potential for a Major New Economic and Social Role* (Washington, D.C.: Exploratory Project for Economic Alternatives, 1977), 37.

20. See D. Schweickart, *Capitalism or Worker Control?* See the discussion by Peter Burns, "The Problem of Socialism in Liberation Theology," in *Theological Studies* 53, no. 3 (September 1992): 509.

21. Gregory Baum, *The Priority of Labor,* 84.

22. See a thorough discussion of this movement by G. D. H. Cole, *A Century of Co-operation* (London: George Allen and Unwin, 1944).

23. Philip Backstrom, *Christian Socialism and Cooperation in Victorian England* (London: Croom Helm, 1974).

24. Eugene Forsey, "A New Economic Order," in G. Vlastos and R. B. Y. Scott, eds., *Towards the Christian Revolution* (first published in 1936 by Willett Clark and Company; Kingston, Ont.: Robert P. Frye and Co., 1989), 127–28.

25. G. D. H. Cole, *A History of Socialist Thought* (London: Macmillan, 1960), vol. 3, pt. 1, 243–45.

26. Ibid., 222–23, 242–46.

27. Forsey, "A New Economic Order," 129–30.

28. Ibid., 129–31.

29. Ibid., 138–39.

30. Severyn T. Bruyn, "Beyond Market and State," in S. T. Bruyn and J. Meehan, eds., *Beyond the Market and State* (Philadelphia: Temple University Press, 1987).

31. Chuck Matthei, "A Community to Which We Belong: The Value of Land in Economics," in *Sojourners,* November 1993, 12–17.

32. E.g., the Don Quixote housing cooperative in Burlington, Ontario, supported through provincial government taxation and initiated by members of East Plains United Church.

33. Matthei, "A Community to Which We Belong," 15.

34. See the analysis of David P. Ross and Peter J. Usher, *From the Roots Up: Economic Development as if Community Mattered* (Toronto: James Lorimer & Co., 1986), xi.

35. Ibid., 32.

36. Ibid., 69.

37. See the discussion of Catholic involvement in the search for alternatives in Quebec, by Gregory Baum, "The Catholic Left in Quebec," in Colin Leys and Marguerite Mendell, eds., *Culture and Social Change* (Montreal: Black Rose, 1991).

38. See the articles about local community organizations in Toronto and Montreal in ibid.

39. Ibid., 19.

40. Ibid., 25. A similar point is made by Gregory Baum, in "Community and Identity," in Marc H. Ellis and Otto Maduro, eds., *The Future of Liberation The-*

ology: Essays in Honor of Gustavo Gutiérrez (Maryknoll, N.Y.: Orbis, 1989), 220–28.

41. Boyte, *The Backyard Revolution,* 26, 31.

42. Ibid., 42.

43. Don Alexander and Judy Beange, "Beyond Capitalism and Socialism: The Communitarian Alternative," paper for the Society for Socialist Studies, Victoria, B.C., May 1990, available from the Society for Socialist Studies.

44. Richard J. Barnet and John Cavanagh, *Global Dreams: Imperial Corporations and the New World Order* (New York: Simon and Schuster, 1994), 430.

Chapter 9: Christian Socialism: A Tradition Not to Be Abandoned

1. Cedric Mayson, *Christians and Southern Africa in Transition* (Johannesburg: South African Council of Churches, 1994), 9.

2. Richard J. Barnet and John Cavanagh, *Global Dreams: Imperial Corporations and the New World Order* (New York: Simon and Schuster, 1994), 423.

3. T. K. Hopkins and I. Wallerstein, *Processes of the World-System* (Beverly Hills, Calif.: Sage Publications, 1980), 3:174.

4. Immanuel Wallerstein, *Unthinking Social Science: Limits of Nineteenth-Century Paradigms* (Cambridge: Polity Press, 1991), 167.

5. Immanuel Wallerstein, *The Capitalist World-Economy* (Cambridge University Press, 1979), 91.

6. Barnet and Cavanagh, *Global Dreams,* 429.

7. Rosemary Radford Ruether, *Disputed Questions: On Being a Christian* (Maryknoll, N.Y.: Orbis, 1989), 88–89.

8. Herb Gamberg, "What Is Socialism?" in Jos. Roberts and Jesse Vorst, eds., *Socialism in Crisis? Canadian Perspectives* (Winnipeg: Society for Socialist Studies/ Fernwood Publishing, 1992), 94.

9. Ibid., 104.

10. See Letty Russell, *Household of Freedom: Authority in Feminist Theology* (Philadelphia: Fortress Press, 1987).

Index